Staff–Student Partnerships in Higher Education

Edited by Sabine Little

continuum

Continuum International Publishing Group

The Tower Building   80 Maiden Lane
11 York Road   Suite 704
London SE1 7NX   New York NY 10038

www.continuumbooks.com

© Sabine Little and Contributors 2011

First published 2011
Paperback edition first published 2012

British Library Cataloguing-in-Publication Data
A catalogue record for this book is available from the British Library.

ISBN: 978-1-4411-8715-4 (hardcover)
       978-1-4411-1993-3 (paperback)

Library of Congress Cataloging-in-Publication Data
Staff-student partnerships in higher education / edited by Sabine Little.
    p. cm.
   Includes bibliographical references.
   ISBN 978-1-4411-8715-4 (hardcover)
    1. College teaching—Great Britain. 2. Teacher-student relationships—Great Britain. 3. Group work in education—Great Britain. I. Little, Sabine. II. Title.
   LB2331.S6925 2011
   378.1'76—dc22   2010024380

Typeset by Pindar NZ, Auckland, New Zealand
Printed and bound in Great Britain

To all students and staff who work together to explore each other's ideas and perspectives, and especially to the student ambassadors I have had the honour and pleasure of working with over the years – thank you for your ideas, enthusiasm, drive and dreams.

Contents

Notes on Contributors

Chapter 1

Philippa Levy was the Academic Director of CILASS, the Centre for Inquiry-based Learning in the Arts and Social Sciences, and a member of the Department of Information Studies at the University of Sheffield before taking over as Head of Department of Information Studies in 2010. Her research interests are in the areas of learning, teaching and learning support in higher education, with particular interests in: inquiry-based pedagogies; networked learning; educational roles of information specialists, including for information literacy development; educational development and change facilitation in universities; and the scholarship of teaching and learning.

Sabine Little is a qualified secondary school teacher, and has worked both as a lecturer of education and an educational developer for a number of years. Her research interests involve the way group members relate to each other and communicate, and the facilitation of groups to enable them to construct their own agendas and knowledge. She has created and co-facilitated (with a number of students over the years) the CILASS Student Ambassador Network, one of the largest and longest-term group of students involved in learning and teaching enhancement in the UK. After the end of the UK CETL Programme, she now works as an independent educational consultant.

Natalie Whelan was first the CILASS Student Ambassador for Geography in 2007–08, and then co-facilitated the Student Ambassador Network in 2008–09, while in the final year of her geography degree. During this time, she has presented on her work at a number of conferences and events. Following her graduation, she is currently completing a graduate trainee manager programme with a large retail group.

Chapter 2

Emma Barnes began working with the Centre for Excellence in Enquiry-Based Learning (CEEBL) while studying for a Masters in Linguistics in 2008. Her role as Student Intern for Humanities was promoting and supporting enquiry-based learning within the faculty through provision of focus groups, workshops and events. She currently works with children with additional needs and disabilities and has a long-standing interest in personalized learning.

Alison Bestwick has been a Student Ambassador in the CILASS at the University of Sheffield since 2006. She began her involvement with CILASS while studying for her BA in Archaeology, and is now in the second year of her PhD studies in the same department. Her role within CILASS included being part of a working group that produced films exploring the concept of inquiry-based learning (IBL) and its impact on the institution. She also liaised with the Department of Archaeology to raise awareness of the usefulness of IBL from a student perspective.

Louise Goldring started working for CEEBL in 2006, as a student intern, while completing her MA in Post-1900 Literatures, Theories and Cultures at the University of Manchester. In 2007, she became the Sabbatical Officer, coordinating the intern programme at CEEBL. In 2008, she took on the position of Student Engagement Officer, responsible for training and supporting students and managing the interns. Her role includes designing and facilitating workshops for staff and students and supporting the development of enquiry-based learning across the University of Manchester and further afield.

Jamie Wood worked as a student intern at CEEBL while completing his PhD in Classics and Ancient History at the University of Manchester. In 2007 he moved to Sheffield to take up a position as a Learning Development and Research Associate at CILASS and worked there for just over two years. His role involved supporting and evaluating curriculum development projects and researching the impact of inquiry-based learning on staff and students, and maternity leave cover for the co-facilitation of the Student Ambassador Network for eight months. In October 2009, he took up a position as a Leverhulme Early Career Postdoctoral Fellow in Religions and Theology at the University of Manchester.

Chapter 3
Kay Sambell is a National Teaching Fellow and Director of Assessment for Learning Enhancement in Northumbria University's Centre for Excellence (CETL) in Assessment for Learning.

Linda Graham has acted as a CETL Student Liaison Officer, Student Development Officer and MA student in Northumbria University's Centre for Excellence (CETL) in Assessment for Learning.

Together, Kay and Linda have worked to establish a range of student communities targeted at improving teaching and learning. Nationally, they helped establish the Student Learning and Teaching Network, and in their own university they have supported the launch of a student-led learning hub, large-scale peer-learning schemes and student-led publications, conferences and events.

Chapter 4

Jo Badge is a Web Resources Development Officer, and provides support to academic staff for online educational technologies and has conducted research into the use of electronic detection software for plagiarism. She is the project leader for the Plagiarism and Academic Integrity research project at the University of Leicester.

Nadya Yakovchuk was the main researcher on the Plagiarism and Academic Integrity project at the University of Leicester. Her doctoral research (undertaken at the University of Warwick) focused on plagiarism in the academic writing of international students. Her academic interests include applied linguistics, academic writing, study skills and plagiarism prevention.

Alysoun Hancock is the Education Officer at the University of Leicester's Students' Union. Alysoun taught English in a comprehensive school for a number of years. She left education to work on film production and script writing in a new media company. She returned to full-time education and to the university she attended to encourage and support students rather than teach them.

Aaron Porter was a sabbatical officer at the University of Leicester Students' Union and is now NUS Vice-President (Higher Education). Aaron is a non-executive director of the Office of the Independent Adjudicator, an observer to the UKICSA Board, the National Student Steering group and the Academic Council of the Higher Education Academy.

Chapter 5

Katherine Harrington is Director of the Write Now Centre for Excellence in Teaching and Learning, led by London Metropolitan University and run in collaboration with Liverpool Hope University and Aston University. She holds a PhD in Victorian Studies from the University of Keele and a BA in Economics and English Literature from the University of California, Davis. She conducts qualitative and quantitative research into student writing, learning and assessment, and, in cooperation with colleagues, develops programmes for students and staff that facilitate the growth of institutional writing and research culture.

Peter O'Neill overviews the operations of the London Metropolitan University Writing Centre. In particular, he is responsible for the new 'writing mentors' programme, which has delivered around 1,600 one-hour writing tutorials in its first two years of operation. He also works with a wide variety of lecturers on 'Writing-in-the-Disciplines' initiatives. He is co-editor of a planned volume entitled 'Writing in the UK Disciplines'. Other interests include ancient rhetoric.

Lynn Reynolds is an undergraduate student of Psychology at London Metropolitan University. Before her return to higher education she worked for the NHS and in the IT industry. She now practises as a student writing mentor at the university's writing centre, collaborating with fellow students to improve their experience of the writing process. Also a writer of poetry and fiction, she is especially interested in using creative techniques in academic writing and in applying insights from cognitive psychology to her role as a writing mentor.

Chapter 6
Jane Williams is the Director of e-learning for the Centre for Medical Education at the University of Bristol. She leads the e-learning and IT development for the undergraduate medical programme. Her main interests include the role of technology in teaching and learning, including students as partners in the delivery of medical education, and legal, technical and ethical issues surrounding the reuse of clinical recordings.

Dominic Alder works as the e-learning support officer for the Centre for Medical Education at the University of Bristol. Among other things, he is responsible for e-learning materials development, website management and bespoke applications development, and manages the student e-learning programme.

Rachel O'Connell, while working on this chapter, was a Foundation 2 doctor at St George's Hospital. She graduated from the University of Bristol's Medical School in 2007, and participated in the e-learning tutorial project in 2004–05. She currently works as a trainee surgeon at the Kent, Surrey and Sussex Deanery.

Will Duffin, while working on this chapter, was a Foundation 1 doctor. He participated in the e-learning tutorial project in 2005–06. He is currently finishing his Foundation 2 year and plans to be a general practitioner.

Miranda Whinney worked on the project described in this chapter as a consultant on copyright and patient permission.

Julian Cook, while working on this chapter, was a research fellow at the Education Support Unit, University of Bristol. He supported the e-learning initiative, and currently works as a counsellor. He continues to provide consultancy on e-learning to the university.

Philippa King, while working on this chapter, was a final-year medical student at the University of Bristol. She participated in the e-learning tutorial project in 2007–08.

Chapter 7

Jacqueline Potter currently works at Edge Hill University as Associate Dean for Teaching, Learning and Academic Development. She started her academic career as an ecologist and lecturer. She became increasingly interested in student learning, and took on a range of departmental, faculty and then central institutional roles to promote quality enhancement and curriculum innovation. This chapter was written while she was working in Ireland as the manager of an academic practice unit. The chapter is a change from other forms of publishing student voices that she is involved with as one of the instigators of Bioscience Horizons, an undergraduate research journal – http://www.oxfordjournals.org/our_journals/biohorizons/.

Niamh Collins is a PhD candidate in the School of Medicine at Trinity College Dublin. She qualified as a medical doctor from Trinity College in 2004 and began working towards a PhD in medicine in 2005. During her PhD studies she worked as a clinical tutor, teaching undergraduate medical students, and she will shortly complete a Masters in Medical Education run by Queen's University Belfast and the Irish College of General Practitioners. In 2007 she was Health Science Faculty Officer on the Trinity College Graduate Students' Union and became involved in developing support for postgraduate students who teach.

Chapter 8

Alan Dordoy is the Head of Learning and Teaching Support at the University of Northumbria. He is responsible for the implementation of the university's Learning and Teaching Strategy, management of quality assurance processes in relation to programme approvals, collaborative ventures approvals, annual and periodic review of taught programmes, regulations and frameworks, external reviews including QAA, staff development for learning and teaching quality and enhancement, and management of the e-Learning portal, graduate school office. Alan's previous roles include undergraduate programme director for sociology programmes, director of a HEFCE FDTL project, and QAA institutional auditor.

Pat Gannon-Leary is a qualified information professional who worked in HE libraries for some 18 years in the UK and USA prior to becoming a researcher. She has conducted research in a number of areas including electronic information services, multi-agency information sharing, user information-seeking needs, diverse student needs, e-learning and the research–teaching nexus.

Sophie McGlinn began working for Northumbria Students' Union in July 2006 as Representation and Democracy Coordinator. Since then she has been actively involved in promoting and developing student representative systems across the institution. This has included introducing and supporting school-level representation for taught and research students, extending provision for students across university campuses and supporting the first ever Learning and Teaching Awards in 2007. She is currently working in the advice-based role of Education Caseworker.

Fiona Baldam was in her final year of a joint honours Childhood Studies and Early Years Education degree at Northumbria University while working on this chapter. Together with Gemma Charlton, she won the university's Learning and Teaching Awards in 2008 and thoroughly enjoyed the experience of collaborating with others during the writing process.

Gemma Charlton was a third-year student in the School of Health, Community and Education Studies at the University of Northumbria while working on this chapter. Together with Fiona Baldam, she won the university's Learning and Teaching Awards in 2008 and really enjoyed the experience of collaborating with others during the writing process.

Chapter 9
Elena Zaitseva is a research officer at the Liverpool John Moores University Centre for Excellence in Teaching and Learning (CETL), responsible for evaluating and researching CETL initiatives and developing staff pedagogic research and scholarship capacity. Her research interests include collaborative and peer learning, intercultural aspects of learning and academic identities.

Elizabeth Clifford is Coordinator of the Liverpool John Moores University Centre for Excellence in Teaching and Learning which has a focus on employability, enterprise and leadership. Her main professional and research interests relate to the promotion of work-based and work-related learning – both as a means of enhancing graduate employability and supporting professional development.

Sarah Nixon is a principal lecturer and CETL Leader within the Centre for Sport, Dance and Outdoor Education at Liverpool John Moores University. Her main teaching area is sports management and her pedagogic research interests lie in student learning experience, with a particular focus on personal development planning and the development of individual potential.

Elizabeth Deja has a health psychology background focused on coping strategies and social support in chronic illness. She currently works as a research assistant at Liverpool John Moores University Centre for Excellence in Teaching and Learning, evaluating and researching teaching and learning innovations, graduates' employability and leadership, and is involved in development of staff pedagogic research capacity.

Andrew Murphy graduated with a first-class degree in Sport Development and then successfully completed his postgraduate certificate in Physical Education (PE). He now works as a PE teacher at secondary level.

Chapter 10
Rebekka Kill is a Senior Lecturer in Creativity, Enterprise and Engagement, University Teaching Fellow and Faculty Enterprise Pioneer at Leeds Metropolitan University. She spends half her time lecturing and working on new curricula and half her time working on projects, brokering cultural partnerships on behalf of the university and research. She teaches across a range of disciplines in the university including Fine Art, Performance and Entertainment Management. In terms of curriculum development, she specializes in interdisciplinary pathways and curriculum innovation, and is currently developing an MA in Creative Enterprise. She is also currently involved in a cross-faculty project on audio/podcast feedback for students and an 'engagement' project related to her partnership work.

Michael Thorne is a mature-age full-time postgraduate student studying for an MA in Performance Practice at Leeds Metropolitan University, where he also gained a first-class degree in Contemporary Performance. He has performed in many situations and locations, including devised works at festivals in England and Europe. He is interested in discovering ways of establishing dialogue with audiences in non-conventional spaces. As part of his learning he has been working on co-authored projects based around research-informed performance. An example of this is running workshops for other faculties within the university using performance to help students develop management and interpersonal skills.

Keeley McDonnell is an MA student at Leeds Metropolitan University. She gained her first-class undergraduate degree in Contemporary Performance.

She is a performer and has an artist residency at Speed Queen, a flamboyant nightclub. She is interested in the notion of an event, and works as an events manager at a bar. Once a month she curates a multidisciplinary event where performers, bands, artists, poets and film makers come together to share their practice. She considers herself a multi-skilled practitioner and aims to share her pedagogy throughout her journey.

Chapter 11

Mark Manning, a registered psychologist, has been a lecturer in psychology at both Griffith University, Queensland and the University of Western Australia, a lecturer in Research Methods at Southern Cross University, and is currently a lecturer in Management at the University of the Sunshine Coast, Queensland. He has conducted research in the area of neuroscience and, more recently, in organizational climate in the tourism and hospitality industry. He has received over A$730,000 in research grants and has published this work in journals such as *Theory & Psychology*, *Vision Research*, *Journal of Nervous and Mental Disease*, *European Journal of Marketing* and *Tourism Analysis*.

Lesley Willcoxson has worked in an academic staff development role at Sydney University and designed and led Murdoch University's academic staff development program. At the University of Southern Queensland and the University of the Sunshine Coast she has lectured in Human Resource Management. She is currently working on AACSB accreditation for the Faculty of Business at the University of the Sunshine Coast and is also Teaching and Learning Coordinator for the faculty. Her research interests lie in the areas of student retention and attrition (for which she has received a Carrick Institute Competitive grant), organizational change, organizational culture, leadership, teaching and learning.

Katrina Gething completed a combined degree in Business and Arts at the University of the Sunshine Coast in 2007, majoring in marketing and public relations. She commenced an honours year in February 2008. Katrina has a background in small business and media relations, and has recently launched a market research business as a direct outcome of the skills she developed from the research methods course described in this chapter.

Natasha Johnston is currently completing an undergraduate Business degree at the University of the Sunshine Coast, with a major in marketing. Concurrent with her studies, Natasha has worked in a Sunshine Coast-based advertising and marketing consultancy owned and run by a former creative director of Saatchi and Saatchi. In this role she has been involved in a

number of key advertising campaigns and undertaken market research for
local and international clients.

Chapter 12

David Metcalfe graduated from the University of Warwick with a first-class
BSc(Hons) in Biological Sciences (2006) and MB ChB (2010). He won more
than fifteen bursaries, scholarships and prizes for research as an undergraduate and was Founding Editor of *Reinvention: A Journal of Undergraduate
Research.* He is now a junior doctor working in London.

Caroline Gibson graduated in 1994 with a BSc Honours degree in Geography
and Geology and is now based at the University of Warwick as managing editor of *Reinvention: a Journal of Undergraduate Research.*

Cath Lambert is Lecturer in Sociology at the University of Warwick and
Academic Coordinator for the Reinvention Centre for Undergraduate
Research, a Collaborative Centre for Excellence in Teaching and Learning.
She also serves as a subject editor and academic advisor for *Reinvention: a
Journal of Undergraduate Research.*

Chapter 13

Brad Wuetherick is a former student leader at the undergraduate and postgraduate level as well as the former Director of the Research Makes Sense
for Students initiative at the University of Alberta, Canada. Currently, he is
the Program Director of the Gwenna Moss Centre for Teaching Effectiveness
at the University of Saskatchewan in Saskatoon, Canada.

Lisa McLaughlin is a former Vice-President (Academic) of the Students'
Union at the University of Alberta (UofA). She is currently a School Health
Facilitator with the APPLE Schools project at the UofA's School of Public
Health, working with an elementary school to improve students' physical
activity and eating habits and to create a healthier school environment.

Chapter 14

Heather Sharp is a lecturer at the University of Newcastle Australia, Centre
for Teaching and Learning, in the area of academic development. Prior to
this, she was a lecturer in the Faculty of Education, University of Southern
Queensland, where she taught in the Bachelor of Education (primary and
middle school and secondary). Her research interests are in the area of
curriculum design and development, pedagogical approaches in school
and tertiary contexts, historical studies, beginning teacher experiences, and
building capacity in students. She is currently researching her PhD in the
area of Australian history curriculum in schools.

Linda Stanley is a third-year undergraduate student enrolled in a Bachelor of Education (Honours) degree at the University of Southern Queensland's new Springfield campus. Her areas of interest are cultural diversity, social justice and equity in education. These areas of interest, and her previous experience co-authoring a book chapter focused on Studies of Society and Environment (SOSE), have inspired a more profound understanding of the importance of SOSE education. Her current honours research is focusing on the issues of cultural diversity found in Australian classrooms, and how practising teachers choose to approach these issues.

Marie Hayward is a third-year undergraduate student at University of Southern Queensland, Springfield Campus. She is currently enrolled in the Bachelor of Education (Honours) Program. Her interests are spread over various fields including sporting activities and disability services. She enjoys drama and partakes in two productions a year in a volunteer position with a disability performing group. As a first-year undergraduate, she co-authored a SOSE textbook, which gave her confidence and a keen interest in collaboration and cooperation with both students and academics alike.

Preface

When the journey towards this book began, back in July 2007, little did I know it would be nearly three years before I would be writing the preface to the final volume. That summer, I attended the Higher Education Academy (HEA) Conference in Harrogate, in order to present with Tim Fiennes, then my co-facilitator of our Student Ambassador Network, the work we had been doing over the last year (Fiennes and Little, 2007). With the overarching theme of 'Engaging Students in Higher Education', we were both looking forward to talking to other students and staff who had worked in partnership in the area of educational enhancement. By the end of the event, Tim and I were sure of two things: we hadn't been able to find any other full-time, undergraduate students involved in learning and teaching enhancement at the event; and the delegates we had met and spoken to were desperate for there to be more 'Tims'. Together, Tim and I discussed how we might encourage other practitioners with examples of staff–student partnerships – which we were sure existed – to come forward and jointly tell their story. Unfortunately, the HEA conference was Tim's last act as student network co-facilitator, as he left university and began his working career.

I picked the idea of a book on staff–student partnerships up with Laura Jenkins, Tim's successor. Together, we puzzled over the chicken/egg conundrum. We knew we had a topic worthy of a publication, but how could we ensure contributions of a high standard, without a publisher – and how could we get a publisher to agree to a book co-authored by staff and students, and be reassured about the academic quality of the final publication? We wanted to ensure that whatever we were proposing would be more than a collection of case studies. In the end, we decided to put out a call for chapters, warning contributors that we had not yet found a publisher. Over the course of the next academic year, we pulled together chapter summaries – and found a publisher shortly after Laura left the university. Her successor, Natalie Whelan, is the co-author of Chapter 1. She, too, has now graduated, and her successor, in turn – Su Arnall – is continuing the work that Tim started what seems a long time ago, working to facilitate staff–student partnerships for learning and teaching enhancement. The story of how the book came into existence is only one example of the difficulties members of staff–student partnerships face in order to facilitate change in education, and each chapter in this volume will add to this story. All have been co-authored by students and staff, and all have shared their journey here.

The partnership models described in this book are diverse, and so are the styles author teams have chosen to document these partnerships. Rather than trying to impose one homogeneous structure, which would attempt to shoehorn these multifaceted approaches into a one-size-fits-all neat little template, the book celebrates such diversity, deliberately keeping the variety of styles intact. It will be up to the reader to decide whether they prefer to read about staff–student partnerships in the form of an almost scientific report, a think piece or a script.

The book falls loosely into two sections, the first focusing mainly on staff–student partnerships in education enhancement, the second on staff–student partnerships in learning and research. This compartmentalization, however, is not exclusive, and the book is very much intended as a 'dipping in' volume.

Chapter 1 sets the scene by giving some of the historical background to staff–student partnerships in learning, research and education enhancement. It questions the role of students as partners in education enhancement from the supposedly increasing 'marketization' of higher education. Within a context where inquiry-based learning (IBL) was both the message and the method of staff–student partnerships, the chapter suggests IBL as an approach that 'challenges staff and students to rethink and reconfigure conventional relations of power and control in the classroom' (p. 4). Chapter 2, at least in part, picks up where Chapter 1 left off, illustrating two examples of long-term staff–student partnerships for educational enhancement in more detail. Both networks that are discussed existed for a number of years, allowing their members to grow in a number of different roles and developing 'the credibility and the confidence, individually, collectively and institutionally, to work with staff as partners and to instigate meaningful educational change' (p. 27).

In Chapter 3, Kay Sambell and Linda Graham describe how a whole module engaged students to look at assessment for learning from the students' perspective, involving students to produce materials that could then be rolled out as an educational enhancement resource throughout the university. The students' work explicitly sees staff and students working in partnership as the way forward, sharing, with mutual responsibility, the effort it takes to make assessment work. Chapter 4 also discusses the creation of student-friendly materials – on plagiarism this time, and many points on 'creating a community of trust and a strong ethos to encourage good scholarship' (p. 59) echo those from the previous chapter. The focus, here, is on an institutional movement to change the 'us and them' attitude, and to work together as peers striving for academic integrity.

In Chapter 5, Lynn Reynolds describes how she, as a student, took the lead and worked with staff in making explicit the struggles students face when faced with academic writing. By writing an entire essay online, and sharing her thoughts and emotions around the process as she went along, Lynn invited comments from other students and the general public. The understanding gained from the process has, in turn, informed the practices of a peer-mentoring scheme for students' academic writing. Chapter 6, too, discusses students involved in the creation of materials, in the shape of e-learning resources produced by medical students, for medical students. The chapter acknowledges the many different relationships students engage in during such a process – partnerships between staff and students, the medical community, educational or e-learning developers and their student peers; and the benefits that can be gained when students are 'not only by educating other students but in educating us as educators' (p. 89).

In Chapter 7, the staff and student authors align their project – to integrate a teaching recognition scheme for postgraduate students into the existing institutional award system – with Lucas' Eight-Step (Lucas, 2000) model for collaborative academic change. An interesting thread running through from other chapters is the students' confusion at the internal workings of the institution, and how working in partnership with staff can help students understand how change might be facilitated within the institutional context. Niamh Collins and Jacqueline Potter did not have an easy ride, and their open discussion of challenges encountered sheds interesting light on staff–student partnerships. While Chapter 8 also looks into teaching awards, the context is very different from that of Chapter 7. Here, students from all levels are invited to put forward their teaching ideas, and the chapter analyses the types of submissions received, and what this might tell us about the ways in which students might prefer learning and teaching to take place.

Involving students as peer tutors is the focus of Chapter 9, where drama students helped sport students to improve their presentation skills. The chapter gives interesting insights into students' perceptions of peer teaching, and throws open the question of how students might best be trained and supported in order to teach their peers. The performing arts also play a large part in Chapter 10, albeit from a different perspective. Here, Rebekka Kill, Keeley McDonnell and Michael Thorne explore the boundaries of staff and student identity when both come together to research and perform. Their use of a script to illustrate their ideas and identities documents their journey through a number of research projects and performances, and charts the formation of their partnership.

In Chapter 11, Mark Manning, Lesley Willcoxson, Katrina Gething and Natasha Johnston describe how students were actively involved in research, as part of a Level 3 undergraduate module on advanced research methods. Staff and students jointly explored the research question 'What factors influence students' decisions to drop out of university?', and the chapter outlines the way the module was taught, as well as some unexpected outcomes. Where students might publish outcomes of their own research is discussed in Chapter 12, which outlines the creation of *Reinvention: a Journal of Undergraduate Research*. Written by David Metcalfe, Caroline Gibson and Cath Lambert, the chapter problematizes the existence of such journals – as opposed to students publishing in the same journals as staff, and illustrates their journey with responses from students and staff from the academic community. In Chapter 13, Brad Wuetherick and Lisa McLaughlin explore students' perceptions of research in the learning environment. The partnership described here is between the university administration and the students' union, and the chapter, like many others in this volume, challenges existing hierarchies and draws on Brew (2006) and her call for universities as communities of inquiry. The breaking down of boundaries and existing hierarchies is also very much the focus of Chapter 14, where staff and students collaborated to write and publish a chapter for a Level 1 textbook. Heather Sharp, Linda Stanley, and Marie Hayward look in detail into existing barriers and how these might be overcome, and continue that discussion in Chapter 15, which summarizes and expands on some of the common threads that appear throughout this volume, including those of power, transience and the benefits of working in partnership.

To most readers, these benefits may well only reiterate what they already know, and yet I hope that the various journeys, ideologies, viewpoints and ideas described throughout the book will provide a point of inspiration, and encouragement for those looking to work with students or staff, in a move towards a community where all members knowingly and willingly share the responsibility for learning, teaching and research.

References

Brew A. (2006), *Research and Teaching: Beyond the Divide*. New York: Palgrave MacMillan.

Fiennes, T. and Little, S. (2007), *Beyond Consultation: Creative Student Partnerships in Educational Development and Innovation*. Paper presented at Higher Education Academy Conference, Harrogate, UK, July 2007.

Lucas, A. F. (2000), 'A collaborative model for leading academic change', in A. F. Lucas and Associates (eds), *Leading Academic Change*. San Francisco: Jossey-Bass.

Chapter 1

Perspectives on Staff–Student Partnership in Learning, Research and Educational Enhancement

Philippa Levy, Sabine Little and Natalie Whelan

This chapter arises out of our work together for CILASS, the Centre for Inquiry-based Learning in the Arts and Social Sciences, at the University of Sheffield. CILASS is a Centre for Excellence in Teaching and Learning (CETL) that was awarded to the university by the Higher Education Funding Council for England (HEFCE) in 2005 as part of a large-scale national initiative in learning and teaching enhancement in higher education (HE). It ran a five-year programme supporting further development in inquiry-based learning (IBL) at Sheffield and worked on this theme with other HE institutions nationally. Staff–student partnership was an important principle in the CETL's approach to educational development and knowledge-building, as it is in the pedagogical rationale that informed its exploration of the practice and impact of IBL and undergraduate research.

The idea of staff–student partnership implies shared responsibility and cooperative or collaborative action, in relation to shared purposes. In this chapter, we discuss this in relation to learning, teaching, research and educational enhancement. We begin by briefly considering the theme of partnership in the light of the discourse of consumerism that runs through contemporary HE and the hierarchical nature of the social structures embedded in university life. We then move on to consider its meaning in relation to the ideal of the university as an inclusive, democratic community of learners and scholars based on the integration of learning, research and teaching. Against this background of competing 'versions' of HE, we offer an overview of forms that staff–student partnership can take in learning, research and educational enhancement, with comment from our personal perspectives as academic and educational developer-researcher staff (Philippa Levy and Sabine Little) and undergraduate student coordinator of the CILASS student ambassador network (Natalie Whelan).

Learning, research and the research/teaching nexus

We believe that the theme of staff–student partnership reaches to the heart of debates about the values and role of the twenty-first century university. One widely-recognized effect of the increasing marketization of HE in western economies since the 1980s has been the positioning of students as consumers of education, reflecting and reinforcing their broader social identity and power as customers in a consumer society (Molesworth et al., 2009). Commentators draw attention to the way in which consumerist discourse frames students as powerful agents in the shaping of HE. For example, Naidoo and Jamieson (2005) argue that many of the characteristics of educational provision and teaching quality assurance in the sector, such as the focus on educational choice through modularization and on student satisfaction in the evaluation of courses, can be seen as an illustration of this. While students' status as customers does not seem contentious in relation to the many services provided by universities – such as libraries and accommodation – problematic issues do arise in relation to their mission in learning, teaching and research. An often expressed concern is that where education is framed as a product or service, teaching is recast as a delivery mechanism and student learning as a passive experience (McCulloch, 2009). Widely espoused desired outcomes for HE, such as independence of thought, critical judgment, self-belief and initiative, depend on opportunities for active student engagement and shared responsibility between educator and student.

If the discourse of consumerism is a powerful element in the mix of structural factors that shape the experience of learning and teaching in HE, the 'academic capital' possessed by academic staff, as conceptualized by Bourdieu (1988), is perhaps more powerful still. Bourdieu's analysis illustrates how hierarchical distance between teacher and student remains deeply entrenched in the patterns of thought, identity and practice of the traditional university. This is reflected in academic language that often is inaccessible to students until they have progressed through a number of 'levels' of study and that constrains genuine staff–student dialogue (Northedge, 2003). Brew (2006) suggests that it is also reflected in the hierarchical positioning of 'scholarship' and 'research' above 'learning' (and teaching) and that the practice of keeping students 'at arms' length' from research for several years can be seen as a means of shoring up the higher status of staff in the institution. Seeing students, including undergraduates, as full partners in the academy's research mission represents a radical challenge to this conventional hierarchy (Lambert, 2009).

Thinking along these lines, it is not difficult to paint a rather bleak picture of the structural characteristics of the staff–student relationship in contemporary HE. Alongside the progressive educational values and practices of many individual staff and the commitment of many institutions to 'student-centredness' in learning and teaching, it seems clear that there is considerable tension between the ideal of partnership and the effects of consumerist discourse and academic hierarchy, not to mention those of a wide range of other factors. Yet sector-wide interest in the theme of partnership is growing. In the UK the former Chief Executive of the Higher Education Academy argues that the future of HE must be based on 'engaged partnership and shared responsibility between academics and students' (Ramsden, 2008, p. 8). The 'student as consumer' discourse increasingly is being challenged, not least by students themselves. A recent President of the UK's National Union of Students recently has argued that genuine enhancement of the HE experience will depend on the creation of much stronger collaborations between staff and students built on a 'communities of practice' rather than a 'consumer-provider' model (Streeting and Wise, 2009). McCulloch (2009) proposes the alternative concept of 'co-production' as the basis for reconfiguring staff–student relations in the direction of cooperative engagement in a shared enterprise, in pragmatic recognition of the mutual expectations and demands that arise from the resourcing of HE by both student and university.

New perspectives on staff–student partnership are also emerging from ongoing re-thinking of the 'research-teaching nexus' in HE. The idea of the modern university as a community of learners and scholars engaged in the pursuit and building of knowledge through collective inquiry reaches back at least as far as the vision put forward in the early nineteenth century by Wilhelm von Humboldt, founder of the University of Berlin. More recently, the work of the Boyer Commission on Educating Undergraduates in the USA in the late 1990s has lent momentum to international interest in strengthening the role of inquiry and research in the undergraduate experience in both research-intensive and teaching-intensive universities. In arguing for students' full inclusion in the research cultures of universities, through IBL in the curriculum and provision of co-curricular research opportunities, the Commission's vision challenges both the didactic style of teaching that it observed in much undergraduate education in America's research universities and the conventionally dichotomous relationship between teaching and research (Boyer Commission, 1998). As Rowland (2005) points out, when inquiry is seen as the common link between what students do as learners, and what teachers do as scholars and researchers, exciting possibilities for more integrated approaches to higher learning emerge in which students may be brought into fuller participation in the scholarly communities of their discipline and into identities as co-learners, not only with peers, but with more experienced scholars and researchers. Examples of initiatives to strengthen the relation between teaching and research include the large-scale 'student as scholar' curriculum redesign project at the Miami University, Ohio (Hodge et al., 2008) and the work of the Reinvention Centre CETL hosted by the University of Warwick and Oxford Brookes University. In the latter, in an explicit rejection and reversal of consumerist discourse, students are seen as 'producers' (Taylor and Wilding, 2009). Extending this perspective, at the University of Lincoln Neary and Winn (2009, p. 216) envisage 'undergraduate students working in collaboration with academics to create work of social importance that is full of academic content and value'.

Partnership in learning and research

Contemporary educational theory and research offer an underpinning rationale for staff–student partnership in learning and teaching. The principle of partnership is especially to the fore in theoretical perspectives that emphasize the role of intersubjectivity, or the social negotiation of meaning, in the learning process. These include the socio-cultural view that teaching is essentially concerned with facilitating students' access to, and participation in, the discourses and practices of an academic community. Partnership models envisage educators bringing their discipline-based knowledge and educational expertise, and students their prior learning experiences, their existing academic or professional knowledge, and their status as legitimate participants in their disciplinary communities, to share authority in the process of jointly constructing meaning. The ideal of partnership is particularly explicit in the 'constructivist-developmental' model of undergraduate education proposed by Baxter-Magolda (2009). Her Learning Partnerships model is based on three principles: validating learners' ability to know, situating learning in learners' experience and defining learning as mutually constructing meaning (p. 150).

These principles articulate well with IBL, and pedagogies based on student inquiry and research open up a range of possibilities for strengthening staff–student partnership. IBL challenges staff and students to rethink and reconfigure conventional relations of power and control in the classroom and to find new forms of interaction that fit with the values and purposes of inquiry in the production of different forms of knowledge. In IBL, students are encouraged to take a significant amount of responsibility for their learning, and to use the scholarly and research practices of their academic or professional disciplines to move towards autonomy in creating and sharing knowledge. Some IBL approaches involve students in large-scale, 'whole-cycle' research projects while others involve them in exploring a smaller-scale question or theme and developing understanding of, and skills in, specific elements of a larger research process. Academic and other staff provide guidance, and often students are encouraged to share the results of their inquiries with each other and wider audiences, including through peer-reviewed publication where appropriate.

From the perspective of the IBL educator, a key challenge is to establish conditions in which students' inquiries are stimulated and can flourish, and in which students are supported effectively in developing relevant inquiry skills. In relation to IBL we believe that it is important to emphasize *shared* staff–student responsibility in learning to counter the misconception that full responsibility is 'handed over' to students. Staff–student partnership in IBL will include, for example, staff working with students to help them formulate and pursue their own lines of inquiry, or assisting students in the development of information literacy skills of relevance to their research. Support takes the form of tasks, assessments, resources, facilitation and environments that are designed to scaffold the inquiry process. Our experience in CILASS has convinced us of the value of taking a holistic and institutional perspective on designing for staff–student partnership in IBL, including where possible in relation to the physical spaces in learning and teaching. Impact evaluation showed that flexible, technology-rich 'collaboratory' spaces – spaces that were designed specifically to support IBL in humanities and social sciences disciplines by the CETL – fostered opportunities to reconfigure learning and teaching relationships in the direction of collaboration around shared practices of inquiry. Other evaluation findings from CILASS IBL development projects chime with those in the wider evidence base (as summarized, for example, by Healey and Jenkins, 2009), including enhanced student engagement with learning and their intellectual and personal development in areas such as changed beliefs and understandings about their own roles in learning and knowledge creation.

IBL can be seen as a form of active learning in which students engage in 'research-like' activities (Elton, 2009). But in allowing for students to engage with authentically open-ended lines of investigation, IBL in some modes also offers students the potential to engage in 'real' scholarship and research, in ways that extend learning into the realms of new insight or discovery and therefore connect students with academic staff in the production of genuinely new knowledge. Bereiter's (2002) distinction between knowledge construction and knowledge building – the former understood as personal conceptual development (learning) and the latter as contribution to the improvement of ideas in an academic or professional domain – offers a useful point of reference for differentiating between different modes and experiences of IBL according to intended or actual outcomes. From the staff perspective, IBL with an open-ended, knowledge-building orientation offers potential for close integration between teaching and research (Spronken-Smith and Walker, in press). The nature of staff–student partnership in IBL differs, therefore, in different contexts of knowledge creation. When staff and students work together on problems or questions designed primarily to engage students actively with an existing knowledge-base ('inquiry for learning') the partnership is grounded in shared responsibility for the co-construction of meaning. When they work together on lines of inquiry that offer opportunities for the development of new disciplinary insights and discoveries ('inquiry for knowledge-building'), perhaps in the context of a course with a direct relation to a staff member's personal research interests, there is an additional element of potential for joint discovery. Perhaps in undergraduate education it is still the third-year research dissertation, or equivalent, that most often offers the potential for staff and students to experience the partnership of co-inquiry, as described by Natalie:

> Sitting in [my supervisor's] office with a mathematical problem in front of us I felt nothing but equal, as we both thought our thoughts out loud and drew upon each other's suggestions to find a solution to the problem: a moment of pure partnership where two heads were better than one. This moment that I experienced can be captured in a more prolonged partnership, although it is a lot rarer.

The challenge is to find ways of making this kind of experience more central to the experience of learning in our universities. Co-curricular opportunities have a role to play here; in addition to embedding IBL in the curriculum, staff–student partnership in knowledge-building also can be taken forward through research enrichment schemes that enable some students to carry out research in partnership with academic staff through vacation scholarships. There is a well-established tradition of this activity in the USA in particular, where schemes historically have been more common in the sciences than in other discipline areas. Evaluations of undergraduate research opportunity programmes (UROP) have shown highly positive impacts on students' intellectual, personal and professional development, including enhanced identification with departmental research cultures and more collegial relations with academic tutors (Healey and Jenkins, 2009). John and Creighton (2010) comment that this body of research confirms the benefit of UROP for student apprenticeship in a research community of practice.

Current initiatives in the UK and beyond suggest how developing an integrated focus on inquiry and research across both curriculum and co-curriculum can enrich universities' provision for a 'research-led' or 'research-engaged' student experience, incorporating the principle of staff–student partnership. CILASS's initial focus as a CETL was solely on IBL in the curriculum. In response to trends in the wider sector, combined with internal institutional interest, in 2008–09 it instigated a pilot initiative for the (co-curricular) Sheffield Undergraduate Research Experience (SURE) scheme. This enabled staff and students to work together on research projects that were proposed either by staff or by students, and it included a student-facilitated peer-support network and a culminating poster conference. Benchmarking against similar national and international schemes showed that benefits experienced at Sheffield were in line with those identified elsewhere. Students reported enhanced research skills and understanding, improved subject knowledge, increased intellectual confidence and a rewarding sense of enhanced participation in, and contribution to, their discipline. Staff feedback was also highly positive, with many projects directly supporting their own work and some resulting in peer-reviewed publications, jointly by staff and students or single-authored by students targeting peer-reviewed journals for student work. Research collaboration tends to be the norm in science and engineering but is less frequent in the humanities and social sciences, so a scheme that was open to these latter disciplines provided valuable opportunities for students to experience partnership with more experienced scholars and researchers and for both parties to benefit.

Partnership in educational enhancement and inquiry

Universities in the UK are increasingly seeking to involve students more actively in the continuous improvement of the student experience in areas including curriculum planning, learning and teaching innovation, assessment and quality assurance (Ramsden, 2008). For example, Healey et al. (2010) describe a new initiative to involve students in the development of institution-wide learning, teaching and assessment strategy in one UK university. The 'partnership' trend in enhancement has been given considerable momentum by the national CETL programme, with CETLs having been encouraged to involve students fully in their governance, as well as in the development, evaluation and dissemination of new learning and teaching practices. However, institutional attempts to engage students in shaping the learning experience historically have rested more on the discourse and practices of representation and consultation than on those of partnership and collaboration; for example, as Bovill et al. (2007) point out, when it comes to input into curriculum design, employers may be consulted far more often than students. A recent report to HEFCE shows that while there is growing interest and activity in this area, the bigger picture in the UK is little changed: models of student engagement in enhancement are, in the main, limited to feedback questionnaires, committee representation and liaison officer roles (Little et al., 2009). Moreover, institutional rationales for placing emphasis on these processes and practices appear to be more about viewing students as customers than about trying to involve them as partners in a learning community (p. 58). The report concludes that there is a need for broader discussion across the sector on models of engagement that focus on notions of learning partnerships within a learning community context.

If staff–student partnership in educational enhancement is at a relatively early stage of development in HE, this contrasts with the considerable amount of funding and interest that has been invested in involving school pupils in decision-making processes in their institutions, and in engaging them in the research process leading to educational change (Atweh and Burton, 1995; ESRC, 2001–2004; Fielding, 2004, 2006, 2007). One model taking into account issues regarding staff–student partnerships in the school context was introduced by Hart (1992). Hart proposed a hierarchy (or 'ladder') of pupil participation in which the first three rungs (labelled 'manipulation', 'decoration' and 'tokenism') are identified as standing outside genuine pupil participation. The other rungs ('assigned but informed', 'consulted and informed', 'adult-initiated and shared decisions', 'child-directed' and 'child-initiated with shared decisions') can be taken out of the ladder's hierarchical structure and adapted in order to highlight various forms of staff–student partnership as these may occur in the HE context (see Figure 1.1).

Figure 1.1 illustrates the complexities that may arise, once we look at the staff–student partnership model in more detail. The various stages of bringing about change in education – instigating action, deciding action and taking action – may be led by staff or students, or indeed jointly. The lines between the 'waypoints' thus illustrate potential pathways through educational change, but they also function as a continuum, rather than links between defined fix-points. 'Leadership', in this case, is not an absolute concept. Within our work at CILASS, for example, a module leader (staff) might invite their departmental student ambassador to listen to and advise on plans for a new module [Staff Instigate Action]. Following the student ambassador's input, both staff and students would discuss ways in which the module might be improved [Staff and Students Decide Action], which the member of staff would then implement [Staff Take Action]. In a different example, student ambassadors decided to offer a range of workshops to help staff engage students about inquiry-based learning. They created a bank of seven workshops on different themes [Students Instigate Action]. When a member of staff showed interest (strictly speaking, this could also be classed as [Staff Instigate Action]), student ambassadors would meet with them and discuss tailoring the workshop to the department's needs [Staff and Students Decide Action]. The student ambassadors would then run the workshop for the department's students, with the member of staff as an active participant in discussions [Staff and Students Take Action].

While the model allows the pathway up either the 'staff only' or 'student only' side, we have decided to represent this journey with 'broken' lines, since they are not part of a 'partnership' model.

An interesting question, perhaps, is to ask who, historically, is more likely to initiate educational change and in what ways. Student satisfaction surveys and a focus, in staff–student committees and similar contexts, on students raising 'issues' rather than ideas may lead to a 'customer complaints' model of student participation. Developing pathways that foster more collaborative approaches is important in taking student involvement in enhancement beyond representation and consultation to a more

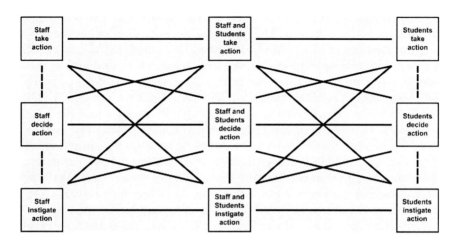

FIGURE 1.1   Initiation, decision-making and action regarding educational change
through staff–student partnerships

meaningful and productive interaction. We believe that, in part, this will
necessitate a change in perception among both staff and students away
from the customer-provider model of HE. Moreover, if we want to transform
the notion of student voice (Lincoln, 1995) into the idea of staff–student
dialogue, then the question of language needs to be considered. From our
own experience, involving CILASS student ambassadors in learning and
teaching discussions at departmental and institutional level often puts them
face-to-face with policies and procedures in a language not intended for a
student audience and based on a 'backdrop of unspoken assumptions, which
provides the frame of reference within which it is meaningful' (Northedge,
2003). To ensure that students are not discouraged, and staff treat students
as partners, careful facilitation of staff–student partnership is required,
to create a 'holding environment' (Kegan, 1995) in which both staff and
students can safely grow and develop, while challenging each other along
the way.

In the course of our work on this chapter, Natalie raised the question
'why',

> Students go to university to learn about something that interests them.
> They are also paying a high price for their education, and so why shouldn't
> they have a say in what and how they learn?

Here she is asking how students can be encouraged to recognize and
embrace their 'right' to get involved in partnership-based enhancement
activity in a way that recognizes the implications of the part-financing

of HE through student fees but also moves beyond the framework of customer-provider relations. The 'students as partners in enhancement' initiative developed by CILASS – described in more detail in Chapter 2 of this book – was an exploration of a new approach to student engagement in our institution. It took the form of a student ambassador network comprising a cohort of 28 undergraduates (one from each of the CETL's 'core' academic departments in the university) operating under the joint facilitation of a member of staff and a student. From the point of view of the staff co-facilitator (Sabine), what was most interesting was the upward spiral of confidence and ambition over the four years of the network's existence. As the network grew in confidence, new, incoming students accepted the current stage of its development as the 'status quo' and built further on it. This suggests the potential of a 'community of practice' involving staff and students alike, as well as a type of 'communal consciousness' that may exist independently from the individuals who participate. The idea that such a 'communal consciousness' may carry a partnership model forward, however, does not mean that the practical logistics of student transience can be overlooked. Any long-term change facilitation involving staff and students is complicated by students leaving the institution, necessitating continuous induction of incoming students. Maintaining a critical mass that allows work to progress is a balancing act that, in Sabine and Natalie's experience, is made easier by having a large group of students involved.

At Sheffield, the CILASS student ambassador network model is perceived to have made a strong contribution to cultural change at the university in relation to institutional practice in educational enhancement, inspiring the development of similar networks in three faculties and new forms of partnership work in a range of professional services. Students are becoming more involved in curriculum design and evaluation. As Natalie put it, 'two heads are better than one' and this approach yielded successful solutions in educational development, with academic staff and undergraduates working together productively to enrich the educational experience of students. Partnerships led to more informative evaluations, new departmental initiatives and the redesign of some areas of undergraduate curricula in ways that proved highly productive.

Evaluation of student ambassador network activities provided evidence that when students are involved and enthused by educational enhancement, they can move the institutional agenda forward with energy and in creative ways. In order to maintain such energy, students need to feel appreciated and valued. The co-facilitation model (by one member of staff and a student) was found to be a useful means of ensuring continued motivation, while giving academic staff who engage with the network a stable point of contact over time. As well as a financial resource to pay students for their time, ongoing staff resource was needed to facilitate and develop this approach to student partnership work and this included, but was much more

than, provision of organizational support. For example, Sabine offered training for students in the conduct of educational evaluation and research, as
well as support for their familiarization with strategic and operational issues
relating to the CETL's work and with educational issues relating specifically
to IBL.

Such support not only helps to ensure that students feel equipped for
their role as partners with staff in educational enhancement, but also makes
explicit the experience skills and skills that they gain through their involvement and take away with them. As part of a study conducted by Su Arnall,
Natalie's successor as student network co-facilitator, student ambassadors
past and present were invited to highlight the main memories, experiences
and skills they had gained from their work for CILASS. Skills mentioned
invariably included those for which 'official' training had been provided
but also included organizational and teamwork skills developed as part of
the experience of partnership work. Ambassadors' memories and highlights
were as varied as their different roles in the network, but 'being treated as
equals' by staff and 'understanding more about how the university works'
often featured. In further evaluative feedback, some students reported that
through their involvement in enhancement activity they had gained better
understanding of their own experiences of learning and teaching, and
that this had contributed to their own engagement with their programmes
of study.

We have noted already that student partnership in enhancement may
well involve them not only in the day-to-day groundwork of educational
change facilitation (for example, discussing course development with
staff or engaging with other students to promote educational resources
or approaches) but also in the evaluation and scholarship that surrounds
educational practice. By involving students in the scholarship of teaching
and learning (SoTL), and in institutional research relating to teaching and
the student experience, they occupy the position of co-researchers with
academic and other staff. In the broad definition of SoTL offered by the
Carnegie Foundation for the Advancement of Teaching, four core practices
are identified: 'framing questions, gathering and exploring evidence, trying out and refining new insights in the classroom, and going public on
what is learned in ways that others can build on' (Huber and Hutchings,
2006, p. 20). Although participatory models of SoTL exist, for example
in the context of educational action research, typically in HE it has been
conducted with student involvement limited to participation as research
'subjects'. But the idea that HE students might be involved more widely as
research partners seems to be spreading. For example, Ainley (2008) suggests enlisting students as researchers to explore what he calls 'the $64,000
question' of how students experience HE, and inspiring examples of staff–
student partnerships in scholarly inquiry and institutional research into
learning and teaching are beginning to be documented (e.g. Taylor and

Wilding, 2009; Werder and Otis, 2010). A range of benefits of collaborative approaches to research into educational enhancement have been reported (e.g. Carless, 2006; Zepke et al., 2006). For example, Carless notes in his research on student perceptions of feedback on assessment that student-led focus groups yielded much more, and better, data than that gathered through focus groups run by academic staff. Manor et al. (2010) suggest that benefits include enriching the research field by broadening the types of research question being pursued, enhancing student researchers' sense of power and responsibility within the learning and teaching relationship, and challenging academic staff to 'rethink their assumptions about education and students and to re-envision the classroom as a truly collaborative learning space' (p.11).

Conclusion . . . and further questions

With this chapter we have aimed to offer an overview of some of the current trends and themes in staff–student partnership in HE that have been of particular relevance to our own work, that have stimulated new perspectives in our own thinking, and that we believe have wide significance. Questions we asked ourselves and each other during the writing of the chapter include:

- To what extent can power relations between staff and students be challenged and changed in HE given its prevailing ideological and structural characteristics, or are the barriers such that it is not possible to envisage wide-scale cultural change in the direction of genuine partnership?
- Why should students contribute to changing something that will not matter to them directly in a year? How do we begin to address the need for partnership in educational enhancement and inquiry, bearing in mind the transient trajectories of students in comparison with staff and the other pressures on both students and staff, including time and priorities?

For us, these remain open questions. A wide range of factors militate against close staff–student partnerships in HE and it would be self-defeating to ignore them. We are enthusiastic and optimistic about emergent practices and future possibilities but are wary of idealizing the concept of partnership and the related ideas of community and co-production. We do not assume, either, that consensus on issues of learning and teaching in HE will be reached. HE is a contested arena. However, by working together in ways that allow staff and students to share authority in learning, teaching, research and enhancement, new knowledge and practices will emerge through contestation as well as collaboration. We believe that opportunities for dialogue and debate, persistence in inviting and supporting student participation, and ongoing challenges to the customer-provider model of HE will be central to the progress of cultural change. We look forward to wider sharing in the sector of emergent practices and experiences in staff–student partnership, and to institutions providing further encouragement and resource to support creative, purposeful experimentation in this area.

Finally, a comment on process. Writing this chapter has challenged us, as it has several other author teams who worked on this book (e.g. see Chapter 15). Reaching a shared language that would satisfy us all was no easy task and neither was the weighting of topics or the negotiation of perspectives. Long-term deadlines meant that the original student author's move out of university into a job unrelated to education led, understandably, to a shift in priorities, resulting in a change within the author team. Nevertheless, we have found the experience of writing this stimulating and rewarding and we see the case for reinventing staff–student relationships in HE along the lines of genuine partnership as compelling – and current initiatives in this direction across the sector as hopeful – despite the challenges posed to institutions, staff and students alike.

References

Ainley, P. (2008), 'The varieties of student experience – an open research question and some ways to answer it', *Studies in Higher Education*, 33, (5), 615–624.

Atweh, B. and Burton, L. (1995), 'Students as researchers: rationale and critique', *British Educational Research Journal*, 21, (5), 561–575.

Baxter-Magolda, M. (2009), 'Educating students for self-authorship: learning partnerships to achieve complex outcomes', in C. Kreber (ed.), *The University and its Disciplines: Teaching and Learning Within and Beyond Disciplinary Boundaries*. New York and London: Routledge, pp. 143–156.

Bereiter, C. (2002), *Education and the Mind in the Knowledge Age*. Mahwah, N.J.: Lawrence Erlbaum Associates.

Bourdieu, P. (1988), *Homo Academicus*, translated from the French by P. Collier. Cambridge: Polity Press.

Bovill, C., Morss, K. and Bulley, C. (2007), *First Year Curriculum Design – Literature Review*. QAA Scotland. Retrieved 28 April 2010 from http://www.enhancementthemes.ac.uk/documents/firstyear/CurriculumDesignLit%20ReviewFINAL.pdf

Boyer Commission on Educating Undergraduates in the Research University (1998), *Reinventing Undergraduate Education: A Blueprint for America's Research Universities*. Stony Brook: State University of New York at Stony Brook. Retrieved 28 April 2010 from http://naples.cc.sunysb.edu/pres/boyer.nsf

Brew, A. (2006), *Research and Teaching: Beyond the Divide*. Basingstoke: Palgrave Macmillan.

Carless, D. (2006), 'Differing perceptions in the feedback process', *Studies in Higher Education*, 31, (2), 219–233.

Elton, L. (2009), 'Guiding students into a discipline: the significance of the student's view', in C. Kreber (ed.), *The University and its Disciplines: Teaching and Learning Within and Beyond Disciplinary Boundaries*. New York and London: Routledge, pp. 129–139.

Economic and Social Research Council (ESRC) (2001–2004), *Consulting Pupils About Teaching and Tearning* (ESRC Network Project). Retrieved 28 April 2010 from www.consultingpupils.co.uk

Fielding, M. (2004),'Transformative approaches to student voice: theoretical underpinnings, recalcitrant realities', *British Educational Research Journal*, 30, (2), 295–311.

Fielding, M. (2006), 'Leadership, radical student engagement and the necessity of person-centred education', *International Journal of Leadership in Education: Theory and Practice*, 9, (4), 299–313.

Fielding, M. (2007), 'Beyond "voice": new roles, relations, and contexts in researching with young people', *Discourse: Studies in Cultural Politics of Education*, 28, (3), 301–310.

Hart, R. (1992), *Children's Participation: From Tokenism to Citizenship*. Florence: International Child Development Centre, UNICEF.

Healey, M. and Jenkins, A. (2009), *Developing Undergraduate Research and Inquiry*. York: Higher Education Academy.

Healey, M., Mason O'Connor, K. and Broadfoot, P. (2010), 'Reflections on engaging students in the process and product of strategy development for learning, teaching and assessment: an institutional case study', *International Journal for Academic Development*, 15, (1), 19–32.

Hodge, D., Haynes, C., LePore, P., Pasquesi, K. and Hirsh, M. (2008), 'From inquiry to discovery: developing the student as scholar in a networked world'. Keynote in P. Levy and P. McKinney (eds), *Proceedings of the 3rd Learning Through Enquiry Alliance Conference*. University of Sheffield: Centre for Inquiry-based Learning in the Arts and Social Sciences, pp. 3–18.

Huber, M. T. and Hutchings, P. (2006), *The Advancement of Learning: Building the Teaching Commons. A Carnegie Foundation Report on the Scholarship of Teaching and Learning in Higher Education*. Stanford; Jossey-Bass.

John, J. and Creighton, J. (2010, forthcoming), 'Researcher development: the impact of undergraduate research opportunity programmes (UROP) on students in the UK'. *Studies in Higher Education*.

Kegan, R. (1995), *In Over our Heads: Mental Demands of Modern Life*. Cambridge, MA.: Harvard University Press.

Lambert, C. (2009), 'Pedagogies of participation in higher education: a case for research-based learning', *Pedagogy Culture and Society*, 17,(3), 295–309.

Lincoln, Y. (1995), 'In search of students' voices', *Theory into Practice*, 34, (2), 88–93.

Little, B., Locke, W., Scesa, A. and Williams, R. (2009), *Report to HEFCE on Student Engagement*. Centre for Higher Education Research and Information (CHERI), Open University. Retrieved 28 April 2010 from http://www.open.ac.uk/cheri/documents/student-engagement-report.pdf

Manor, C., Bloch-Schulman, S., Flannery, K. and Felten, P. (2010), 'Foundations of student-faculty partnerships in the scholarship of teaching and learning: theoretical and developmental considerations', in C. Werder and M. Otis (eds), *Engaging Student Voices in the Study of Teaching and Learning*. Sterling, VA: Stylus.

McCulloch, A. (2009), 'The student as co-producer: learning from public administration about the student-university relationship', *Studies in Higher Education*, 34, (2), 171–183.

Molesworth, M., Nixon, E. and Scullion, R. (2009), 'Having, being and higher education: the marketisation of the university and the transformation of the student into consumer', *Teaching in Higher Education*, 14, (3), 277–287.

Naidoo C. and Jamieson I. (2005), 'Empowering participants or corroding learning? Towards a research agenda on the impact of student consumerism in higher education', *Journal of Education Policy*, 20, (3), 267–281.

Neary, M. and Winn, J. (2009), 'The student as producer: reinventing the student experience in higher education', in M. Neary, H. Stevenson, and L. Bell (eds), *The Future of Higher Education: Policy, Pedagogy and the Student Experience*. London: Continuum, pp. 126–138.

Northedge, A. (2003), 'Enabling participation in academic discourse', *Teaching in Higher Education*, 8, (2), 169–180.

Ramsden, P. (2008), *Teaching and the Student Experience*. Report presented to the Department of Innovation, Universities and Skills Debate on the Future of Higher Education. Retrieved 9 November 2009 from http://www.dius.gov.uk/higher_education/shape_and_structure/he_debate/teaching_and_student_experience.aspx

Rowland, S. (2005), 'Intellectual love and the link between teaching and research', in R. Barnett (ed.), *Reshaping the University: New Relationships Between Research, Scholarship and Teaching*. Buckingham: Society for Research into Higher Education/Open University Press, pp. 92–102.

Spronken-Smith, R. and Walker, S. (in press), 'Can inquiry-based learning strengthen links between teaching and research?', *Studies in Higher Education*.

Streeting, G. and Wise, G. (2009), *Rethinking the Values of Higher Education – Consumption, Partnership or Community?* Gloucester: Quality Assurance Agency for Higher Education.

Taylor P. and Wilding, D. (2009), *Rethinking the Values of Higher Education – the Student as Collaborator and Producer? Undergraduate Research as a Case Study*. Gloucester: Quality Assurance Agency for Higher Education. Retrieved 28 April 2010 from http://www.qaa.ac.uk/students/studentEngagement/Undergraduate.pdf

Werder, C. and Otis, M. (2010), *Engaging Student Voices in the Study of Teaching and Learning*. Sterling, VA: Stylus.

Zepke, N., Leach, L. and Prebble, T. (2006), 'Being learner centred: one way to improve student retention?', *Studies in Higher Education*, 31, (5), 587–600.

Chapter 2

A Collaborative Evaluation of Student–Staff Partnership in Inquiry-Based Educational Development

Emma Barnes, Louise Goldring, Alison Bestwick and Jamie Wood

This chapter explores how students have been involved in curriculum development at two universities in the United Kingdom. At both universities undergraduate and postgraduate students are paid by educational development and research units to work in partnership with academic and learning support staff to improve the student learning experience. The chapter uses a series of case examples to illustrate the methods that have been used to pursue this aim and to demonstrate some of the learning that has happened as a consequence. It is argued that staff need to create meaningful partnerships with students if the inclusivity and effectiveness of educational change is to be maximized. We suggest that students have a positive effect on the curriculum when they are treated as partners by staff in academic and service departments and their roles and responsibilities are clearly defined. The chapter closes by making a number of recommendations relating to implementation and transferability of practice.

In 2005 two Centres for Excellence in Teaching and Learning (CETL), with a special focus on inquiry-based learning (IBL), were established by the Higher Education Funding Council for England (HEFCE).

Pedagogical literature refers to both 'enquiry-based learning' (e.g. Khan and O'Rourke, 2004; Hutchings, 2007) and 'inquiry-based learning' (e.g. Brew, 2003; Healy, 2005). These differences in spelling have historical and linguistic roots; they do not reflect inherent pedagogical differences (Hutchings, 2007). We have chosen to utilize the term 'inquiry-based learning' (IBL) throughout this article.

The Centre for Excellence in Enquiry-Based Learning (CEEBL) was set up at the University of Manchester and the Centre for Inquiry-based Learning in the Arts and Social Sciences (CILASS) was established at the University of Sheffield, in recognition of institutional excellence in inquiry-based learning and with remits to further develop and disseminate that expertise.

Beyond their focus on IBL there are strong similarities between the two CETLs and the institutions to which they belong. The universities of Manchester and Sheffield are broadly comparable: both are large research-intensive institutions located in the north of England. In the field of student engagement, both CETLs placed active student involvement at the centre of their educational development activities and adopted similar approaches in doing so. This included the formation of networks comprised of students who were paid to develop, promote and support IBL in their departments, faculties, at an institutional level and externally through a range of activities.

Background

Bocock and Watson (1994a) suggest that one of the essential prerequisites for successful university reform was the establishing of 'common cause' between all those with a stake in the success of the institution. Scott and Watson (1994) concur, arguing that teachers needed to become increasingly active and willing partners in the enterprise of educational reform. While Bocock and Watson (1994a) include students in their vision of those participating in the common cause, there have been few systematic efforts to involve them, with some notable exceptions in recent years (Streeting and Wise, 2009; Taylor and Wilding, 2009).

The literature on student engagement in curriculum reform at the pre-university level is relatively rich, and represents a growing field (see Thiessen, 2006 for a survey). Studies have demonstrated that change initiatives in which students are embedded effectively benefit both the students and the schools concerned. Students are more engaged, develop their skills and knowledge, possess greater understanding of and support for the overall reform process, and can contribute much to 'improving what happens in classrooms and schools' (Thiessen, 2006, p. 352).

Regrettably, research into the role and impact of student educational development activities in higher education is thin, although some studies have been carried out. These studies support the proposition that student involvement in such initiatives provides similar benefits as in the better documented cases at pre-university level (Visser et al., 1998). Wood et al. (2009) examine the impact on students of involvement in the two student networks discussed here, and students reported numerous positive benefits, including the development of skills, knowledge and values. While this chapter focuses on students engaging directly in learning development activities, further research is needed into impact on the wider student body.

As outlined in the introductory chapter of this volume, what Baxter-Magolda (2003) has termed 'self-authorship' has been proposed as one of the most desirable outcomes of higher education in recent years. Self-authorship means that students have developed 'the internal capacity to choose one's beliefs, values, identity and relationships' rather than relying upon external authority to negotiate complex decisions about these issues in life during and after college (Baxter-Magolda and Crosby, 2006, p. 1). In order to exhibit the cognitive maturity, integrated identity and mature relationships expected of them as young adults, students must have opportunities to develop self-authorship at university. Most outcomes of higher education hinge on the capacity for self-authorship (e.g., intercultural maturity, critical thinking, decision-making, responsible citizenship). Engagement in paid employment and/or student affairs initiatives can be as important in the developing of these capacities as experiences situated in the curriculum and on campus. Baxter-Magolda noted that when 'professors and employers engaged participants in sharing authority and expertise, participants became aware of their role in an ongoing dialogue toward truth' and became 'partners with educators in the learning process' (2003, pp. 236, 245). Sharing authority and responsibility for curricular change with students could thus be highly beneficial for the students concerned and the institution as a whole. Such benefits could extend far into the wider community because students play a pivotal 'role in creating, implementing and maintaining standards within their community' through engagement 'in clarifying their own needs and articulating them to peers' (Baxter-Magolda, 2003, p. 239). Networks – including student networks – could therefore play a particularly important role in articulating this process in 'the large and heterogeneous universities of the future' (Scott and Watson, 1994, p. 44).

The concept of 'communities of practice' has been particularly influential in thinking about how educational change might be effected more broadly. Wenger (1999) defines communities of practice as a group or groups of people who have a mutual interest or passion for something in which they already have some knowledge or skill, and who interact regularly in order to further improve that skill or knowledge. Key characteristics of membership of such groups are a sense of active belonging or membership, of being able to make a difference through social action, and of collective meaning-making through common concepts and knowledge (McMillan and Chavis, 1986; Wenger, 1999). The active and participatory nature of the communities of practice theory has powerful potential connections to concepts of self-authorship, with its assumption that students will develop the capacity for independent thought and action in collaboration with educators, fellow students and the broader community.

It has been suggested recently that a communities of practice approach might be a good way of moving beyond models which understand learning not as production or delivery, but as induction (Coffield, 2008; Streeting and Wise, 2009). The emphasis would be on building relationships between students and staff, and with other students at all levels of study. It would require open debate at the level of policy among all members of the higher education community. At the practical level of implementation it would similarly involve collective, flexible and organic action and reflection from all concerned (Streeting and Wise, 2009). CEEBL and CILASS sought to adopt this kind of approach, promoting partnerships between students at all levels of study, and between students and staff, including educational development staff.

Although a collaborative approach that promotes the engagement of the full range of stakeholders offers benefits in terms of meaningful educational change and student learning, it is not unproblematic. Streeting and Wise (2009) suggest that issues of power and responsibility stand at the centre of efforts to implement more communal, participatory and partnership-based modes of education. Put bluntly, power creates opportunities for change but it can also build barriers. Critical theorists and educationalists such as Pierre Bourdieu (Bourdieu and Passeron, 1990), Paulo Freire (1996) and Michael Apple (1985) argue that traditional educational structures create very unequal power relationships between teachers and students. Such educational structures both represent and reproduce established social power relations and thus there may be powerful governmental, institutional, disciplinary, departmental, personal and professional pressures against participatory models of educational change. For example, individual members of staff may not be willing to give over some of their power (and responsibility) for decision-making at the level of the curriculum. Power relations are highly significant factors underpinning the ways in which staff envisage teaching, education and therefore educational change (Trowler and Cooper, 2002). Academic staff hold a number of different and often tacit assumptions about 'the nature of students in higher education (including their abilities and preferences)' (Trowler and Cooper, 2002, p. 229), and this may restrict their ability and disposition to act in partnership with students. Institutions may also find it hard to provide the resources necessary to support the creation of a system of truly collaborative educational development. It is also debatable whether the majority of students actually want to be engaged actively in improving their learning experience. This is due, at least partly, to preconceived, deeply held and socially constructed ideas about what a university education entails. Taylor and Wilding (2009) have thus argued persuasively that students should be given 'informed choices' in relation to their education: they do not have to be engaged in educational change or even participate in innovative educational activities, but they should be given the opportunity and information to decide for themselves.

In what follows we examine the operation of the student networks at CEEBL and CILASS in the light of the opportunities and challenges outlined in this literature review. First, however, it is necessary to describe the functioning of the two schemes.

The networks

The networks shared a range of characteristics (see Table 2.1). CILASS ambassadors and CEEBL interns worked with academic staff on educational and curriculum development projects and with members of the core teams at each CETL on strategic priorities. At both CETLs the initiative for staff–student collaboration could come from either party. The approach taken by the staff members with whom the students engaged was largely facilitative, but provided a constant focus within the comparatively rapid turnover of students.

The way in which the students worked, whether in groups or individually, was often inquiry-based: students might be given a task or have generated it for themselves, but were granted a relatively large degree of freedom in determining how to complete the task. One difference between the two networks is the students' level of study: whereas the majority of ambassadors at CILASS were undergraduate students, within the CEEBL intern body there was more of a mix between undergraduate, taught postgraduate and PhD students.

Supporting and inducting the networks

Students in the two networks were given many opportunities for personal and professional development as well as a great deal of choice over the focus of their work and a lot of flexibility with working hours. This ensured that students remained engaged, and enabled each member of the respective networks to work to their strengths.

Both CETLs wrote clear guidelines for incoming students and, as a continuously evolving community, relied on past network members to provide advice, hints and tips for new members. At CILASS, before becoming an ambassador, students would shadow a current ambassador's activities to find out more about the role. At CEEBL, interns attended a two-day practical induction at the start of the internships, where the focus was on training and team bonding before projects began. CEEBL also negotiated clear goals and deadlines for the interns by asking them to focus on a specific project throughout the year, which was chosen by the intern in conjunction with CEEBL staff. Interns were asked to produce a project plan and a timeline, with support from the CEEBL team. CILASS achieved much the same result with its working groups, each of which focused on specific outputs, such as a journal or a film. Each working group received specific training depending on its requirements and the needs of the project.

At both CETLs the staff coordinator played an important role as an intermediary between the members of the network, the core staff team and academic project leaders in departments. At CILASS facilitation was shared between a member of staff and a full-time student, working alongside each

Table 2.1 A comparison of both networks

CEEBL student intern programme	CILASS student ambassador network
Centre for Excellence in Enquiry-Based Learning, University of Manchester	Centre for Inquiry-based Learning in the Arts and Social Sciences, University of Sheffield
Ran from 2005–2010	Ran from 2006–2010
Developed out of the university's 'Students as Partners' model	Remit co-developed with first cohort of student ambassadors
Current students were recruited on an annual basis from a range of disciplines and degree levels with at least one student from each of the four faculties of the university (4–6 total per year)	CILASS ambassadors were recruited from the 26 departments that make up the Faculties of Arts and Social Sciences (up to 28 ambassadors interns per year)
Paid position	Paid position
Interns worked roughly five hours a week on a flexible basis	Each ambassador was budgeted to work for 60 hours over the academic year, roughly two hours per week on a flexible basis
Interns acted as co-consultants working with members of teaching staff in the development, delivery, evaluation and dissemination of IBL modules	Ambassadors worked with IBL staff 'champions' in their departments, in working groups, and with members of the CILASS core team
Interns also contributed to core CEEBL activities including research and evaluation	Ambassadors were involved in CILASS research and evaluation, including conference presentations and publications
Interns came together as a whole team for larger events such as workshops or conferences	Ambassadors worked in working groups on a number of activities, and as a whole network to organize an annual conference
Originally coordinated by a Sabbatical Officer, working closely with the Associate Director at CEEBL. In 2008, to increase consistency and support for the intern team, a full-time member of staff, the Student Engagement Officer, was appointed to manage the programme	Co-facilitated by a member of the CILASS core team and a student coordinator; a current student at the university who worked for 135 hours over the course of the year

other to organize and manage the activities of the network as a whole, to set priorities and plan for the future. The student co-facilitator also had a role in the governance of CILASS, sitting on a variety of committees, including the Steering Group and other decision-making bodies. Each student co-facilitator was encouraged to carry forward their own individual research project during their year in post. At CEEBL, as well as regular monthly meetings with all interns, the Student Engagement Officer held twice-yearly individual meetings with each intern as a way of recognizing and supporting their work and providing a time for reflection and improvement. There was also a strong focus on extensive and continuing development for the interns, including regular training sessions during the internship. At CILASS the sense of continuation and support was also achieved through turnover of ambassadors throughout the year rather than all at the start of the academic year. This meant that there were always some experienced ambassadors on hand to guide, train and support those who were less experienced.

Evaluation

In order to write this chapter we drew together all of the evaluative material on the two networks and critically reflected on what it told us about the operation and impact of the networks. There has been substantial evaluation of both networks throughout the time in which they have been operational, meaning that a wealth of evidence already existed. This material included:

- reflective self-evaluation reports completed by the CEEBL interns on a twice-yearly basis
- reflective focus groups that the CILASS ambassadors engaged in at the end of each year
- research presentations and publications that have been prepared, or are being prepared, that investigate specific aspects or impacts of the activities of the ambassador and intern networks (e.g. Wood et al., 2009).

In order to present the key findings of these processes in a digestible format we decided to pick out the main themes and illustrate them by reference to case examples. Where necessary, additional data were collected in order to flesh out the cases. We would like to thank past and present ambassadors and interns for their input into the development of the cases.

All four authors of this chapter have experience of being members of the student networks described and two have experience of coordinating the networks. We wanted these experiences, and as such our ethos of student–staff partnership, to be reflected in the genuinely collaborative way we approached the writing of this chapter. We worked as an equal and supportive team, dividing up all aspects of the research, writing and editing processes. We used an online document sharing tool (Google Docs) to write the chapter. We have not included many quotes from students in this chapter and that is because the student voice is not inserted into sections, rather it runs throughout the chapter and this reflects our definition of student–staff partnership.

In the following section we outline the main types of educational development activity in which students have engaged at CEEBL and CILASS. Particular attention is devoted to instances where students played an integral role. These are presented as case examples in the text. Following each example we draw out and summarize the key points that contribute to successful and productive staff–student collaboration. These points will then be discussed collectively in the concluding section.

Student educational development activities and their impacts
1. Developmental partnerships

As part of their efforts to incorporate inquiry-based learning into a range of courses, both CETLs encouraged members of academic and educational development staff to collaborate with students on the development of their modules. The students employed at both CETLs had considerable input at this level, as the following examples illustrate.

Project: Developing Inquiry-Based Learning Careers Sessions

Student(s): Faculty of Medical and Human Sciences (MHS) Intern (2008–09) at CEEBL

Context: Students within the Medical School are required to specialize relatively early in a particular field of medicine and it was felt by students that not enough support or information was available in the first year of their course to guide them through these decisions. Some work had already been undertaken on career awareness development in the school and as a result, the MHS intern was put in contact with the member of staff who was leading work in this area. Together, the intern and the staff member drew up the goals of the project.

Impact: The main project was to work with professionals in the School of Medicine, the Careers Service and the Students' Union, in order to create inquiry-based learning careers awareness sessions. This was followed by the creation of a student society, the Medical Careers Society, which has now taken ownership of the drive for increased careers awareness, including the inquiry-based learning modules, and will continue to raise careers awareness in the medical school. Through the student society staff 'have found a group of students being more proactive about effective change' (MHS CEEBL Intern 2009). Future plans include the creation of a user-led website where MHS students can advise each other on different careers within medicine and provide feedback on work placements.

Key points:
- The intern, as a student expert in his field, was able to take ownership of the content of the careers sessions and use student feedback to identify areas where input was needed.
- The intern had more freedom to be innovative and more time to commit than a member of staff might. His lack of official affiliation to the school as a member of staff meant that he was less constrained by internal bureaucracy and politics.
- The intern was able to utilize his academic contacts and connections within the Careers Service and the Students' Union to create the infrastructure

for a continued and broader partnership between students and staff within the school for years to come.

Project: Small Change, Big Difference Project

Student(s): CILASS ambassador for the Department of Sociological Studies (2008–09)

Context: The ambassador's aims were twofold: first, to connect students in the department both within and between years; and second, to increase student engagement in their modules. Drawing together suggestions from fellow ambassadors and her peers within the department, she arranged a staff–student collaboration meeting and presented her proposals. This led ultimately to the delivery of a more detailed presentation to the departmental teaching committee. The presentation outlined three main suggestions – the introduction of a blog to ease the transition of incoming students, establishing dissertation presentations, and setting up reading groups in modules. The suggestions had evolved from the ambassador's own experiences as a dual honours student, and included initiatives already present in her 'other' department. The ambassador wanted to replicate these positive experiences for students in other departments.

Impact: All three of the ambassador's ideas were well received. Staff investigated the possibility of starting a blog for the 2009 intake. Dissertation presentations were already under discussion, in the context of a departmental curriculum review, although the ambassador's work reaffirmed the commitment to this idea. Staff also began to think about introducing reading groups into particular modules for the subsequent academic year. The ambassador continued to work with staff members to take these developments forward. Some negative reactions from staff were more focused on the feasibility and practicality of the suggestions than a reaction against the involvement of students in the developmental process. The framework of 'Small Change, Big Difference' has been so successful that the session has been run on several more occasions as a discussion session, where staff and students come together to discuss what 'small changes' towards IBL can be integrated to achieve a 'big difference' in the learning experience.

Key points:
- Being a dual honours student helped the student ambassador to generate new ideas and think outside of the disciplinary context, while the input of ambassadors from other departments was also influential.
- The initiative had the initial support of CILASS in the context of a push for greater ambassador engagement with their departments; this gave the ambassador the impetus and support to take the initiative, generate some new ideas and attempt to get buy-in from staff in the department.
- Teaching staff in the department were open to these new ideas and to the concept of student partnership; it was especially significant that the

project secured the support of an influential figure such as the Director of Teaching and Learning.

- It was fortuitous that the Department of Sociological Studies was in the midst of a curriculum review, which meant that staff were open to new ideas.

2. Developing resources

In both institutions, students and staff work together to develop resources and exercises relating to IBL. These resources can be used to promote understanding of IBL, showcase best practice, provide basic information and provoke discussion and interaction between staff and students. Such resources include basic printed resources such as guides and newsletters, and web resources such as blogs, Facebook groups and website pages relating to IBL, all of which are aimed at both staff and students. The specific training and skills that the students have developed in their roles are also used to create resources such as films, as the following example shows.

Project: The Film Group

Student(s): CILASS Student Ambassador Network (SAN) Film Group

Context: The SAN was divided into working groups, which each had different aims, methods and projects to do with the research, promotion, implementation and evaluation of IBL. The SAN Film Group created films that explored concepts of IBL. This ranged from small projects, such as recording students in the Music Department interacting with professional musicians, to larger projects, such as making a 13-minute film researching student perceptions of information literacy. The student perspective that was the focus of all films provided a unique opportunity for staff and students to understand each other, and to use the films as a basis for discussion.

Impact: The films the group produced were often used as catalysts for discussion among staff and students, both within CILASS, across the University of Sheffield, and within the higher education community as a whole, via national conferences. The fresh perspective provided by the students has resulted in a greater dialogue between staff and students. For example, staff responded to a student film ('What is IBL?'), which was shown at an away day, by producing their own film on the subject for presentation to the students, which in turn was used to initiate further dialogue.

Key points:

- The members of the film group gained skills they would not normally have had a chance to develop, namely that of the filmmaking process, as well as gaining more transferable skills such as working in a team, working to a brief and working to a deadline.
- They also gained a greater understanding of, and sense of place within, the university community as a whole, resulting in a better position for

them to communicate with other students and staff – generating an upward spiral of skill and benefit.

3. Events, workshops and training

In both CETL networks, staff and students worked together to implement new training or events to engage students in IBL. Both networks have organized conferences: CILASS ambassadors organized an annual conference where staff and students present together, while CEEBL interns initiated a student-led conference in March 2009. Students from both networks are also involved in IBL training sessions for other students and have frequently been asked to run and facilitate workshops on the student perspective.

Project: IBL and Employability Workshop

Student(s): CILASS ambassadors

Context: In December 2008, members of the CILASS network visited Manchester Metropolitan University at the invitation of a member of staff who had been impressed by the SAN during a visit to CILASS. He wanted to inspire and motivate his students to realize the potential of IBL in their own studies. As a result, three SAN members visited to run two workshops for Level 2 Business Studies students, on the topic of 'IBL and employability'. Activities included asking the students to fill in a real application form for a graduate business scheme while encouraging them to think about how the skills they gain from IBL may set them apart in such a situation.

Impact: The workshops were judged to be a success, with the students responding well to the fact that other students were running the session, rather than members of staff. The session was so successful it has since been rerun several times, both within the university and externally. In all cases staff as well as students were present, providing the basis for future discussions and collaboration where appropriate.

Key points:

- The member of staff trusted the ambassadors to devise and conduct the session, realizing that the ambassadors would potentially inspire and enthuse other students.
- The session was transferable to other contexts, and actively demonstrated the benefits of students taking initiative, both to staff and students.

Reflective conclusion: what makes student and staff partnerships work?

In what follows we summarize and discuss some of the key findings from the evaluations we have carried out and our collective experiences as members and coordinators of the student networks at CILASS and CEEBL.

As was noted above, issues around power create both opportunities for and barriers to promoting student engagement in educational change initiatives. It has been suggested that one of the ways in which such challenges might be negotiated successfully in order to improve practices is through focusing on the social roots of frameworks and beliefs about power and responsibility in the classroom and curriculum (Trowler and Cooper, 2002, p. 236). By making explicit what is currently implicit, staff and students could become aware of the pervasiveness of power. This is often the first step in being able to work more democratically and cooperatively with students and colleagues (Brookfield, 1995, p. 237). By working as networks and in partnership with staff and students at a number of different levels and on a range of different projects, including scholarly research activity, interns and ambassadors have been able to interact with staff on an equal level. With the support and partnership of staff at CEEBL and CILASS, they have developed the credibility and the confidence, individually, collectively and institutionally, to work with staff as partners and to instigate meaningful educational change. Individually and collaboratively, students have developed the expertise, skills and culture of a community of practice. In many cases, it is now existing members of the networks who take care of the induction of new members, for example, when prospective members shadow outgoing interns or ambassadors. At the same time, students have retained their 'expertise' as a student, allowing them to form a bridge between staff and the wider student body.

Research has shown that open and democratic communication between all members and levels of an institution is key to successful change initiatives (Bocock and Watson, 1994b) and, similarly, that an open attitude to student involvement in curriculum change and a willingness to share responsibilities is essential for successful staff–student partnerships (Visser et al., 1998). This has significant implications for those seeking to reconceptualize the role of the contemporary university, the role of staff and students within the institution, and the relationship between the two (Taylor and Wilding, 2009). The case examples we have presented in this chapter have demonstrated how successful initiatives have instigated, promoted and supported ongoing dialogue between staff and students. As mentioned earlier, both networks have often adopted an inquiry-based approach to tasks. Since inquiry-based learning requires students to take responsibility for their individual and collaborative working arrangements as they engage in research and problem-solving activities, this has resulted in collaborative decision-making and shared responsibilities in both the processes and outcomes of educational development. The increased flexibility and responsibility which is encouraged by inquiry-based learning has heightened the motivation of the students involved in the networks, improving individual projects and, more broadly, learning itself.

We feel that the coordination and facilitation of the networks was key to their successful implementation, so in the next section we present a series of practical recommendations for establishing and facilitating a network which allows for staff–student collaboration.

Practical conclusion: recommendations for setting up and facilitating a network

The experiences of students and staff at CEEBL and CILASS point to some practical and important considerations for anyone wishing to instigate a network of students similar those described above.

1. Ensure students are not overloaded or overwhelmed
Students can be inundated with exciting opportunities for collaboration when working in these types of networks. It can be difficult to achieve a balance between the opportunities that are open to them at departmental, faculty, institutional and national levels. Clarity of expectations and support from network coordinators are key factors for ensuring that students do not become overwhelmed.

2. Ensure clarity of remit, objectives and priorities from the outset
Designing and developing projects takes time, confidence and training. It is important to ensure that students are supported from the outset by clearly defining roles, goals and deadlines. This should be negotiated with the students, not imposed upon them. Such clarity avoids the confusion that can occur through abstract remits and unclear priorities. Sometimes it is appropriate for a student to be fully integrated into a project from start to finish; this is an ideal situation for both staff and student partners. This is not always possible, however: CEEBL interns, for example, are only employed for one academic year whereas projects may go on for longer. As both CETLs pay students, budgetary and time constraints must be factored in.

3. Think carefully about who is coordinating the network
Many of the potential problems surrounding clarity of objectives and priorities can be overcome by deploying a staff coordinator. The ideal staff coordinator is in a position to understand and relate to students on the networks, while also acting as a mediator, framing the interaction with staff for the students and bridging the gap between 'student initiatives' and 'staff responsibility'. For example, we have recognized that it is important that the coordinator makes it clear to academic staff at the outset of the project that the CETL expects the students to be treated as true partners rather than 'cheap labour'. Clarity of expectations is thus vital on both sides.

Employing a staff coordinator does not negate valid and active partnership between the coordinator and students on the networks, or students and academic staff. Rather, the staff coordinator can empower students, by ensuring a smooth induction and maintaining support throughout the partnership processes. Co-facilitating a network together with a student combines the advantages of having a 'constant' facilitator with the benefit of demonstrating staff–student partnerships to the institution and involving students at coordinator level. As students on the networks develop skills and confidence, the staff coordinator may have a smaller role to play and it should be the responsibility of all members to negotiate these changing relationships.

These practical considerations are an important step on the way to achieving effective staff–student partnership for educational development on the level of a whole network. However, we believe that a genuine interest and belief in partnership, and mutual respect, from both the staff and students, are just as significant. Effort and resource should thus be expended in order to cultivate these dispositions if success is to be sustained and engrained across institutions and even the sector as a whole.

References

Apple, M. W. (1985), *Education and Power*. London: Ark.

Baxter-Magolda, M. B. (2003), 'Identity and learning: student affairs' role in transforming higher education', *Journal of College Student Development*, 44, (2), 231–247.

Baxter-Magolda, M. B. and Crosby, P. (2006), 'Self-authorship and identity in college: an interview with Marcia B. Baxter-Magolda', *Journal of College & Character*, 7, (1), 1–2.

Bocock, J. and Watson, D. (1994a), 'Common cause: prospects for renewal', in J. Bocock and D. Watson (eds), *Managing the University Curriculum: Making Common Cause*. Buckingham: The Society for Research into Higher Education and Open University Press, pp. 129–137.

Bocock, J. and Watson, D. (1994b), 'Introduction', in J. Bocock and D. Watson (eds), *Managing the University Curriculum: Making Common Cause*. Buckingham: The Society for Research into Higher Education and Open University Press, pp. 1–9.

Bourdieu, P. and Passeron, J.-C. (1990), *Reproduction in Education, Society and Culture*. 2nd edition. London: Sage.

Brew, A. (2003), 'Teaching and research: new relationships and their implications for inquiry-based teaching and learning in higher education', *Higher Education Research & Development*, 22, (1), 3–18.

Brookfield, S. (1995), *Becoming a Critically Reflective Teacher*. San Francisco: Jossey-Bass.

Coffield, F. (2008), *What if Teaching and Learning Really Were the Priority?* London: LSN.

Freire, P. (1996), *Pedagogy of the Oppressed*. London: Penguin.

Healy, M. (2005), 'Linking research and teaching to benefit student learning', *Journal of Geography in Higher Education*, 29, (2), 183–201.

Hutchings, B. (2007), *Enquiry-Based Learning: Definitions and Rationale*. Manchester: CEEBL, University of Manchester. Retrieved 28 April 2010 from www.campus.manchester.ac.uk/ceebl/resources/papers/hutchings2007_definingebl.pdf

Kahn, P. and O'Rourke, K. (2004), *Guide to Curriculum Design: Enquiry-Based Learning*. York: Higher Education Academy. Retrieved 28 April 2010 from http://www.campus.manchester.ac.uk/ceebl/resources/guides/kahn_2004.pdf

McMillan, D. W. and Chavis, D. M. (1986), 'Sense of community: a definition and theory', *Journal of Community Psychology*, 14, (1), 6–23.

Scott, P. and Watson, D. (1994), 'Managing the curriculum: roles and responsibilities', in J. Bocock and D. Watson (eds), *Managing the University Curriculum: Making Common Cause*. Buckingham: The Society for Research into Higher Education and Open University Press, pp. 33–47.

Streeting, W. and Wise, G. (2009), *Rethinking the Values of Higher Education – Consumption, Partnership, Community?* Gloucester: The Quality Assurance Agency for Higher Education. Retrieved 28 April 2010 from http://www.qaa.ac.uk/students/studentEngagement/Rethinking.pdf

Taylor, P. and Wilding, D. (2009), *Rethinking the Values of Higher Education – The Student as Collaborator and Producer? Undergraduate Research as a Case Study*. Gloucester: The Quality Assurance Agency for Higher Education. Retrieved 28 April 2010 from http://www.qaa.ac.uk/students/studentEngagement/Undergraduate.pdf

Thiessen, D. (2006), 'Student knowledge, engagement, and voice in educational reform', *Curriculum Inquiry*, 36, (4), 345–358.

Trowler, P. and Cooper, A. (2002), 'Teaching and learning regimes: implicit theories and recurrent practices in the enhancement of teaching and learning through educational development programmes', *Higher Education Research & Development*, 21, (3), 221–240.

Visser, K., Prince, K. J. A. H., Scherpbier, A. J. J. A., Van Der Vleuten, C. P. M. and Verwijnen, G. M. M. (1998), 'Student participation in educational management and organization', *Medical Teacher*, 20, (5), 451–454.

Wenger, E. (1999), *Communities of Practice: Learning, Meaning, and Identity*. Cambridge: Cambridge University Press.

Wood, J., Little, S., Goldring, L. and Jenkins, L. (2009), 'The confidence to do things that I know nothing about: skills development through extra-curricular inquiry activity', in P. Levy and P. McKinney (eds), *Proceedings of the 3rd Learning Through Enquiry Alliance Conference*. Sheffield: CILASS, University of Sheffield, pp. 117–122.

Chapter 3

Towards an Assessment Partnership Model? Students' Experiences of Being Engaged as Partners in Assessment for Learning (AfL) Enhancement Activity

Kay Sambell and Linda Graham

This chapter explores second-year undergraduates' experiences of an option module, designed by the lead author, which enabled them to explore the topic of Assessment for Learning (Black and Wiliam, 1998). The module was created to offer students a chance to learn about the body of scholarly work investigating the impact of assessment on student learning in higher education. Since its inception in 2005, the module has been offered annually, as part of a portfolio of options on the Joint Honours programme in the School of Health, Community and Education Studies at Northumbria University. On this particular joint honours programme, students choose two part-routes which have an applied social focus (such as Early Years, Childhood Studies, Disability Studies, Advice and Guidance). The routes take an analytic, discursive approach to these subject areas, rather than offering a licence to practice.

Having explicitly studied various philosophies, principles and debates surrounding the Assessment for Learning (AfL) agenda, students choosing the option (about 20 each year) were then invited to produce enhancement materials designed to enable other students and staff to engage with relevant concepts. Some of their materials, which are discussed in this chapter, have subsequently been used to help staff and students at course and university level begin to interrogate and enhance their own assessment practices.

Our chapter draws attention to students' perceptions of the relevance of getting 'behind the scenes' of university assessment. It suggests that these students' experiences of the module:

1. strongly resonate with Baxter-Magolda's (2004) Learning Partnerships Model (LPM)
2. suggest that involving students extensively in an Assessment Partnerships Model (APM) could offer a useful way forward for AfL enhancement activity.

To highlight key aspects of the students' viewpoints the chapter draws heavily on the published material of two students (Wake and Watson, 2007). Their *Assessment for Learning: A Student Survival Guide* has continued to make tangible developmental contributions to communities of staff and students beyond the boundaries of the module. We supplement this with in-depth interview data with a number of other students on the module. In this sense, then, although the chapter has, technically speaking, been written by two people, and the theoretical inferences remain largely the views of the lead author, the main body of the chapter has been produced by the insights and experiences of several of the students on the module. The specific contributions of individual students, where appropriate, are thus duly acknowledged in the biographical information at the end of the chapter.

Context: staff perspective

The lead author of this chapter is currently Director of Assessment for Learning Enhancement in Northumbria University's Centre for Excellence in Learning and Teaching: Assessment for Learning (CETL AfL). She also teaches Childhood Studies on an interdisciplinary joint honours programme at the university. She, in collaboration with other staff at Northumbria, has a long track record of using and researching innovative assessment and its impact on students' approaches to learning (Sambell et al., 1997; Sambell and McDowell, 1998; Sambell et al., 2006). This culminated in the establishment, in 2005, of the HEFCE-funded Northumbria CETL, which acts as a national centre for expertise in AfL and a home for innovation, development and research into the integration of assessment, learning and teaching across the university. It aims to accelerate a transformation in assessment practice, so that students are able to benefit from assessment which does far more than simply test what they know. To this end, dissemination and enhancement activity targeted on AfL is central to the CETL's aims. The co-author of this chapter is a student undertaking postgraduate work in support of AfL. She is also the CETL Student Development Officer, liaising between staff and students across the university to enhance students' experiences of assessment.

Recent developments in the scholarship of assessment: assessment for learning

Strong arguments have been put forward in recent years about the need for a paradigm shift in thinking about assessment (Segers et al., 2003). Birenbaum (2003) suggests that conceptions and approaches to assessment must change radically if assessment environments are to keep in step with shifting views of the nature of effective learning and teaching environments. Learning has been largely reformulated along constructivist-based principles. From this viewpoint, the view of the teacher shifts from an authority who transmits knowledge ('the sage on the stage') to the role of a mentor or facilitator who guides learning ('the guide on the side'). Likewise, views about the role of the student shift from being a passive consumer of knowledge to an active constructor of meaning. This means that learners and teachers become viewed as jointly responsible partners in the learning process, with dialogue between both parties seen as vital (Bloxham and Boyd, 2007). From these perspectives, learner-focused pedagogic environments such as those offered by enquiry-based learning (Hutchings and O'Rourke, 2002), which jointly engage staff and students in communities focused on research activity, reflection and conversation, become highly prized.

Concepts of assessment, however, have been slower to change. As assessment scholarship develops in the higher education community, though, enhancement activities focus on developing assessment approaches that are in sympathy with constructivist-based views of learning. These approaches are formulated in conceptual opposition to the conservative 'testing culture' (Birenbaum, 1996) which has tended to dominate thinking about assessment. By focusing predominantly on the measurement function of assessment – the assessment *of* learning – testing cultures position the student as a passive, powerless, even oppressed victim of the assessment process. Research has shown, for example, that the standards and criteria for judging work often remain a mystery to students, preventing learners from making effective evaluations for themselves (Carless et al., 2007). Further, if students see assessment tasks simply as hurdles that teachers require them to jump this can damage or, at worst, undermine deep approaches to learning (Sambell et al., 1997).

Efforts to challenge, or at least ameliorate, some of the damaging effects of testing cultures on student learning have resulted in what Boud and Falchikov (2007, p. 4) have dubbed an assessment *for* learning 'countermovement.' This broadly aims to promote new assessment cultures which foster learning (Boud and Falchikov, 2006; Bryan and Clegg, 2006). While approaches to AfL vary, they often involve the design of specific activities as part and parcel of everyday curriculum design and delivery. These might, for instance, involve self and peer assessment activities that offer students insight into assessment standards and criteria within a discipline, supporting them to effectively make judgements about the quality of their own work (e.g. Boud, 1995; Brown and Knight, 1994; Nicol and Macfarlane-Dick, 2006; Orsmond et al., 2006; Rust et al., 2005; Sadler, 1989; Sluijsmans et al., 2001). Other enhancement activity has concentrated on helping students gain more timely feedback and engage productively with it (e.g. Gibbs and Simpson, 2004; Knight and Yorke, 2003; Nicol, 2009), or on developing assessment so as to foster the skills and dispositions of learning for the longer term (e.g. Boud and Falchikov, 2006; Bryan and Clegg, 2006; Carless et al., 2007; McDowell et al., 2006).

As awareness about the impact of assessment on students' approaches to learning spreads across the sector, 'assessment for learning' (Gipps, 1994) has become a popular term and a great deal of enhancement activity is centred on it. A number of universities now include assessment for learning in their learning and teaching strategies or have developed initiatives and projects, with a view to enhancing student learning.

AfL enhancement activity

Increasingly, then, university staff are learning about and debating assessment, via conferences, induction, courses, research and their continuing professional development. In our CETL, for instance, we are keen to foster research, enquiry and exploration, so that we can investigate and learn more about the possible impact of assessment for learning, rather than simply promote it as a 'motherhood and apple pie' idea. In order to help achieve this aim, our CETL explicitly engages novice and experienced staff across the university in formal and informal learning opportunities to learn more about assessment (Reimann and Wilson, 2009), with a view to interrogating and hopefully improving assessment practice by promoting awareness, reflection, conceptual development and change. These learning opportunities include, for instance, the chance for staff to read and discuss their views of assessment-related research by participating with other lecturers in an informal monthly reading group. Others participate in courses that address the theories and principles of assessment as part of the raft of continuing professional development programmes on offer at the university.

It struck me, however, that while students were often being offered ways of becoming engaged in assessment for learning activities as an integral part of their courses, I hadn't come across many instances in which undergraduates, outside of those studying to become educators themselves, were explicitly offered the chance to learn about, debate and become engaged with concepts of assessment per se, in the ways that are increasingly on offer to our staff. Further, the extensive literature on AfL is almost exclusively produced by staff, so it seemed timely to engage students as partners in AfL enhancement activity. To this end I validated a module on AfL, which students on a non-vocational joint honours programme could select as a second-year option.

How did the module work?

The aim of the module was, primarily, to enable students to engage in some depth with the scholarship of assessment (Rust, 2007). At the outset of the module, I explained my enhancement role in the CETL, and suggested students might want to work with me on an AfL project, in which we would try to develop materials that would encourage others to reflect on the key issues. Students were asked to author guides to AfL, or develop other authentic materials of their own choosing, such as workshops or interactive games. These were to be suitable for new students coming onto the joint honours programme or for members of staff at our own university.

While the student-authored enhancement materials were, on the one hand, submitted for summative assessment, students knew that, with relevant permissions, they subsequently could be used 'in real life' in assessment enhancement activity. In this sense the module sought to offer students an authentic (Gulikers, 2006) summative assessment experience, so that they could actively apply what they learned about AfL throughout the module. Students could choose to work individually or in small self-selecting groups to produce their guides or learning materials. Teaching sessions were used to support students in building up appropriate knowledge, skills and theoretical insights to produce their materials effectively.

I hoped that being immersed together in a collaborative process of active enquiry about AfL would afford students the 'substantial investment of time and effort [needed] to participate generatively and with convergent understanding in the central forms of the knowledge community' (Northedge, 2003, p. 21), extending their repertoire of knowing about assessment issues, and bringing their own internal voices into dialogue with others in the field. As part of the project, then, learners engaged with other students, with CETL staff, on published work of assessment research and the literature on educational development. Exemplars of educational development materials were shared during the course, including, for example, Brown's 'Assessment Manifesto' (2005); Brown et al's '500 Tips on Assessment' (2005); and Gibson's 'Tome Reader' (2007) (a guide for PhD students written in the style of video-game 'cheats' pages). Students were also introduced, (via, for example, the Higher Education Academy, university and conference websites), to the world of professional development and scholarship in learning and teaching. This, in itself, was an eye-opener for my students, as none had realized this world existed, despite it being a major aspect of my own professional life, because until then they had only encountered me as a lecturer/researcher within my substantive area, Childhood Studies. Furthermore, the module inevitably opened up lengthy discussions about university assessment processes, which otherwise exist 'behind the scenes' from the student viewpoint. This enabled students to build a larger picture of the competing demands and different stakeholder views of assessment than they previously had met through personal experience.

Students' views of their engagement in the module

In what follows, we will highlight some of the key themes and issues to emerge from the students' perspectives. It was striking that, while many staff see AfL as a set of classroom techniques to improve student perform- ance (Davies and Ecclestone, 2008, p. 72), the students saw AfL in a much more holistic way. For them, AfL did not simply offer the means to gain better marks. Instead, the enhancement materials they developed focused predominantly on issues relating to the stances, dispositions and actions of staff and students. From these students' viewpoints, then, AfL represented improved staff–student partnerships in academia.

As we will highlight below, the aspects of AfL that the students sought to promote resonate strongly with the dynamics of Baxter-Magolda's (2004) Learning Partnerships Model (LPM). The LPM offers teachers a frame by which to steer their pedagogic thinking. For Baxter-Magolda this frame helps students to develop appropriate attributes, because ultimately society will expect graduates to 'assume positions of responsibility,' 'manage complex- ity and engage multiple perspectives,' 'gather and judge relevant evidence . . . to make decisions,' and 'act in ways that benefit themselves and others equitably and contribute to the common good' (p. xviii). Educators working within the frame seek to provide learners with carefully balanced levels of support and challenge to facilitate 'self-authorship', which Baxter-Magolda defines as 'the internal capacity to define one's beliefs, identity, and relations with others' (p. 8). These include support which respects and affirms the value of student voices, engages in learning with them and helps them to view their own experiences as opportunities for learning and growth. The challenges include expecting students to: attend to complexity and avoid simplistic decisions; and develop their personal authority by listening to their own voices in deciding how to act; and encouraging them to share their authority and expertise by working interdependently on thorny issues (Baxter-Magolda, 2004).

AfL: Mutual trust and shared responsibility

Having studied and discussed different stakeholders' views of the purpose of assessment, students were aware of the complexity of the issues. They were keen, however, to develop AfL enhancement materials which prompted others to consider, challenge and confront some commonly held subject positions that assessment might imply. Issues of power and authority were played through very explicitly in the student guides, offering telling critiques of the significant cultural gap that students perceived might exist between staff and students.

For the students, this gap was important to consider, because it repre- sented a barrier to AfL and partnership working, rooted in a lack of mutual trust and responsibility. This was not, however, represented as just the teachers' problem, but, interestingly, was framed as a matter of mistrust and misconception emanating from both sides. The following lengthy extract from a student guide to AfL (Wake and Watson, 2007) illustrates the point. It offers a powerful indictment of both staff and student identities. The student authors of the guide use stereotypes of learners as well as teachers to satirize what they see as dysfunctional learning environments, which AfL seeks to challenge.

In the extract the students are trying to explain the concept of deep and surface approaches to learning to the implied student reader of their guide. They use heavy irony to draw attention to the unsatisfactory nature of pedagogic relationships that are not based on mutual respect, trust and partnership. To introduce these ideas, the guide initially satirizes the view of the lazy student who won't take control of their own learning, and who sees knowledge as a commodity.

Spotting a Surface Learner

- Only does the bare minimum to get by
  (well that's **me** off to the pub)

- Just memorises, when more is needed
  (yeah just cram, don't think)

- Puts non-academic activities first
  (yep, they're off to the pub again!)

- Often misunderstands what is expected of them
  (Oh! You meant *that*)

- Are often fighting boredom
  (just wake me up when they've finished)

- Loves to 'cut corners'
  (a few lists to pad out that essay will do the job)

The narrative continues:

Now, if we are going to be really honest, I bet most of us recognise ourselves in at least one of those statements . . . You don't? . . . Whoops, sorry, our mistake!! (p. 7)

The student guide immediately moves on to conceptually link these learner identities to factors in the learning environment, which include the construction of teacher identities:

> The truth is that all too often (but, of course, not always) certain factors encourage students to be a surface learner . . . one of them being the Surface-Learning Lecturer . . . OK. We're kidding. There's no such term. But if there was, here's how they would conduct their lectures . . .

How to Spot the Surface-Learning Lecturer
. . . who will always strive to provide:

(Wake and Watson, 2007, p. 8).

Within this representation, mistrust and misconceptions on both sides, then, dictate the types of subject positions on offer. Over-exaggeration is used to make funny, but serious, points about the need for dialogue and partnership working on both sides. As one student explained in interview:

The thing I was trying to get at doing that bit was [that with some teachers] there was not negotiation here, this is non-negotiable, this is the way I teach and this is it, it was very much I'm in control and you're not, with no say in it. The person you can imagine standing at the front of the class, [saying] don't ask me questions: just do it. The Anti-Christ of AfL!

By contrast, AfL was represented as partnership and shared responsibility, as the following extract, still aimed at students, makes plain.

Do you want an alternative? Then read on, help is at hand!

The Idea of Constructive Alignment
Basically Constructive Alignment is an approach to what you learn that gives you opportunities for higher quality learning!
   It involves two aspects:
1. CONSTRUCTIVE = the student bit! You construct meaning through the learning activities you do. You must create the meaning and understanding for yourself, gone are the days where your lecturer tells you what it is!
2. ALIGNMENT = the lecturer's part. Will provide you with activities and tasks that will help you achieve the desired learning goals or outcomes.

Gone are the days of inappropriate mundane tasks that leave you bewildered.

(Wake and Watson, 2007, p. 12).

It is especially interesting that the concept of constructive alignment (Biggs, 2003), which is usually understood as the teacher's responsibility to effectively engineer learning, teaching and assessment so as to 'trap' the student into learning what the teacher desires, is recast in the student version as a matter of working in partnership with mutual responsibility.

Developing personal authority
In developing their enhancement materials, students formed a strong sense of addressing a particular audience. This seemed important in helping them to feel that their own thoughts, feelings and voices were respected and valued. They strove to make points and communicate their ideas effectively, which, interestingly, they saw in stark contrast to the ways in which they approached 'normal' assignments.

We were conscious that we wanted to use different ways of getting the point over rather than just a load of writing that would have bored me rigid. The pictures were deliberately chosen to illustrate the point.

Being asked to focus on enhancing others' conceptual engagement appeared to foster creativity, rather than routine compliance with assessment tasks that others have mandated (Torrance, 2007). The following student, for instance, describes how she chose to mix genres in her guide, as a more familiar and natural way of expressing her views and ideas in order to persuade others to develop their thinking about assessment:

> I thought if we had done a 500-word guide with a 1,500-word reflective commentary it would have ended up another assignment and I am sick of doing assignments! The terminology you use, the formality of the words and the formality of the sentence structure. Your audience wouldn't have understood it. They wouldn't have got as much from it as they would get from our guide. But I was quite conscious that we are still writing to an academic standard because we read a lot and I read stacks of stuff.

Voice and alienation

When developing their enhancement materials, students chose to use alternative formats from the traditional academic essay or report. As has already been seen in the extracts above, they rooted their guides in informal and diverse textual practices, which allowed them to express their ideas in alternative genres and modes of exchange. With some relish, they chose to employ informal vernacular multi-literacy practices grounded in peer community and popular culture, but which are seldom engaged in their formal assessment (Ivanic et al., 2007).

They found the opportunity to use these culturally and linguistically diverse literacy practices surprisingly liberating, helping them feel they could build on what they already brought to learning. This could be seen as an instance in which university culture adapts to embrace the culture brought by the student, respecting the diverse voices they bring, rather than habitually expecting the student to become assimilated into university culture (Ramsden, 2009).

Further, the module inevitably opened up many lengthy discussions of what makes a 'good' assignment. This gave rise to considerable debate about academic discourse and questions of voice, which, from students' viewpoints, seemed closely linked to the themes of belonging and ownership of the world of ideas. From students' perspectives, 'normal' assessment experiences were associated with feelings of not belonging, of not feeling part of something which you are supposed to feel at home with (Mann, 2001). One student, for example, talked of searching for personal meaning while preparing her guide to AfL, rather than her usual experience, which involved trying to simply produce what she thought someone else was expecting or wanted to hear: 'Normally I don't write it for me. I don't think I write my academic assignments for myself, I'm writing them for the person who is reading them.'

Producing her guide became viewed as an opportunity to engage holistically with issues of personal identity, rather than performing a task in an atomistic way, by 'putting in' material that others appear to demand:

> I used it to think through the things with assessment that had happened to me. It was about me, which my assignments aren't normally. I just normally check what they're asking and put bits in on each criteria.

Sharing expertise and authority

In interview, the students' sense of having something to offer to the academic community in relation to AfL enhancement activity was palpable. In part, they felt this was connected to their growing recognition, via the module, that communities of assessment scholars tend to share and debate their ideas, rather than work in isolation. They could also see that views about 'good' assessment relate strongly to stakeholders' values, attitudes and assumptions about the purposes of assessment, meaning that ideas about assessment are contested, rather than absolute. In this sense, they began to appreciate that assessment knowledge can be viewed as situated within and distributed across communities (Lave and Wenger, 1991; Knight, 2002), rather than being possessed by the individual.

This had the capacity to challenge and change the way that they saw themselves as learners. One talked, for instance, of the ways in which working and producing assignments collaboratively with peers afforded enhanced opportunities for dialogue about assessment issues, and impacted positively on her own learning experience, by enhancing her own sense of achievement:

> We definitely discovered working together you're giving so much more. You're pulling things out of each other you didn't realize you had. I don't class myself as a creative person, but when I looked at that final product it worked really well. Whereas, writing a normal academic assignment, it's very isolating.

This 'natural', collaborative way of working contrasted starkly with most students' prior experiences of doing assignments, which was characterized by a sense of estrangement, and a requirement to fulfil assessment for purely functional, rather than personal ends (Mann, 2001).

'Usually there is no obligation, you're writing for a set task and set thing and once it has been achieved then that's it.' By contrast, this student continued to talk about producing her enhancement materials in a very different way.

The sense that someone would read this – I think that helped us create it, especially after seeing the guides that they handed out as examples and they had said it might [be displayed]. People might pick it up, have a look through it.

Here the student invests meaning in terms of making a difference to others. In other words, her work is undertaken partly for the good of the community, not just for individual marks:

It is not just a pass or a fail or a number in a box, there's other important things like satisfaction, there's recognition, there's the feeling that it is going to help other people.

From this perspective the student has a sense of contributing to the assessment community in a more reciprocal relationship than is usually the case, which the learner experiences as empowering and enthusing. Another student spoke of suddenly seeing how, as a more experienced learner, she had something of value to say and to offer to others: in this case the first-years. This led her to recognize and value her own authority and she subsequently volunteered, with her co-author, to take her materials into Study Skills sessions as part of the academic induction of the next cohort of learners:

We'll go and show the first-years. It's peer learning, isn't it? It is proof that there is life after a 2,000-word assignment, that there is something fun and you can achieve something.

The sense of supporting the development of others, here by showing them an 'assessment survivor', was valued as a meaningful way of sharing the expertise that they had developed. Moreover, some students' work on AfL was published as part of the staff development series at the university. These students were energized, surprised and somewhat amused by their new identity, as they suddenly recast themselves as authors who might be read and cited by the academic community:

It was just so mega and was just so funny! We've had our names in brackets, me and you. Plebs can make it! . . . They'll say who's this new [author, date]? A sense of achievement and recognition isn't it? As students you feel, we're not quite there yet, 'cos we're still a student. But we are!

The sense of suddenly belonging as partners in an academic community throws issues of identity and status into sharp relief.

Conclusions

Carless (2009) suggests that mistrust is one of the main barriers impeding the development of assessment cultures in universities. In his view trust could be enhanced by heightened communication about the purposes of assessment between university staff. Further, he argues that students need to be shown and helped to understand some of the tacit assumptions of the assessment process, via increased collaboration and dialogue, rather than shrouding assessment processes in secrecy. This, too, boils down to a question of trust.

It certainly seems that the student viewpoints we have discussed in this chapter seem to agree. Their materials advocate strong staff–student collaboration and trust surrounding assessment. Of course it is perfectly possible that the materials the students in our case study produced simply paid lip service to the spirit of AfL, if they felt they were themselves in thrall to the power of an assessor with whose ideological position they felt duty-bound to agree (Tan, 2004). The sheer enthusiasm and energy of the texts they produced seem, however, to suggest that the ideas being expressed moved beyond simple lip service. They illuminate and focus upon issues of culture, power and identity that seem to resonate powerfully with students' lived experience, making visible some hugely important aspects of our learning, teaching and assessment cultures. They also clearly challenge deficit models of the contemporary student as somehow 'lacking' (Wilson and Scalise, 2006), blamed for not engaging properly (Harper and Quaye, 2008), or as viewing education as a commodity rather than an experience. They argue, instead, for moving towards an Assessment Partnership Model, framed by dialogue, mutual trust and the development of more conceptually informed assessment communities.

While the AfL option module continues to be offered to second-years each academic year, and students who choose it continue to come up with inventive, creative and innovative new formats for the development of materials that aim to engage others with the scholarship of assessment, we are now looking at ways of building versions of the model into core modules, so that all students on the course might benefit from the approach. The year-long Study Skills module, offered to enable students to make an effective transition to university study, is an obvious starting point, as it is taken by all (approximately 140) students coming onto our Joint Honours programme. It is currently being redeveloped, so that not only will all new students be introduced to the materials that second-years have produced for them to help them learn about the scholarship of learning, teaching and assessment, but everyone will become involved in a 'Making Connections' project, in which they will have the opportunity to produce, as well as use, authentic enhancement materials. The hope is that gaining academic credit for work on the scholarship of learning will make learning-to-learn come to life from the outset of the course, develop students' own conceptions and self-conceptions around learning, and, moreover, have the potential to make a genuine contribution to the university.

Postscript by the CETL student development officer

As Student Development Officer in the CETL it's my role to liaise directly with groups of students and staff in order to try and improve the student experience. This entails developing ideas about AfL on both sides. In my experience, students grasp its principles very quickly – they can readily see how it benefits them. Staff, for a whole host of understandable reasons, can seem more sceptical. Indeed, Carless (2009) suggests that, in relation to assessment, it's very difficult to get 'the right kind' of professional development for staff.

I have found, however, that the student-produced materials have, somehow, helped to encourage staff and students alike to engage with and discuss relevant issues. Perhaps it's something to do with the enthusiasm and energy of the materials, which proves, if proof were needed, that, students can be witty, inventive, creative, altruistic, committed and funny, as well as well-informed. I have used the guides and interactive games with a range of experienced staff from many universities, as well as on induction programmes for new lecturers, and people often tell me how useful they are in helping them get to grips quickly with the key ideas from the student perspective, without too much intrusive jargon getting in the way. The student guides continue to fly off the shelves and I receive requests for the interactive materials on a regular basis, from as far away as Nepal, so the AfL students continue to have quite an impact, some years after developing their enhancement materials.

Maybe hearing about the issues straight from the horses' mouths really helps, too. I am continually impressed about the lengths some of our student officers, once they become more informed about assessment issues, will go to in order to convince staff to trust their students, and to risk trying AfL approaches. Students come with me, for instance, to talk to big groups on our new lecturers' course, or to stand up and discuss their viewpoints at learning and teaching conferences, even if it feels quite daunting. I'll leave the last word about that with one of the students:

> I was really up for it, actually. It's not often that you get the chance to sit and talk to your lecturers about what we think and stuff. It is beneficial to both sides and it helps to better the relationship. Next time I'll try and do it without shaking!

Acknowledgements

The students whose published materials directly contributed to this chapter include Bernice Wake and Holly Watson, although many others' ideas, too numerous to name individually here, have deeply influenced our thinking about and approaches to AfL. Without their generous and creative contributions, we'd definitely be lost.

References

Baxter-Magolda, M. (2004), 'Learning partnerships model: a framework for promoting self-authorship', in M. Baxter-Magolda and P. King (eds), *Learning Partnerships: Theory and Models of Practice to Educate for Self Authorship*. Sterling, VA: Stylus, pp. 37–62.

Biggs, J. (2003), *Teaching for Quality Learning at University*. Buckingham: Society for Research into Higher Education.

Birenbaum, M. (1996), 'Assessment 2000: towards a pluralistic approach to assessment', in M. Birenbaum and J. F. R. C. Dochy (eds), *Alternatives in Assessment of Achievements, Learning Processes and Prior Knowledge*. Boston, MA: Kluwer, pp. 3–30.

Birenbaum, M. (2003), 'New insights into learning and teaching: their implications for assessment', in M. Segers, F. Dochy, and E. Cascallaer (eds), *Optimising New Modes of Assessment: In Search of Qualities and Standards*. Dordrecht: Kluwer Academic, pp.13–36.

Black, P. and Wiliam, D. (1998), 'Assessment and classroom learning', *Assessment in Education*, 5, (1), 7–74.

Bloxham, S. and Boyd, P. (2007), *Developing Effective Assessment in Higher Education: a Practical Guide*. Maidenhead, UK: Open University Press.

Boud, D. (1995), *Enhancing Learning Through Self-Assessment*. London: Kogan Page.

Boud, D. and Falchikov, N. (2006), 'Aligning assessment with long-term learning', *Assessment and Evaluation in Higher Education*, 31, (4), 399–413.

Boud, D. and Falchikov, N. (eds) (2007), *Rethinking Assessment in Higher Education: Learning for the Longer Term*. London: Routledge.

Brown, S. (2005), '*An Assessment Manifesto*', Deliberations. Retrieved 28 April 2010 from http://www.londonmet.ac.uk/deliberations/assessment/manifesto.cfm

Brown, S. and Knight, P. (1994), *Assessing Learners in Higher Education*. London: Routledge.

Brown, S., Race, P. and Smith, B. (2005), *500 Tips on Assessment* (2nd edn). London: Routledge.

Bryan, C. and Clegg, K. (eds) (2006), *Innovative Assessment in Higher Education*. London: Routledge.

Carless, D. (2009), 'Trust, distrust and their impact on assessment reform', *Assessment & Evaluation in Higher Education*, 34, (1), 79–89.

Carless, D., Joughin,G. and Liu, N. (2007), *How Assessment Supports Learning: Learning-Oriented Assessment in Action*. Hong Kong: Hong Kong University Press.

Davies, J. and Ecclestone, C. (2008), 'Springboard or strait-jacket? Formative assessment in vocational education learning', *Curriculum Journal*, 19, (2), 71–86.

Gibbs, G. and Simpson, C. (2004), 'Does your assessment support your students' learning?', *Learning and Teaching in Higher Education*, 1, 1–30.

Gibson, M. (2007), *Tome Reader*. Retrieved 28 April 2010 from http://www.dr-mel-comics.co.uk/tomereader/index.html

Gipps, C. V. (1994), *Beyond Testing: Towards a Theory of Educational Assessment*. London: Falmer Press.

Gulikers, J. (2006), *Authenticity is in the Eye of the Beholder: A Five Dimensional Framework for Authentic Assessment*. Heerlen, The Netherlands: The Open University.

Harper, S. R. and Quaye, S. J. (eds) (2008), *Student Engagement in Higher Education: Theoretical Perspectives and Practical Approaches for Diverse Populations*. London: Routledge.

Hutchings, W. and O'Rourke, K. (2002), 'Problem-based learning in literary studies', *Arts and Humanities in Higher Education*, 1, (1), 73–83.

Ivanic, R., Edwards, R., Satchwell, C. and Smith, J. (2007), 'Possibilities for pedagogy in further education: harnessing the abundance of literacy', *British Educational Research Journal*, 33, (5), 703–721.

Knight, P. (2002), 'Summative assessment in higher education: practices in disarray', *Studies in Higher Education*, 27, (3), 275–286.

Knight, P and Yorke, M. (2003), *Assessment, Learning and Employability*. London: Open University Press.

Lave, J. and Wenger, E. (1991), *Situated Learning: Legitimate Peripheral Participation*. London: Cambridge University Press.

Mann, S. J. (2001), 'Alternative perspectives on the student experience: alienation and engagement', *Studies in Higher Education*. 26, (1), 7–19.

McDowell, L., Sambell, K., Bazin, V., Wakelin, D. and Wickes, H. (2006), *Assessment for Learning: Current Practice Exemplars from the Centre for Excellence in Teaching and Learning*. Newcastle: MARCET, Red Guide Paper 22.

Nicol, D. (2009), *Transforming Assessment and Feedback: Enhancing Integration and Empowerment in the First Year*. Scottish Quality Assurance Agency (QAA) for Higher Education.

Nicol, D. and Macfarlane-Dick, D. (2006). 'Formative assessment and self-regulated learning: a model and seven principles of good feedback practice', *Studies in Higher Education*, 31, (2), 199–218.

Northedge, A. (2003), 'Rethinking teaching in the context of diversity', *Teaching in Higher Education*, 8, (1), 17–32.

Orsmond, P., Merry, S. and Sheffield, D. (2006), 'A quantitative and qualitative study of changes in the use of learning outcomes and distractions by students and tutors during a biology poster assessment', *Studies in Educational Evaluation*, 32, 262–287.

Ramsden, P. (2009), *The Future of Higher Education Teaching and the Student Experience*. UK: Department for Innovation, Universities and Skills.

Reimann, N. and Wilson, A. (2009), 'HE teachers' learning about assessment: engaging with formal and informal learning opportunities'. Paper delivered to the EARLI 13th biennial conference for research on learning and instruction, '*Fostering Communities of Learners*', 25–29 August, Amsterdam.

Rust, C. (2007), 'Towards a scholarship of assessment', *Assessment & Evaluation in Higher Education*, 32, (2), 229–237.

Rust, C., O'Donovan, B. and Price, M. (2005), 'A social constructivist assessment process model: how the research literature shows us this could be best practice', *Assessment & Evaluation in Higher Education*, 30, (3), 231–240.

Sadler, D. R. (1989), 'Formative assessment and the design of instructional systems', *Instructional Science*, 18, 119–144.

Sambell, K. and McDowell, L. (1998), 'The construction of the hidden curriculum: messages and meanings in the assessment of student learning', *Assessment and Evaluation in Higher Education*, 23, (4), 391–402.

Sambell, K., McDowell, L. and Brown, S. (1997), '"But is it fair?" An exploratory study of student perceptions of the consequential validity of assessment', *Studies in Educational Evaluation*, 23, (4), 349–371.

Sambell, K., McDowell, L. and Sambell, A. (2006), 'Supporting diverse students: developing learner autonomy via assessment', in C. Bryan and K. Clegg (eds), *Innovative Assessment in Higher Education*. London: Routledge, pp.158–168.

Segers, M., Dochy, F. and Cascaller, E. (eds) (2003), *Optimising New Modes of Assessment: In Search of Qualities and Standards*. Dordrecht: Kluwer Academic.

Sluijsmans, D., Moerkerke, G., Dochy, F. and Van Merriënboer, J. (2001), 'Peer assessment in problem-based learning', *Studies in Educational Evaluation*, 27, (2), 153–173.

Tan, K. (2004), 'Does student self-assessment empower or discipline students?' *Assessment & Evaluation in Higher Education*, 29, (6), 651–662.

Torrance, H. (2007), 'Assessment as learning? How the use of explicit learning objectives, assessment criteria and feedback in post-secondary education and training can come to dominate learning', *Assessment in Education: Principles, Policy and Practice*, 14, (3), 281–294.

Wake, B. and Watson, H. (2007), *Assessment for Learning: A Student Survival Guide*. Northumbria: MARCET. Red Guide series, Paper 33.

Wilson, M. and Scalise, K. (2006), 'Assessment to improve learning in higher education: The BEAR Assessment System', *Higher Education*, 52, (4), 635–663.

Chapter 4

Working Together to Reduce Plagiarism and Promote Academic Integrity: A Collaborative Initiative at Leicester

Jo Badge, Nadya Yakovchuk, Alysoun Hancock and Aaron Porter

Plagiarism in higher education is said to be on the increase (Eaton, 2004; Hart and Friesner, 2004). It is difficult to know the cause of this rise, but it is probably linked to an increase in detection through the use of electronic detection mechanisms and exacerbated by an increasing reliance by students on internet resources (Lancaster and Culwin, 2005; Hayes, 2009). Studies have shown that students who plagiarize do so for a variety of reasons, from failing to understand the importance or mechanism of referencing and paraphrasing to poor time management and study skills to deliberate attempts to obtain an unfair advantage (Park, 2004; Bennett, 2005).

Recent years have also seen an evolution in policies to deal with plagiarism across the Higher Education Board. However, the two UK-wide surveys conducted by Joint Information Systems Committee (JISC) Plagiarism Advisory Service (PAS) that benchmarked the policies and penalties in place for dealing with plagiarism across UK higher education institutions (Tennant, et al., 2007; Tennant and Duggan, 2008), highlighted substantive differences between institutions in their approaches to plagiarism. This means that students 'committing' the same offence are likely to be treated differently by different institutions, something that former Adjudicator for Higher Education, Baroness Deech (Baty, 2006), saw as a major problem facing higher education institutions. The concern that plagiarism threatens the quality of the degrees awarded by higher education institutions has led to considerable media attention on the subject and research and discussion of how the problem of plagiarism can be addressed in higher education (Larkham and Manns, 2002; Park, 2003; Fielden and Joyce, 2008). A holistic approach to dealing with plagiarism that places major importance on plagiarism prevention has been emphasized by respected researchers in the area (Carroll and Appleton, 2001; Park, 2003).

Anecdotally, it seems that when a student is introduced to plagiarism in their early days of higher education, the induction is normally that of the 'it's-bad-so-don't-do-it-or-you'll-be-punished' type. Strict warnings, a range of punishments and accounts of students who have fallen foul of accidental or deliberate slips in scholarship are typical examples of how plagiarism is often framed in the academic world – in very negative terms. These observations find support in more systematic empirical research. Park (2003, p. 472), for example, collected different metaphors for referring to plagiarism, among which are 'the unoriginal sin', 'a writer's worst sin' and a 'cancer that erodes the rich legacy of scholarship'. Pecorari (2001) compared institutional anti-plagiarism policies in three countries, the USA, UK and Australia, stating that, overall, they 'appeared to assume a universal view of plagiarism as an academic crime' (p. 243). In her UK-based overview of student-oriented plagiarism prevention guidelines, Yakovchuk (2004) concluded that most institutions in her randomized sample referred to plagiarism as '(intellectual) dishonesty and cheating' (p. 5).

It is perhaps unsurprising, therefore, that from their early days onwards, students tend to treat plagiarism with a great deal of caution and concern. While source attribution enhances student work and gives them an opportunity to demonstrate their knowledge and learn to weave their emerging voices into the existing academic scholarship (essentially very positive aims), in reality it often becomes a burden and a source of worry for students. A patronizing and moralistic attitude on the part of academics seems to widen the gap between them and their students, rather than provide encouragement and a warm welcome into the academic world. Students join the academic community when they become undergraduates and may ultimately become academics themselves. An approach to academic integrity that involves both staff and students working in a responsible partnership may enable students to feel more confident that their voices will be heard.

In his report to the Secretary of State, Paul Ramsden, as Chief Executive of the Higher Education Academy (Ramsden, 2008) called for students to be engaged in a partnership with staff to shape their own education. He pointed out that

> there is growing recognition that students have a major role to play in the enhancement of teaching and assessment. Universities and colleges are increasingly positioning students as engaged collaborators rather than inferior partners in assessment, teaching, course planning and the improvement of quality, and are using student representatives as central contributors to the business of enhancing the student experience.
>
> (Ramsden, 2008, p. 5)

He called for creating 'learning communities' in which students' role would be that of 'responsible partners who are able to take ownership of quality enhancement with staff and engage with them in dialogue about improving assessment, curriculum and teaching' (p. 16). By doing this, Ramsden believes, students will be able to 'understand themselves as active partners with academic staff in a process of continual improvement of the learning experience' (ibid.). There are signs that the national bodies and influential policymakers are beginning to look at this role of partnership with students in making decisions about the future of higher education. The Office of the Independent Adjudicator for Higher Education (OIAHE) is examining its future role as the arbitrator in disputes between students and their higher education institutions (see www.oiahe.org.uk). Part of this role is to issue guidance and recommendations to institutions on how they deal with complaints, which includes those associated with penalties for plagiarism. A recent consultation exercise by the OIAHE specifically sought feedback on whether there should be increased student representation on their board (at present limited to representatives from the National Union of Students).

This chapter reports on a project carried out at the University of Leicester that attempts to frame the issue of plagiarism in more positive terms and increase student involvement in the promotion of academic integrity and good academic scholarship. After providing some background information about an alternative value system for dealing with plagiarism, we describe our staff–student cooperation project in more detail, outline its outcomes, reflect on the process of collaboration and offer ideas of how this partnership can be taken further.

Background

When faced with similar problems of increasing rates of plagiarism, some higher education institutions in the USA implemented radical solutions that have led to a transformation of staff and student views on the issue (McCabe et al., 2002). Over the past few decades, a growing number of US institutions have been adopting an '*honour code*' system, which has been reported to have a positive effect on the level of academic misconduct among their students (McCabe and Trevino, 1997; McCabe et al., 2002). This value-based system places campus-wide emphasis on academic integrity, student involvement in promoting good academic practice and mutual responsibility of staff and students for adhering to academic values and maintaining academic standards. Collaboration between staff and students and student-led initiatives were shown to be instrumental to this model's success (McCabe and Trevino, 1997).

The University of Virginia is believed to have the oldest honour code system of its kind that is entirely student-run. It was founded in 1842 following a period of unrest between staff and students. The basic principle of this system is a *community of trust* – 'a community where each student acts honourably and lives up to an ideal standard of conduct' (Honor Committee, 2002), that is, students are trusted to uphold the principles of academic integrity. It is also assumed that the ethical principles exercised on the university campus are carried over to life outside in the community. As one of the students observed:

> To truly understand the honor system you have to live with it. And I think once you live with it, you begin to see how honor will inevitably become a part of everything that you do, not just now when you're a student, but every day of your life. When you're an honorable person, people know it.
>
> (Honor Committee, 2008)

Staff members of the university also see the benefits of such a system: 'I've taught at other universities, and the system here liberates me and my faculty colleagues. They concentrate on what's important in the classroom – learning – and not policing the students' (Honor Committee 2008). This focus on 'learning and not policing' has informed our collaborative efforts to change the angle from which plagiarism can be viewed in the context of our university.

Our collaboration

Our staff–student collaboration has developed as a spin-off from a university-wide academic integrity project run by a staff research team from the School of Biological Sciences and the Genetics Education Networking for Innovation and Excellence (GENIE) Centre for Excellence in Teaching and Learning (CETL). The project aimed to explore staff and student views on plagiarism, academic integrity and the US honour code system. The Students' Union was initially contacted to discuss best approaches to setting up a consistent procedure for recruiting student participants across different subject disciplines. The Academic Affairs Office at the time, Aaron Porter (sabbatical) saw an opportunity to widen the Students' Union involvement beyond providing participants for the focus groups in the research study. A partnership was formed between the Students' Union employed Education Officer, the sabbatical officer responsible for education and the university research staff working on the academic integrity project (Jo Badge and Nadya Yakovchuk). Once the focus groups for the research project were completed, a new Students' Union Education Officer was appointed (Alysoun Hancock) and joined the partnership. Together with support from the partnership, she led a review of the Students' Union's approaches to educating students about plagiarism.

The aim of the partnership was to explore how changing the Students' Union's approach to plagiarism (and academic dishonesty in general) could lead to a transformation of staff and student views on the issue, and could help students make the most of their academic potential through embracing core academic values and mastering correct academic conventions. We see our staff–student partnership as an evolving process of collaboration between the team members (and the wider groups they represent), through which perspectives have been developed and enriched (and perhaps in some cases altered) and joint efforts have been made to instigate changes to educational practice in light of the current developments in pedagogic research.

Students' union concerns

The Education Unit is one of the services that the University of Leicester Students' Union provides for students. It offers a free and impartial service to help and advise students. All kinds of requests for guidance are made and frequently students approach the Education Unit for advice about plagiarism.

The Students' Union Education Unit were involved in recruiting students from across the institution to take part in focus groups for the previously mentioned staff-led academic integrity research project. The main participants were those students who were already Students' Union course representatives. Their involvement in the project and the recruitment of a new Education Officer, Alysoun Hancock, led to a discussion on how the Students' Union Education Unit gave advice on the avoidance of plagiarism and supported students in this area.

The Education Unit took the opportunity to gain some feedback on this topic and asked a range of students, some who had been found to plagiarize, about their experience of plagiarism. Between January and June 2009, 20 students visited the Education Officer for advice and guidance on how to proceed after being found to have plagiarized. Each case varied in the extent of plagiarism, and it was interesting to note that the responses from departments were also varied. Some departments were more positive in their dealings with the student concerned than others. For example, students may have been provided with one-to-one support to discuss good citation practice and paraphrasing whereas others had been given penalties without further explanation or guidance. Student experience of learning about plagiarism also varied enormously. Generally, the introduction reinforced the negative connotations of plagiarism, focusing on penalties and poor academic practices. Many students were able to give only a partial definition of the word usually along the lines of 'using the ideas of someone else and pretending they were your own' but were unclear of the wide range of activities that plagiarism encompassed.

A wider consultation with students was achieved through the student course representative system. The undergraduate and postgraduate Students' Union coordinators took the topic to their course representatives for discussion and collated their responses. The feedback was wide-ranging. Students reported various experiences of being informed about plagiarism and the consequences for them. The following examples illustrate the inconsistencies found by students.

Some found their course induction clear, helpful and reassuring. They were offered plenty of help and advice and encouraged to seek clarity and guidance from staff. One first-year student said, 'We had an informative lecture at the beginning of the first semester. The message has been reinforced before every written assignment. Occasionally we are given additional information about other aspects of plagiarism e.g. Turnitin' (Turnitin is a service which searches for non-original text in student work, see www.turnitin.com). Another student said, 'My department held a lecture on this in the first year and we also have information in our departmental handbook. We are taught how to reference work correctly and how to take notes from an academic's work and to use these ideas to expand and develop our own ideas. The handbook also refers to the Student Learning Centre for further information'.

Others were less positive and felt advice given to them was inadequate. A third-year student said, 'I had no explanation of plagiarism until my third-year dissertation model was presented'. A postgraduate student said, 'we were warned about plagiarism and told to reference correctly. We were not taught about the different things that could be classed as plagiarism'. One first-year student who came to the Student Support Centre to see the Education Officer for advice said 'I'm always worried about referencing when I hand in a piece of work'.

The Students' Union's findings corroborated the outcomes of the staff-led academic integrity project. Although there has been a wealth of information targeted at students to tell them that they should not plagiarize, a gap in students' understanding still exists. They seem to be confused about the wide range of activities that constitute plagiarism and do not always know how to avoid plagiarizing. The national picture of inconsistency in dealing with plagiarism (Jones, 2006; Tennant et al., 2007; Tennant and Duggan, 2008) was also found to be reflected *within* the institution.

This evidence obtained from both staff- and student-led systems of enquiry led to the Students' Union-initiated process of redesigning their materials on plagiarism prevention and referencing. Since the results of the staff-led academic integrity research project demonstrated acceptance of a more positive and educational approach to plagiarism, the Students' Union took on board some principles of the academic integrity approach in their work to support students.

How has the Students' Union improved what advice and help is available?
The Student Support Centre based within the Students' Union produces advice leaflets on a variety of topics. One leaflet, 'What is Plagiarism & Academic Dishonesty', gives specific advice with regard to plagiarism. This leaflet was centred on warning students that plagiarism had severe consequences. The language was very negative and much attention was

given over to 'offences' that would result in 'penalties' and 'cheating'. Very little of the text was given to defining plagiarism or making it clear where students could seek help. It was felt that the leaflet in its original form was no longer acceptable.

A redesign of the leaflet (see Figure 4.1) was based on the principles of academic integrity and honesty. It was developed by the Students' Union Education Officer in consultation with the research staff involved in the academic integrity project and the Students' Union sabbatical officers. The original leaflet was an A5 booklet; this was changed to a single-sided A4 sheet to provide a clear, simple layout. The emphasis is now on providing a *student guide* and assisting *student understanding*. Sources of help are clearly listed and this section includes links to interactive guides available from the Student Development Centre and to the university policy on plagiarism.

The earlier consultation done through the Students' Union provided quotations from students about their experiences and thoughts on plagiarism, which helps to emphasize an empathetic point of view. The aim here

FIGURE 4.1   Redesigned leaflet produced by Students' Union after collaboration with staff and students with emphasis on academic integrity

is to begin to break down the barriers between staff and students and move our student culture away from an 'us and them' system to a single unified academic 'community of trust'. This also introduces the concept of peer education, students giving advice to other students, an important part of an honour code system. The phrase 'no student wants to find out that they have unwittingly fallen foul of the rules' was deliberately included to encourage students to recognize that they needed to take responsibility for their own work. Finally, a clear definition of plagiarism was included to educate and inform.

Another Students' Union's initiative was to introduce the concept of plagiarism visually. It is said that the word 'plagiarism' originates from the Latin *plagiaries* 'kidnapper' and further down from the Greek *plagion* 'a kidnapping'. This somewhat sinister origin and the semantic field surrounding the word 'plagiarism' do little to promote a positive view of good academic practice. The illustration developed by the Student Support Centre is aimed at alerting students to the topic in a lively and engaging way by attempting to depart from the overly negative connotations of the term. The illustration (see Figure 4.2) may be used in a forthcoming poster campaign and other Students' Union's activities.

FIGURE 4.2 Illustration for awareness campaign based on the origin of the word plagiarism from the Greek plagion, 'a kidnapping'

How has the institution improved what help is available?
The Student Learning Centre has a new Student Learning Zone based
in the university's David Wilson Library. Before the start of the academic
integrity project, advice on plagiarism was available as a paper-based leaflet
entitled 'Avoiding Plagiarism'. As part of the improvements to the Student
Learning Zone and a wish to provide more relevant and positive resources
on this topic, an online subject-specific tutorial was developed. The tutorials
deliver high-quality, interactive learning materials to students in a format
that allows them to work at their own pace and review and consolidate their
learning as often as necessary. The tutorials are publicly available at http://
tinyurl.com/plagiarismtutorial.

The tutorial was developed using the rationale that if students could learn
the study skills to enable them not to plagiarize, they would not simply be
avoiding getting penalized but they would be developing the academic skills
required to improve the quality of their work. This rationale also supported
the essential principles of academic integrity, promoting the positive aim to
educate students in the goals of good scholarship rather than force punitive
measures upon them.

While generic advice on study skills is valuable, it is enriched when
subject-specific examples are used. The tutorial was inspired by a study skills
tutorial from Acadia University in Canada and the intention was to include
an adaptation of a subject-specific exercise developed at the University of
Leicester by Willmott and Harrison (2003). It was structured on a core of
generic content that could be re-versioned. The discipline-specific elements
were designed as discrete entities so that their adaptation would not inter-
fere with the pedagogical integrity of the rest of the resource.

Since its development the first tutorial written for biological sciences
has been adapted for 14 further subjects at the University of Leicester
including: Computer Science; Criminology; Engineering; English and
American Studies; Geography; Geology; History; Labour Market Studies;
Law; Management; Medicine; Museum Studies; Occupational Psychology;
and Psychology. Feedback from staff and students on the tutorial has been
overwhelmingly positive, the vast majority identifying it as interesting, easy
to understand and informative.

Work in progress: Students' Union's recommendations
Most students would like to avoid plagiarism. It is clear from the discussions
with students groups within the Students' Union that more could be done to
educate and inform students about the pitfalls of plagiarism. It is important
that they know what plagiarism is, how to avoid it and where to go for help if
it becomes an issue for them. The Students' Union and the University want
to promote the topic of plagiarism in a positive way and avoid the connotations of it being a punishable 'crime'. The Students' Union is keen to work

in partnership with staff at the University of Leicester to promote academic integrity and reduce plagiarism.

The Students' Union has formally approached the institution with a set of recommendations, which will be considered by the university's academic policy committee in conjunction with recommendations from the research project looking at academic integrity. These recommendations seek to improve student awareness of plagiarism:

Students' Union Recommendations:

- Plagiarism covered at the beginning of each academic year in departmental induction activities
- Topic revisited at key points in course (e.g. before a dissertation) if necessary
- Examples showing a range of types of plagiarism provided either in a departmental handbook, or as part of initial induction or refresher tutorials
- Induction specific to the needs of particular student groups (e.g. postgraduate students, international students)
- Departmental check that the topic of plagiarism has been covered and that students understand it
- Consistency of approach between departments to plagiarism induction
- Consistency of approach across the university to plagiarism-related penalties and outcomes
- Avoidance of punitive language when giving back work to a student who has been found to plagiarize
- More publicity around the university (e.g. on departmental noticeboards, in the library) about the importance of good academic practice
- More understanding of electronic devices used e.g. Turnitin
- Guidance on the interactive tutorials on offer from the Student Learning Zone
- Involvement of the Students' Union in running workshops, publicity campaigns and distributing student guides to understanding plagiarism
- Information about the Education Officer in the Students' Union and where to go for help if plagiarism has been found
- Plagiarism awareness week and partnership between university and Students' Union
- Student forum asking students what would be helpful to them.

This joint approach by staff and students to make coherent and concordant recommendations to the institution is a direct product of the staff–student partnership project.

The university has already begun to subtly change its approach in this area. During the planning phases of the academic integrity project, the learning and teaching strategy was updated in 2006–07 and included the phrase 'academic integrity' as a core value of the strategy: '. . . that students should appreciate and demonstrate the importance of displaying high standards of academic integrity in every aspect of their studies'.

It is this shift in emphasis in terms of policy, the language of instruction and the language of policy that are the seeds of change for a cultural shift in the institution away from plagiarism detection towards the promotion of academic integrity. The wider academic integrity research project led by staff demonstrated that the values and overarching ethos of the honour code system could be adopted in the UK. We believe that by discussing these issues openly and in partnership we are leading by example in respecting each other and working together towards the ideal of good scholarship and practice by staff and students alike.

How can this practice be transferred and carried forward in other institutions?

The problem of plagiarism can be turned around into positive learning experiences. Discussion about good academic practices and a focus on key skills can start to offer reassurance to students and assist their development into mature, critical and analytical graduates. Staff and student partnerships working together on this area will help to embed the cultural changes required to break down the division between staff and student as 'mentor' and 'disciple'. While the concept of using positive reinforcement for academic integrity rather than punitive measures against plagiarism is relatively new, our experience shows that this cultural change could be instigated at other institutions. We make the following recommendations:

- Development of an academic code of conduct that seeks to use positive language, clearly define terms and conduct, and include examples of different types of plagiarism. This should help clarify the concept of plagiarism and its scope.
- Institutions should seek to provide a single point of information for staff and students on plagiarism and the skills necessary for good academic scholarship. This will help to promote a consistent approach across the institution.
- Active Students' Union involvement in all aspects of work relating to plagiarism prevention and dealing with suspected cases of plagiarism. This should encourage students to take more responsibility for their own learning.

Future trends

This staff–student partnership has focused on creating a community of trust and a strong ethos to encourage good scholarship. In our discussions about academic integrity, it is clear that the issue goes to the heart of the purpose of higher education. For this reason we believe that, in the future, an increasing number of higher educational establishments will move towards a positive response to academic scholarship and move away from projecting a threatening and punitive view of plagiarism. Some institutions, such as Northumbria University, have already begun this process by setting out the institution's core values for students to engage with from the beginning of the students' university careers (Shepherd, 2007).

Students recognize that the value of their degrees is related to the quality of education they receive. The National Union of Students in the UK has a renewed focus on matters of scholarship and recently held their first national conference on higher education, looking at the purpose of higher education. The student voice is increasingly being heard in quality assurance audits and through the National Student Survey. A movement towards not just incorporating the views of students, but further engaging them in peer learning and commitment to their own learning must surely follow. This involvement by students as equal partners in the higher education community of trust is at the heart of the values that underpin the academic integrity movement.

Conclusion and reflections

The staff–student partnership at the University of Leicester is an example of a research-led initiative to instigate changes to educational practice. It is hoped that this may be the beginning of a cultural shift towards a focus on good academic scholarship. Students who become aware of how to avoid plagiarism will also be developing their writing skills and critical thinking abilities.

There is considerable scope for continued cooperation as student-led initiatives can potentially extend to student engagement in peer mentoring or tutoring schemes or even a judiciary system. Involvement in the judiciary process, for example, could promote leadership skills and provide responsibilities essential for good citizenship and employability.

The process of working on this project has been informative for both staff and students, with both gaining an appreciation of the other's point of view. Participation in the project itself raises awareness of the issues surrounding good scholarship. This was one of the implicit aims in conducting such a research project.

One of the difficulties faced by the author team was the transient nature of the student population. One of the original members of the author team graduated and moved to a new position. This transiency serves to remind us of how new policies and initiatives must be self-sustaining to be successful. Each new intake of students needs to be successfully engaged in good academic practice anew and the experiences of graduates need to be captured before they leave the confines of the institution.

Framing the issue of plagiarism in more positive terms and increasing student involvement in the promotion of academic integrity should hopefully get students thinking less about plagiarism 'horror stories', and more about establishing themselves in a new and stimulating academic world. Achieving this through a working partnership, to create a more positively focused community of trust is surely a sustainable answer to the problem of plagiarism.

References

Baty, P. (2006), 'Inconsistent penalties raise risk of legal action, Deech says'. *The Times Higher Education Supplement*, 23 June 2006.

Bennett, R. (2005), 'Factors associated with student plagiarism in a post-1992 university', *Assessment & Evaluation in Higher Education*, 30, (2), 137–162.

Carroll, J. and Appleton, J. (2001), *Plagiarism: A Good Practice Guide*. UK: Joint Information Systems Committee PAS.

Eaton, L. (2004), 'A quarter of UK students are guilty of plagiarism, survey shows'. *British Medical Journal*. Retrieved 1 August 2009 from http://www.bmj.com/cgi/content/full/329/7457/70-c

Fielden, K. and Joyce, D. (2008), 'An analysis of published research on academic integrity'. *International Journal for Educational Integrity*, 4, (2), 4–24. Retrieved 4 June 2009 from http://www.ojs.unisa.edu.au/index.php/IJEI/article/viewFile/411/291

Hart, M. and Friesner, T. (2004), 'Plagiarism and poor academic practice – a threat to the extension of e-learning in higher education?' *Electronic Journal of e-Learning* 2, (1).

Hayes, N. (2009), 'A cheat, moi? That's unfair'. *Times Higher Education Supplement*, 29 January 2009.

Honor Committee. (2002), *On my Honor: An Introduction to Your Honor System*. Retrieved 29 June 2009 from http://www.virginia.edu/onmyhonor/

Honor Committee. (2008), *Introduction*. Retrieved 29 June 2009 from http://www.virginia.edu/honor/

Jones, M. (2006), 'Plagiarism proceedings in higher education – quality assured?' *Proceedings of the Second International Plagiarism Conference*, Gateshead. Retrieved 15 June 2009 from http://www.plagiarismadvice.org/images/stories/old_site/media/2006papers/MartinJones.pdf

Lancaster, T. and Culwin, F. (2005), 'Classifications of plagiarism detection engines', *Italics e-Journal*, 4, (2).

Larkham, P. J. and Manns, S. (2002), 'Plagiarism and its treatment in higher education', *Journal of Further and Higher Education*, 26, (4), 339–349.

McCabe, D. L. and Trevino, L. K. (1997), 'Individual and contextual influences on academic dishonesty: a multicampus investigation', *Research in Higher Education*, 38, (3), 379–396.

McCabe, D. L., Trevino, L. K. and Butterfield, K. D. (2002), 'Honour codes and other contextual influences on academic integrity: a replication and extension to modified honour code settings', *Research in Higher Education*, 43, (3), 357–378.

Office of the Independent Adjudicator for Higher Education (OIAHE) website. Accessed 12 January 2010 at http://www.oiahe.org.uk/

Park, C. (2003), 'In other (people's) words: plagiarism by university students – literature and lessons', *Assessment and Evaluation in Higher Education*, 28, (5), 471–488.

Park, C. (2004), 'Rebels without a clause: towards an institutional framework for dealing with plagiarism by students', *Journal of Further and Higher Education*, 28, (3), 291–306.

Pecorari, D. (2001), 'Plagiarism and international students: how the English-speaking university responds', in D. Belcher, and A. Hirvela (eds), *Linking Literacies. Perspectives on L2 Reading-Writing Connections*. Ann Arbor, MI: The University of Michigan Press, pp. 229–245.

Ramsden, P. (2008), 'The future of higher education: teaching and the student experience', *Report to the Secretary of State*. Retrieved 10 December 2009 from http://www.nus.org.uk/PageFiles/350/The%20Future%20of%20Higher%20 Education%20(Teaching%20and%20the%20student%20experience).pdf

Shepherd, J. (2007), 'An Idea Worth Imitating'. Retrieved 25 June 2009 from http://www.guardian.co.uk/education/2007/mar/20/highereducation. students

Tennant, P. and Duggan, F. (2008), *Academic Misconduct Benchmarking Research Project: Part II. The Recorded Incidence of Student Plagiarism and the Penalties Applied.* HEA JISC. Retrieved 16 November 2009 from http://www.heacademy.ac.uk/ assets/York/documents/AMBeR_PartII_Full_Report.pdf

Tennant, P., Rowell, G. and Duggan, F. (2007), *Academic Misconduct Benchmarking Research Project: Part I. The Range and Spread of Penalties Available for Student Plagiarism among UK Higher Education Institutions.* JISC Plagiarism Advisory Service. Retrieved 16 November 2009 from http://www.plagiarismadvice.org/ documents/amber/FinalReport.pdf

Willmott, C. J. R. and Harrison, T. M. (2003), 'An exercise to teach bioscience students about plagiarism', *Journal of Biological Education*, 37, (3), 139–140.

Yakovchuk, N. (2004), 'An analysis of on-line student plagiarism prevention guidelines at British universities', *Proceedings of the Plagiarism: Prevention, Practice & Policy 2004 Conference*, Newcastle upon Tyne. Retrieved 15 June 2009 from http://www.jiscpas.ac.uk/documents/papers/2004Papers26.pdf

Chapter 5

Using Wikis and Blogs to Support Writing Development: The Online Evolving Essay Project

Katherine Harrington, Peter O'Neill and Lynn Reynolds

Wherever the workman is utterly enslaved, the parts of the building must of course be absolutely like each other; for the perfection of his execution can only be reached by exercising him in doing one thing, and giving him nothing else to do. The degree in which the workman is degraded may be thus known at a glance, by observing whether the several parts of the building are similar or not; and if, as in Greek work, all the capitals are alike, and all the mouldings unvaried, then the degradation is complete; if, as in Egyptian or Ninevite work, though the manner of executing certain figures is always the same, the order of design is perpetually varied, the degradation is less total; if, as in Gothic work, there is perpetual change both in design and execution, the workman must have been altogether set free.

(Ruskin, 1917, pp. 157–158)

The London Metropolitan University Writing Centre opened in October 2006 as an initiative of the Write Now Centre for Excellence in Teaching and Learning. From the outset, the writing centre saw itself as not only helping students to succeed with the demands and conventions of academic writing. It also wanted to help students – like Ruskin's Gothic workmen – to find an authentic voice as writers in particular disciplines, but also as themselves. Our approach in working with students has been to avoid hierarchical 'teaching' of writing; rather, we have put into place an undergraduate writing mentor scheme where confident student writers work with fellow students in order to give them the confidence to write freely within the context of their academic discipline, as opposed to writing with the aim simply to please a lecturer, which often leads to the undesirable result of written work that looks remarkably and uninspiringly similar to all other assignments executed in this manner (see O'Neill, 2008, for the use of peer tutors in writing in UK higher education). This collaborative ethos helped to inform the evolving essay project, conducted in February and March of 2007 by Lynn Reynolds, one of the London Met Writing Mentors and a third-year undergraduate student in psychology. The aim of the evolving essay was to build an online complementary resource by writing a 1,500-word psychology essay online and in real time. Collaboration was the essence of the project, and it involved London Met Writing Centre and Psychology Department staff as well as London Met student writing mentors. The online nature of the project also meant that this collaboration could be extended worldwide with staff and students contributing to a global conversation.

This chapter – like the evolving essay itself – is written primarily by Lynn. However, it is in a very real sense the result of collaboration: the collaboration that informed the original evolving essay; continuing conversation about the project with London Met staff and with participants at joint presentations at conferences where the project has been discussed; feedback from London Met staff on drafts; and also actual drafting of some of the text by staff. When collaboration is real, although the final product may have multiple sources, all collaborators should be able to stand behind the text. This is certainly the case for this chapter. As with the original project, a wiki was used for some of the drafting, allowing multiple authors to revise the text, although the real collaboration has been the discussion and ongoing attention to the project over the last two-and-a-half years. The collaboration continues with the evolving essay available online at anessayevolves.blogspot.com where it is still possible for people to contribute to the discussion. Readers might like to take a look at this resource, which we hope will be of practical use to staff and students alike, before continuing with this chapter.

The project was inspired by Lynn having been a frequently baffled and blocked student writer throughout the course of her first undergraduate degree in the late 1980s. This was an agonizing state and seemingly resistant to being helped by generic advice on how to write at university. She was not an unconfident student on the whole, and was able to function well when tests were in a multiple choice or short answer format (which, since she was studying Physiology, were mercifully common). Writing-intensive assignments, however, would usually stimulate feelings of confusion and pessimism.

Later, during her time at London Metropolitan, Lynn encountered the writing centre, to which she was immediately attracted. This centre makes use of an approach to student writing development which is already well established in the United States and adapts it to the particular requirements of the UK system of higher education. It is collaborative and non-directive, following the insights of Bruffee (1984) and Lunsford (1991), and aims to help students take ownership of their academic writing. During the first three years of the programme, London Met undergraduate writing mentors have offered over 2,000 one-hour, one-to-one tutorials.

Students who visit the writing centre have the opportunity to work directly with a fully-trained peer mentor to increase their mastery of any aspect of the academic writing process. The underlying assumption driving the scheme is that as the result of close collaboration with their peers, student writers will be able to achieve a level of development greater than that attainable through working alone (Vygotsky, 1978). As a result of the writing centre training (see O'Neill et al., 2009) and after working as an undergraduate writing mentor during the first term of the scheme, Lynn began to sense the power of this model. Discussing academic writing not only seemed to improve the writing confidence of the students she worked with, but it also appeared to bring about a change in their self-perception. Instead of viewing themselves as passive recipients of knowledge, students began to see that they had the potential to contribute to the discourse within their discipline. They began to become, as Scardamalia and Bereiter (2006) put it, active learners and members of a knowledge-building community.

However, Lynn remembered well what it was to be outside such a group, and wanted to create some kind of supplementary example that would be useful for student writers at all levels, especially those struggling to approach square one. After all, they are often those most in need of support and yet perhaps those least equipped to ask for it. She also wanted to establish a source of comfort and inspiration that would be accessible around the clock. Her aim was to reassure student writers that although it often felt otherwise, they were not entirely alone.

The internet seemed the most obvious medium to host this message. Writing centre staff are regular visitors to a number of blogs ('blog' being a contraction of the phrase 'web log'), online diaries offering reflections on an experience or endeavour. In addition to being a simple method of private publishing, blogs also offer readers the option to make comments on each entry. Because blogging software enables so many avenues of communication and is mostly free of charge and easy to use, we decided that it would provide the ideal home for this experiment. Lynn was given the freedom to publish all blog entries without them being reviewed or edited by the team; however, these entries grew out of and were often followed by collaborative discussion with other students and staff in the writing centre.

The project's ethos was to make transparent every step of the writing and thinking process, especially during times of difficulty or confusion. Everything would be published: drafts, notes and reflections. The act of writing so openly on a blog would, we reasoned, encourage others to keep reading and responding to Lynn's thoughts and questions. Their participation would help them reflect on their own experience, which in turn would provide helpful insights to be used in developing the essay. To make the process approximately align with reality, it was agreed that the entire essay would be researched and written over a six-week period. In addition, the final version would be assessed by a psychology lecturer who had not previously been involved with the project or party to the online content. Finally, it was agreed that for ethical reasons the essay title would not be one that had been used for an assessed piece of coursework: it was written by Lynn, based on her experience of the types of questions set as assignments in psychology.

Just before the project was launched, Peter O'Neill, who overviews the London Met Writing Centre, and Kathy Harrington, Director of the Write Now CETL, mooted the idea of deploying yet another piece of internet technology to enhance the collaborative element of the process. This was important because, in addition to being a fundamental element in the writing centre's philosophy, collaboration is a feature of writing in many different kinds of career. It also happens to be an activity that generates much anxiety when it appears in the undergraduate curriculum. Debate around the realities and ethics of collaboration would be stimulated in force, it was felt, by attempting to make the evolving essay a multiple-author venture. Writing centre staff had recently been jointly developing projects using wikis, internet applications that enable a number of remote users to edit a document directly. Excited by the potential of their suggestion, Lynn linked a wiki to the online essay blog. Drafting and note-making would now be carried out on the wiki and participants in the project would be invited to contribute more explicitly to the writing by making direct additions and amendments. Process commentary and off-topic content were still to be posted on the blog. Writing centre staff advertised the venture widely to psychology, academic writing and learning development email lists with international reach and it was clear from the initial response that this project was likely to attract substantial interest.

Models of academic writing and their limitations

It has been Lynn's observation that success in post-1992 higher education requires a more active engagement with the course than was needed in her previous experience of degree-level study. The assessment methods used by lecturers are more diverse; traditional examinations are still present, but a wide variety of writing-intensive assignments such as essays, practical reports, reflective logs, learning journals and posters are also given, prompted in part by a growing interest providing more authentic assessment opportunities for students (McDowell and Sambell, 1999; MacAndrew and Edwards, 2002). At London Metropolitan a significant number of students enter the university via non-traditional routes. Many in Lynn's particular cohort were also from outside the UK and did not have any experience of current academic conventions in this country. Despite being issued with explicit marking criteria, Lynn and a number of her student colleagues found that they lacked a clear conception of what a good essay or report was like.

In the face of this uncertainty, they looked for examples of the kind of writing they aspired to produce. These were plentiful and easy enough to find, but uninformative. It proved difficult to deconstruct a finished text and abstract the essential characteristics of its genre. And having seen these examples, it subsequently became much more challenging to forget them and begin to formulate original ones. In general, fully finished models tended to undermine their confidence as writers rather than serve as a source of inspiration. This experience was echoed by one of the earliest contributors to the evolving essay wiki, who commented,

> When there's a model answer or example essay given to you as a guideline, you can become so paranoid that people might think you plagiarized it that you completely deviate from it. And through this determination not to use the same points or concepts, you leave out key material that you may otherwise have included had you NOT seen the model.

Although several other contributors revealed that they had found model essays helpful, Lynn's personal experience echoes the findings of empirical studies investigating this issue, which suggest that model texts are of limited use to students seeking guidance on how to write in a particular academic genre. Participants in some of these studies were able to do nothing more sophisticated than imitate the diction found in the examples they were given (Gowda, 1983; Church and Bereiter, 1983). Although imitation of the words of others who are already established academic writers can be seen as a legitimate developmental step in the student writer's education, there is also the risk that novice writers will mistake this practice for the more complex and difficult process of writing as a member of a disciplinary community. And if adopted as a general approach to study it clearly has negative implications for the development of student voice and a sense of ownership of their written work.

Similarly, Hjortshoj (2001) has argued that writers reliant on a limited repertoire of strategies acquired early on in their academic career are failing to engage with the true complexities and confusions of scholarship. Of course, a writer who is not thus engaged will not necessarily produce bad writing, but she or he is more likely to encounter writing blocks and other difficulties with the writing process, and these tend to become more probable and more disabling as assignments become progressively more sophisticated and demanding.

There is even some evidence that such a product-oriented approach to writing may be a cause of difficulty in learning. Bereiter and Scardamalia (1987) suggest that the failure to develop a sense of writing as a process may propagate the acquisition of 'inert' knowledge. This is a superficial level of understanding characterized by the ability to recite facts but not perform meaningful operations upon them. To accept the implications of these findings is to accept the idea that mimicry as a writing strategy can impede high-level intellectual development. In Ruskin's parlance, students using this as their principal writing technique may risk becoming enslaved thinkers as well as enslaved writers. Our contention is that scholarship should not be regarded as a performance to be emulated, and indeed approaches that show how non-experts successfully cope with and complete tasks are more likely to promote self-efficacy in students (see Margolis and McCabe, 2006). Students need to take a hands-on stance at an early stage to optimize their university experience. Many do. And yet, for a variety of reasons, this is not an inevitable outcome. The findings of the evolving essay project, as well as our experiences in London Metropolitan's writing centre, confirm our belief that collaboration – especially across the hierarchical divide between staff and students – is a key part of encouraging an active approach to learning at university.

The experience of collaborating online

Interest in the evolving essay project was very high from the outset and included contributions from staff and students across the UK and USA and Canada. A number of 'silent' visits were received from 'lurkers' throughout Europe and Scandinavia. Many of the most active participants were current students studying at either undergraduate or postgraduate level, although some contributions appeared to come from individuals outside academia for whom the process of writing was a purely professional concern. As anticipated, a lively interest was shown by those already connected with writing centres or study support. Substantial subject-specific discussion was contributed by psychology lecturers and researchers, who, together with lecturers in other disciplines, also took part in debates around issues such as question-setting, assessment and research. Contributions were always offered on an informal, usually first-name basis. This is significant. As was discovered after the end of the project, some of the participants were extremely eminent in their particular discipline. For example, 'Michele' turned out to be Michele Eodice, president of the International Writing Centre Association. And yet in the online space there seemed to be an unspoken agreement that rank was an irrelevance. What mattered was that the ideas and feelings generated by each topic be fully and freely explored within the group.

In retrospect it becomes clear that the evolving essay blog and wiki effectively harnessed the power of collective intelligence to construct a project-focused knowledge-building community. This is no mean feat; Lunsford (1991) describes the endeavour to create a truly collaborative environment as '. . . damnably difficult' (p. 5). The key, she comments, to true collaboration is that participants be genuinely reliant upon one another in order to carry out the task in hand. Collaboration must also reject traditional hierarchy, otherwise it merely replicates the passivity of an instructor-led classroom environment or exists in the denial of having done so.

On careful inspection, our project does indeed fulfil the criteria for collaboration. Lynn certainly needed her fellow participants. She felt accountable to them and depended on their input to help her process research findings and guide her writing efforts. In turn, they needed her to convert their discussions into a final essay draft. The extent to which traditional hierarchies dissolved during the active phase of the project has already been discussed. It can therefore be said that the space created was what Lunsford calls a 'Burkean Parlor': one where consensus and difference were equally valued, and where knowledge was arrived at by negotiation.

Traffic to the websites was continual. As of February 2008, the project blog and wiki had received 471 unique visits and 95 contributions, only two of which were negative in tone. A thematic analysis of the comments posted on both media was conducted as part of an evaluation of the project. Of these 95 contributions, 45 per cent referred to the process of writing, 28 per cent referred to the subject content of the essay, 18 per cent provided explicit encouragement for Lynn's efforts, 6 per cent counted as spam, and 3 per cent referred to related work. Of the 45 per cent (n=42) of contributions commenting on the process of writing, 55 per cent related to technical aspects and 45 per cent to emotional aspects of writing.

These observations resonate with those made by Cameron et al. (2009), who identify three distinct elements of a developing competence in academic writing. The first element is 'know-how', which covers the practice of writing from its mechanics (e.g. how to construct a paragraph, how to build an argument) up to a repertoire of attitudes and fuzzy skills such as viewing writing as a process and finding ways to start, continue and finish. Know-how is relatively well represented in study-support literature and academic instruction. Less frequently discussed is the dimension of emotion, which loomed so large on the wiki and blog. And lastly, a very much neglected topic, there is the importance of building an identity as an academic writer. Recognizing that one is in fact a writer appears to be closely linked to the process of a naïve learner becoming empowered as a scholar and gaining the confidence to use writing as a mode of thinking. At this level the individual is able to tolerate the uncertainty of an untidy, recursive approach to writing and use it as a way of formulating original concepts.

Not only have these three themes emerged very clearly from the analysis of the evolving essay project, but also they dovetail precisely with Lynn's own struggles as a student and with her experience of helping others in the writing centre. Each factor has been important, but we would argue that the process of becoming an advanced writer ultimately turns upon the issue of academic identity. This is the critical element enabling students to position themselves as creators of ideas rather than consumers of static knowledge; it marks the point at which the academic writer begins to find their unique voice. Without appropriate and well-timed intervention from others, many students' chances of reaching this point are greatly decreased. As will now be discussed, collaboration – between peers and between staff and student

– has an essential part to play in developing all three dimensions that make up writing competency.

Online collaboration and the development of 'know-how'

Contrary to our expectations, the scenario whereby Lynn's writings on the wiki were directly edited by a multitude of contributors did not materialize. This was initially disheartening and we feared that this lack of direct writing might indicate a failure of collaboration. However, we soon realized that visitors to the sites were participating fully; they just preferred to engage in discussion around Lynn's output rather than making their own changes or offering suggestions of a directive nature. When this became clear, all prewriting and planning activities were moved from the wiki to the blog, which provided a much more suitable environment for active discussion. Given the extent of activity in some discussion threads, collaboration was very obviously taking place.

Bereiter and Scardamalia (1987) describe two ways of assisting with the writing process. During this project we observed both of them. The first mode, termed substantive facilitation, is the kind of collaboration we originally envisaged taking place on the wiki. Through substantive facilitation, a teacher or collaborator reduces the cognitive burden on the learner by actively taking some responsibility for achieving the desired objective. In short, they do some of the work for the student writer – apparently the most direct and straightforward route to enhancing writing know-how. This is a process that occurs quite often in education, but that may not always be in the best interests of the novice writer since it may truncate their experience of the writing process. Once the evolving essay project was fully underway, it is noteworthy that a very small amount of substantive facilitation occurred. One example of this involved a particular collaborator directly editing the punctuation and spelling of the text on the wiki.

Although substantive facilitation may seem potentially disempowering (because the implication exists that the student cannot cope with the full demands of the assignment they face), Lynn reports that it was in this context incredibly helpful. The key to this would seem to be that she felt absolutely free to accept or reject such support as she saw fit. Control, cited by Lunsford (1991) as the antithesis of collaboration, was thereby minimized.

Throughout the duration of the project, the type of assistance in most plentiful supply was that of procedural facilitation. This is the converse of substantive facilitation. It is a type of intervention which takes account of the student's existing writing process then aims to enrich it by introducing additional elements of self-regulation (Bereiter and Scardamalia, 1987). For example, a student who never revises their writing may be encouraged to reflect upon their text and develop their own strategies for revision. It is clearly a more indirect approach to boosting know-how, but one which has potential to make the more profound change to the student's writing abilities, since it identifies the impetus for efficacy as being within the student rather than outside.

During the active phase of our project it was this class of intervention that enabled Lynn to take significant leaps forward with the essay, usually by helping her identify and articulate problems in the manner discussed earlier. As described by Vygotsky (1978), it is a technique which enables the reframing of tasks that lie beyond current abilities, and in doing so extends overall reach. It enabled Lynn to increase her writing know-how far beyond the level she would have achieved working alone. Our experience in the writing centre as well as in this project has been that peers are especially good at determining what Vygotsky termed the learner's zone of proximal development. This zone is the gap between what can be achieved independently and what can be done with outside help and it is important that interventions and advice lie within this area. Even with the best of intentions, academic staff can be so thoroughly acquainted with course material that they find it difficult to relate to the student's less developed understanding. As Corbett (2007) recognizes, this is one of the reasons collaboration (as opposed to tuition) can be such a powerful experience for a student.

Online collaboration and the emotional dimension of writing

As has already been mentioned, many of the blog and wiki contributions point to the emotionally charged nature of writing. This will hardly come as a surprise to anyone with recent memories of engaging in the writing process. Particular emotional states mentioned by participants in the evolving essay project include confidence and its absence, a sense of cognitive overload, confusion, passion, fascination, frustration, enjoyment, depression, paranoia, satisfaction and avoidance. Our findings, like those of Cameron et al. (2009), reveal that negative emotions are in plentiful supply when it comes to talking about writing. Since strong feelings can prove to be quite disabling, contributors frequently expressed a sense of relief at being able to use the blog as an outlet for naming their experience. This was a special feature of the evolving essay project, one distinctly missing from model essays and the normal type of academic writing advice.

The real revelation, though, was not the ubiquity of intense negative feelings but the fact that collaborators had such creative ideas about how to turn them around and co-opt them as aids to the writing process. One participant – a lecturer – described paralysing feelings of perfectionism as a cue to start chanting, 'Any old rubbish, any old rubbish' to herself. She would then take action and begin to write just anything, after which she would inevitably surprise herself with the high quality of this 'rubbish'. Happily, too, although positive emotions in connection with writing were in shorter supply than the negatives, they did exist. Several contributors stated how much they enjoyed writing, although usually not before they had said how difficult they found it! What emerged most from these discussions was that participants' feelings could be worked with instead of being feared and eradicated.

Accounts on the blog of experiencing these intense emotions serve also to remind us that – as Hjortshoj (2001) states – writing is not an exclusively mental process. It is clearly an embodied one, and our physical sensations provide clues which may enhance our insight into it. Gendlin (2004) refers to these sensations as 'felt sense' and argues that they indicate the presence of transitional knowledge which cannot as yet be articulated (on this, see the evolving essay blog entry 'Nailing jelly to the ceiling'). Perl (2004) has developed a methodology for uncovering and expressing this knowledge in writing. It is centred upon attending to the exact nature of the felt sense, and gently interrogating it through a series of writing prompts (or through attending to it during free writing, cf. Elbow, 2000, p. 140). Having used these techniques in the past, by ourselves and with fellow students in the writing centre, we have found that the presence of supportive peers or staff makes it much easier to interrogate felt sense. An attentive collaborator is frequently able to grasp the essence of an elusive thought before it bobs back under the surface of consciousness.

Online collaboration and academic identity

The collaboration forged through the evolving essay project successfully captured the non-directive, non-hierarchical, supportive essence of the London Metropolitan University Writing Centre. This is partly due to the quite exceptional extent of emotional openness encountered during the project. Ben-Ze'ev (2004) asserts that this kind of enhanced emotional disclosure is characteristic of relationships conducted in cyberspace. Perhaps a Burkean Parlor might be more easily created online than in the real world.

This type of candour and openness can serve a special purpose when staff and students collaborate. It can be argued that a sense of ourselves as academic writers will not develop unless we are recognized as such by peers and authority figures. Cameron et al. (2009) cite the work of Althusser (1972) and Butler (1997, p. 160) when they describe a workshop exercise that included the process of tutors hailing students as academic writers. Students thus hailed were then able to accept this call by recognizing *themselves* as writers, a twofold process that was witnessed by the other workshop participants. We have observed a similar process taking place in the writing centre. When a peer mentor takes a piece of writing seriously, its author consequently becomes more serious about writing. Lynn also experienced this for herself during the evolving essay project.

A further way in which staff and peers may foster a change in identity is by helping the student writer bear feelings of doubt and confusion. This is a significant benefit, since tolerating these uncomfortable emotions is essential to the process of learning as much as to the development of academic writing competence (Cousin, 2006). Confusion such as the kind documented by the evolving essay project may be a good thing; it can be a symptom of the transition to a more advanced level of conceptual understanding. Short-circuiting the transition through this kind of liminal state for the purpose of emotional comfort may have negative consequences. Bereiter and Scardamalia (1987) and Hjortshoj (2001) all concur with Cousin on this point. They suggest that the mature writing process is necessarily a complex, non-linear one involving repeated 'microloops' of planning, writing, reading, revising and editing. The first draft is an opportunity for the writer-as-thinker to set down their confusion. Subsequent revisions represent numerous opportunities to recover from this state as they approach an enhanced understanding.

When confronted by the multiple possibilities opened up by this approach, the less confident writer may feel paralysed and seek to escape the liminal state by reverting to the less developed compositional process of 'knowledge telling' (Bereiter and Scardamalia, 1987). The knowledge-telling writer typically responds to the separate components of an assignment title by writing down all the thoughts that come to mind at that time. The end result of knowledge telling may be a perfectly competent, even good, piece of writing, but it will not represent the act of thinking as writing, termed 'knowledge transforming'. It is an academic survival strategy rather than the use of writing to deepen disciplinary knowledge. Of course, knowledge transforming is emotionally and cognitively challenging. The interplay of content and rhetoric must be accommodated and a discomfiting double dose of liminality tolerated.

We are convinced that the struggle to use the knowledge-transforming process in academic writing is worthwhile. Grappling even halfway successfully with this process fosters a faith in one's ability to use learned material in a meaningful, purposeful way. It is the opposite condition to that of labouring under a huge burden of inert knowledge. Meyer et al. (2006) suggest that the mastery of certain 'threshold' concepts within a discipline is an efficient way of developing this kind of confidence. When a learner grasps a threshold concept, it becomes not mere intellectual knowledge, but part of their identity, something which cannot fail to influence their thinking. Threshold concepts, once learnt, are most unlikely to be unlearnt. Cousin (2006) argues that this very irreversibility can make it difficult for educators to empathize with students who are yet to master the threshold concepts within their discipline. She maintains that attending to students' misunderstandings and confusions is a valuable way for staff to facilitate the learning process. The evolving essay project is an example of exactly this kind of collaboration. The provisional nature of the blog and wiki enabled students to communicate their confusions to lecturers and to one another with complete honesty. And the collaboration of peers within the same discipline enabled participants to translate for each other 'at the boundaries between the knowledge communities students belong to and the knowledge communities they aspire to join' (Corbett, 2007). Not only was the ongoing project a way of assisting its participants in developing academic identities, but the completed project now offers a valuable insight into this little-discussed aspect of learning.

Conclusion

Confidence with writing is one of the biggest assets to a student career. For today's student, writing forms a large part of course assessment. It is a prominent activity in academia and the non-academic workplace alike. Yet many students never manage to get really close to the true heart of the writing process. They continue to work at an elementary level, viewing academic writing as a product-oriented activity or one primarily concerned with upholding stylistic conventions. Well-meaning lecturers may unwittingly undermine their students' attempts to develop as writers by encouraging them to consult model answers or essays. This is not a wholly innocuous practice; research findings suggest that novice writers are largely unable to move beyond emulating the writing style of the models they are provided with. Failing to develop a reasonably sophisticated writing process tends to make students vulnerable to writing blocks and other difficulties, especially when they are called upon to tackle demanding assignments. And it may limit their learning potential by favouring the acquisition of inert knowledge over a more active approach to study. It is also a cause for concern in terms of student voice and ownership.

Writing is a social activity. There is considerable irony in the fact that many student writers tend to struggle with written assignments in complete solitude. Collaboration on writing projects rarely occurs at undergraduate level, yet it is commonplace in the higher echelons of academia. It is, we believe, an approach worth practising; true collaboration requires commitment, interdependency of group members and the suspension of established hierarchies. It is consequently tricky to get right, but yields enormous benefits. The most pragmatic and obvious of these is that since academic writing is always created for a reader, it makes sense to obtain preliminary reader feedback before submitting the assignment to an assessor. Collaboration does of course have other advantages. Some of these can be seen in the writing centre at London Metropolitan University, which operates according to collaborative and non-directive principles. Many students who attend the writing centre and work with its trained peer mentors seem to undergo profound changes.

The evolving essay project was conceived as an attempt to replicate this supportive environment online. We aimed to develop a resource that went beyond the usual advice and models of how to write at university. It was an exercise in modelling creation rather than emulation. As a collaborative venture it was a complete success, forging a partnership between staff, students and those interested in the practice of academic writing. From the outset it became clear that the internet was an excellent medium for collaboration. Contributors were exceptionally honest about their relationship with academic writing and supportive of attempts to research and write the essay. Because of this honesty, the project yielded considerable information about the different dimensions of the academic writing experience, contributions that coincided with observations made by other researchers in academic writing development. It was found that our participants' experience of the writing process comprised three elements: their writing know-how, their emotional responses while writing and the extent to which they were able to develop an identity as an academic writer. The outcome of the evolving essay project leads us to believe that each element may be enriched when staff and students collaborate online. The blog and wiki proved invaluable in helping other student writers develop their own identity as creators of knowledge. This is extremely important, as it makes the difference between active, free learners with their own writerly voices and individuals enslaved by inert knowledge. It is our hope that this project will provide inspiration to tutors wishing to enable their students to develop as confident and self-directing academic writers and lead to the development and integration of similar collaborative writing experiences within disciplinary teaching.

References

Althusser, L. (1972), 'Ideology and ideological state apparatuses (notes towards an investigation)', in L. Althusser, *Lenin and Philosophy and Other Essays*, trans. B. Brewster. New York: Monthly Review Press, pp. 127–186.

Ben-Ze'ev, A. (2004), *Love Online: Emotions on the Internet*. Cambridge: Cambridge University Press.

Bereiter, C. and Scardamalia, M. (1987), *The Psychology of Written Composition*. Abingdon, Oxon: Routledge.

Bruffee, K. A. (1984), 'Collaborative learning and the "Conversation of Mankind"', *College English*, 46, (7), 635–652.

Butler, J. (1997), *The Psychic Life of Power: Theories in Subjection*. Stanford, CA: Stanford University Press.

Cameron, J., Nairn, K. and Higgins, J. (2009), 'Demystifying academic writing: reflections on emotions, know-how and academic identity', *Journal of Geography in Higher Education*, 33, (2), 269–284.

Church, E. and Bereiter, C. (1983), 'Reading for style', *Language Arts*, 60, 470–476.

Corbett, S. J. (2007), 'The give and take of tutoring on location', *Praxis: A Writing Center Journal*, 4, (2).

Cousin, G. (2006), 'Threshold concepts, troublesome knowledge and emotional capital: an exploration into learning about others', in J. H. F. Meyer and R. Land (eds), *Overcoming Barriers to Student Understanding: Threshold Concepts and Troublesome Knowledge.* Oxford: RoutledgeFalmer, pp. 53–64.

Elbow, P. (2000), 'Wrongness and felt sense', in P. Elbow (ed.), *Everyone Can Write: Essays Toward a Hopeful Theory of Writing and Teaching Writing.* New York and Oxford: Oxford University Press, pp. 137–141.

Gendlin, E.T. (2004), 'Introduction to "Thinking at the Edge"', *The Folio*, 19, (1), 1–8.

Gowda, N.S. (1983), *An Exploration of the Role of Language Awareness in High School Students' Reading and Writing.* Unpublished doctoral dissertation, Ontario Institute for Studies in Education.

Hjortshoj, K. (2001), *Understanding Writing Blocks.* New York: Oxford University Press.

Lunsford, A. (1991), 'Collaboration, control and the idea of a writing center', *The Writing Center Journal*, 12, (1), 3–10.

MacAndrew, S. B. G. and Edwards, K. (2002), 'Essays are not the only way: a case report on the benefits of authentic assessment', *Psychology Learning and Teaching*, 2, (2), 134–139.

Margolis, H. and McCabe, P. (2006), 'Improving self-efficacy and motivation: what to do, what to say', *Intervention in School and Clinic*, 41, (4), 218–227.

McDowell, L. and Sambell, K. (1999), 'The experience of innovative assessment: student perspectives', in S. Brown and A. Glasner (eds), *Assessment Matters in Higher Education: Choosing and Using Diverse Approaches.* Guildford: Society for Research in Higher Education and Open University Press, pp. 71–82.

Meyer, J. H. F., Land, R. and Davies, P. (2006), 'Implications of threshold concepts for course design and evaluation', in J. H. F. Meyer and R. Land (eds), *Overcoming Barriers to Student Understanding: threshold concepts and troublesome knowledge.* London and New York: Routledge.

O'Neill, P. (2008), 'Using peer writing fellows in British universities: complexities and possibilities' [Special issue on Writing Fellows]. *Across the Disciplines*, 5. Retrieved 17 December 2009 from http://wac.colostate.edu/atd/fellows/oneill.cfm

O'Neill, P., Harrington, K. and Bakhshi, S. (2009), 'Training peer tutors in writing: a pragmatic, research-based approach', *Zeitschrift Schreiben.* Retrieved 17 December 2009 from http://www.zeitschrift-schreiben.eu/Beitraege/o'neill_Training_Peer_Tutors.pdf

Perl, S. (2004), *Felt Sense: Writing with the Body.* Portsmouth, NH: Boynton/Cook Heinemann.

Ruskin, J. (1917), *The Stones of Venice*, Vol. 2. London: J. M. Dent.

Scardamalia, M. and Bereiter, C. (2006), 'Knowledge building: theory, pedagogy and technology', in K. Sawyer (ed.), *Cambridge Handbook of the Learning Sciences.* New York: Cambridge University Press, pp. 97–118.

Vygotsky, L. (1978), *Mind in Society: The Development of Higher Psychological Processes.* Cambridge, MA: Harvard University Press.

Chapter 6

Students and Staff as Educational Partners in the Development of Quality-Assured Online Resources for Medical Education

Jane Williams, Dominic Alder, Julian Cook, Miranda Whinney, Rachel O'Connell, Will Duffin and Philippa King

Many undergraduate medical students at the University of Bristol enjoy developing e-learning materials as part of a student e-learning initiative to produce high-quality online interactive learning materials. These electronic materials are produced as part of the Student Selected Components (SSC) programme, which provides opportunities for independent study within the medical curriculum as required by the General Medical Council (GMC, 2003). Comprising 25 per cent of the medical programme, students undertake a variety of projects (e.g. literature reviews, clinical audits, development of educational and training materials) as they progress throughout their course. The initiative is now in its sixth year with approximately 10 per cent of the student cohort (250) developing e-learning materials.

Students select their e-learning projects based on personal learning experiences; some have such a unique learning experience that they wish to capture and share that learning with others. For others, a subject may not be covered as well as they would like or it may not be covered (e.g. students in the European student exchange scheme, ERASMUS).

Placed within the context of studying medicine at the University of Bristol and the role of e-learning therein, this chapter describes the student e-learning initiative and provides some background on how the practice model developed to support this initiative has evolved. It continues by presenting student reflections from three students who have participated in the initiative over its existence to date. Drawing on these and other student reflections, the authors analyse the different and multiple partnerships that exist and are emerging, identify key factors for success and conclude on the notion of students as educational partners and co-developers of online learning materials for the undergraduate medical programme at the University of Bristol.

Background

The role of e-learning within undergraduate medicine at Bristol University
The medical programme at the University of Bristol uses a distributed model for delivering the clinical component (Years 3–5) whereby teaching is delivered by eight academies across 11 NHS Trusts and several other clinical practice settings (Mumford, 2007). In practice students rotate around the academies receiving all their clinical teaching, clinical experience and pastoral care, and taking assessments. In this way students receive both a breadth and depth of clinical knowledge and exposure providing a rich learning experience. However, provision and opportunity may vary, according to local specialisms and local challenges and can lead to a potential imbalance in access to key teaching or experiences. E-learning through a range of interactive online materials and video resources is therefore a key component of the clinical curriculum and integral to delivering a consistent and high-quality learning and teaching experience across all sites. Furthermore, students find it challenging when first entering the hospital environment and facing the realities of their chosen profession (Eckoldt et al., 2009). A longitudinal study investigating how e-learning materials can support and enhance the learning experience of students studying medicine and surgery in their first clinical year (Year 3) is the subject of a separate research project based at Bristol. Early research findings suggest that the e-learning elements of this course help students prepare for clinical teaching and develop their confidence for both clinical teaching sessions and ward rounds (Timmis et al., 2009).

Student generated e-learning materials
There is a long history associated with student generated electronic-based learning materials at Bristol University since the mid 1990s when first-year veterinary anatomy students developed computer-assisted learning material as part of their course (Garvin and Carrington, 1997). The cognitive benefits from students authoring learning materials are considered and documented well elsewhere (Turner and Dipinto, 1992; Nikolova, 2002 and papers therein). This paper is not about the cognitive benefits of students learning from writing and developing content. What was interesting, and prompted further examination, were the reflections from students in their written assignments accompanying their online product on the rationale behind undertaking an e-learning SSC. Students were reflecting on developing their knowledge of learning and teaching theory and principles and applying these to online materials. It was this that gave rise to the notion of our students as educators.

The practice and education of medicine is governed by a number of agencies including universities, the General Medical Council and British Medical

Association (BMA). The BMA in its 'Doctors as Teachers' say: 'all doctors have a professional obligation to contribute to the education and training of other doctors, medical students and non-medical healthcare professionals on the team' (BMA, 2006). Foundation doctors (two years of training after graduation from medical school in the UK) must demonstrate teaching competencies. In this paper we ask: 'Why wait until a foundation doctor?' The e-learning initiative provides students with opportunities to reflect on good and bad teaching they have been exposed to. Developing e-learning materials and learning exercises allows them to take small manageable steps towards being educators by practising designing their first learning materials – this includes setting objectives, scoping the material, pitching it at the right level and providing a variety of interactive learning exercises.

> I feel that I have been able to apply many of the teaching principles that I developed while making the e-learning SSC when teaching medical students. It showed me the value of making sessions student-led, problem-based, interactive and clinically relevant.
>
> Will Duffin

Student–staff partnerships as communities of practice

This chapter draws heavily on the concepts of Wenger's (1998) 'communities of practice' and social theories of learning. Communities of practice contain three main dimensions:

i)   mutual engagement: membership of participants in different roles acting in mutual benefit
ii) a joint enterprise: the activity which is defined by the participants through the process of pursuing it
iii) a shared repertoire: 'includes routines, words, tools, ways of doing things, stories, gestures, symbols, genres, actions or concepts that the community has produced [. . .] and which have become part of the practice' (Wenger, 1998, p. 83).

Applying this to the student e-learning initiative, students are mutually engaged in the common goal of enhancing the student learning experience and improving medical education, through the joint enterprise of developing innovative online learning materials as part of the student e-learning initiative, and developing a shared repertoire with their peers, teachers and e-learning professionals of common understanding, skills, knowledge and language of technology-enhanced learning and online learning materials development.

Lave and Wenger (1991) introduced the term 'legitimate peripheral participation' to describe how people join and are 'newcomers' in a community of practice. By granting newcomers legitimacy at the periphery they can, without fear of rejection, gain access to the 'masters', experienced expert members. In turn, newcomers contribute to the practice, ensuring its evolution, becoming relative 'old-timers' or masters. Learning to be a doctor is akin to an apprenticeship, where knowledge is applied to real problems combining theory with practice. Students on the e-learning initiative could be said to be beginning their apprenticeship in education. Lave and Wenger (1991) suggest that the concept of apprenticeship be broadened from that of the traditional master/student relationship to one of a community of practice of legitimate peripheral participation where newcomers' and masters' participation changes.

The student e-learning initiative

Learning is the engine of practice, and practice is the history of that learning.

(Wenger, 1998, p. 96)

The initiative began in 2003 when one student who had developed some online learning materials for their SSC encouraged a group of students to undertake similar projects. At this time, the initiative was entirely student-led with support sought from e-learning specialists on an ad hoc basis. The initiative gained considerable interest and an option to develop e-learning materials as an SSC was offered formally in 2005 by the e-learning team based in medical education. Students retain the responsibility of defining their SSC, setting objectives and identifying a supervisor.

The initiative has developed considerably, with each year seeing the products increase in sophistication. Students experiment with several software tools, media and interactive elements to achieve their objectives. A quality assurance framework developed and refined by student feedback supports the initiative and includes: drop-in sessions to discuss educational, legal, ethical and technical aspects of the process (e.g. instructional design, copyright, patient consent and adherence to standards) and to obtain advice and guidance; an online support course including frequently asked questions and a number of how-to guides with top tips for success; and sample forms for requesting to use images and other information.

Developing high-quality e-learning materials is time-consuming. One of the challenges students face is how to achieve this within the four-week SSC period. In 2008, an introductory workshop was introduced prior to deciding whether to undertake an e-learning SSC. Sessions covered educational principles, evaluation, question design and software tools. Students then submitted their project ideas and rationale before being accepted onto the initiative. There were concerns that this might change the dynamic of the initiative but these were unfounded with the usual 10–15 per cent of the student cohort submitting well-thought-out plans. The end products demonstrated the value of this additional step with 13 out of the 19 products submitted now used by students in the academic year 2009–10.

To date, the workshops and drop-in sessions have been run by staff. A further introduction for 2009–10 is the involvement of students in the initial presentation given to all Year 3 students on options for their SSCs. Students present their e-learning materials, acknowledging the strengths and challenges of doing an e-learning SSC. These students will continue to be involved with the initiative by providing peer support; as relative 'old-timers' and 'journeyfolk'.

> There are other inflection points as well, where journeyfolk, not yet masters, are relative old-timers with respect to newcomers, leading to diversified fields of relations among old-timers and newcomers within and across the various cycles, and the importance of near-peers in the circula-tion of knowledgeable skill (Lave and Wenger, 2005, p. 155).

Communities of practice are characterized by having shared histories of learning, life cycles that reflect and strengthen the process of the joint enter-prise, that in turn strengthen and add to the practice (Wenger, 1998). In this way, our community has evolved through the mutual engagement of staff seen here in the steps taken to enhance the underlying support processes provided to the students which in turn has seen an increase in the standard of e-learning materials each year.

Quality assurance
The mutual accountability in the joint enterprise can be seen in the develop-ment of the quality assurance framework. Materials are checked for accuracy of content and coverage before being cleared for permissions and consent for any media not generated by the students. Early years of the initiative saw students selecting a diverse selection of visual elements (video, photographs, diagrams, medical illustrations, clinical materials) with an eye to the message conveyed, without considering the legal and ethical aspects, leaving them unsuitable for publication. Students now show greater awareness of these issues. Some students show their artistic talents and solve copyright and patient consent issues by illustrating their own materials and shooting their own video using their peers as mock patients and doctors.

It is important to ensure all materials have gone through a rigorous and quality assessment process before being integrated into the curriculum. In particular an awareness of when and how to gain informed patient consent is a competency that students must acquire to become a doctor.

To develop a workable approach to clearing permissions, one tutorial was selected as a pilot. With the student's help, a robust and scaleable system was developed to clear permissions, locate alternatives or redraw images if necessary. Finally, other improvements are made to ensure an educationally sound product (e.g. modifying question design). Over time and with continuous refinement of the support processes, the resulting e-tutorials can be turned round very quickly, with students seeing their products incorporated into the curriculum and used by their peers.

Therefore participants, both students and staff, have developed expertise and community-based understandings of the importance and benefits of such a framework.

Voices from the community

This section presents reflections from three students representative of the initiative over time. The students were asked to comment on the rationale behind doing an e-SSC, what they learnt from the experience, whether they considered themselves as a partner in the delivery of medical education and in what capacity. At the time of publication the student authors are a specialist trainee, foundation doctor (Year 2) and fifth (final) year student. The two practising doctors were asked what if anything they had taken into their training years.

All three students tell of: their increasing awareness of the importance and use of online learning in medical education; their interest and personal experiences of e-learning materials, often citing exciting innovative products and some less inspiring ones; their wish to develop new skills – technical, ethical and educational, and their desire to achieve a high level of understanding of a particular subject in order to teach others, or by being inspired to research more by their teachers. They recalled the challenges of keeping content relevant to the audience's need, working independently, the labour-intensiveness of the process and the high commitment of time required to develop a credible product that would motivate and inspire future learners. All reflected on the numerous skills developed: project management, communication and negotiation, evaluation, video production, editing and animation, explaining concepts difficult to do so with books, processes for gaining consent, and so on. Of particular note, was the desire to develop and contribute something unique, taking pride in their achievements.

When the opportunity arose to produce an online tutorial myself I jumped at the challenge. I was interested in understanding a topic to a high level and the process by which it can be learnt to such a standard I could go on to teach others using an online tutorial. I also wanted to acquire new skills in designing user-friendly, interactive web pages and features which conventional text books cannot provide.

Rachel O'Connell

I had always been inspired by the e-learning tutorials available on the university's online learning environment and how much more enjoyable they were to work through in comparison to reading a textbook. The appeal of e-learning – multimedia content, interactive quizzes and user-led navigation through a topic was clear.

Will Duffin

Brew (2007), in understanding what students learn from engaging in research activities, synthesizes similar lists of personal and professional benefits from various studies (Blackmore and Cousin, 2003; Seymour et al., 2004; both cited in Brew, 2007). In particular, she reports that Blackmore and Cousin note the value placed by students on the opportunities of working in a direct relationship with academics in knowledge production within a culture of inquiry. In both these studies students reported they were treated differently as research associates from when they were students on courses. In investigating the relationships between teaching and research and the implications for inquiry-based teaching and learning in higher education, Brew (2003) argues for academic communities of practice in which relationships between teachers and students are renegotiated. In the new model, students and staff are mutually engaged in the production of knowledge and inquiry.

Part of the shared repertoire that our students have developed is the concept of an e-learning tutorial based on their own learning experiences as recipients of online learning of varying quality. One of our challenges is to encourage a wider repertoire by making it open, well informed over time and self-perpetuating. A recent addition to the support framework for the initiative has been a showcase of examples of good practice to help inspire and generate new ideas.

Dr Rachel O'Connell, specialist trainee

I chose examination of the female breast because there had been a lack of formal teaching on the topic during my clinical years. I realized that many medical students, particularly males, found breast examination difficult and perhaps uncomfortable to perform for the first time. The aim of the tutorial was to show students the technique of a breast examination and the possible pathologies associated with the breast. In this way, when they performed breast examinations they would have a framework to follow and would be able to make effective clinical diagnoses rather than 'just going through the motions'.

I always felt in partnership with both my supervisor and the team responsible for establishing e-learning tools. It was always clear that there were two intentions of the tutorial. The first was to increase my own understanding of the topic and to begin to understand the process of being a 'teacher' and the intricacies of providing education to medical students. The second was that if the standard of the end product was high enough then the tutorial could be used as a learning tool for students. This was very exciting and relied upon me having an open and honest relationship with my supervisor.

When I started this project I had not appreciated the expertise that would be required to gain consent and also to gain permission from patients and websites to use their material, as well as producing the web pages. I found this challenging but gained first-hand experience of these things and learnt the importance of presentation and continuity. It was essential that I had the support of the e-learning team behind me to guide me through and help me overcome these challenges; otherwise getting the tutorial online would not have been possible.

The process of researching, learning, designing and creating my own tutorial has provided me with a wealth of experience which I have used in my foundation years as a doctor. I have confidently taught medical students on several occasions, and often use the skills I learnt from researching for my tutorial to produce interesting and interactive slides for teaching sessions.

Dr Will Duffin, foundation doctor

At the time of the SSC, I had developed an interest in radiology and had been inspired by the excellent teaching given by one consultant radiologist. I wondered if I could use e-learning to emulate this teaching in a digital format. I also wanted to make his 'teaching files' – or films from interesting patients he had collected during his career available to more than just the eight students in [. . .] Academy. Furthermore I thought this would be an excellent opportunity to learn about diagnostic radiology and leave something behind from the process that others could benefit from too.

I felt a strong sense of partnership with my supervisor, who as a consultant radiologist could offer the expertise and core knowledge, knowing that I was bringing an idea of what kind of information and learning experience we needed as students. Through creating learning content for the first time, becoming an active contributor rather than just a passive user, I felt a new partnership with the faculty which had previously been a distant, didactic presence in the course at Bristol. I also became involved in partnerships with students in the year below, as they sought my advice on creating an e-tutorial.

The faculty offered technical support with the basics of using software, and an opportunity for others creating e-learning tools to meet and share problems and ideas. This created a healthy sense of community and helped prevent isolation.

Philippa King, final-year medical student
The aim of my e-SSC was to produce a tutorial on stable angina. I was adamant I wanted my tutorial to be individual, creative and to catch people's eye, and so I knew I needed to include additional formats within the tutorial. Therefore I included various extra formats such 'drag-and-drop' and 'fill-in-the-gaps' to complement the tutorial and make it more individual. I also included a video of a patient presenting with angina, as this allows students to appreciate a typical presentation, and also involves a different format of learning, to appeal to all modes of study.

The process of creating an e-tutorial enabled me to produce a finished product of which I am proud. Though at the time I felt progress was slow, it was also very rewarding to see the e-tutorial come together and see parts added as they were made. I also appreciated the chance to come up with creative and individual ideas and then develop them to make a tutorial that is unique. The fact that it is my Grandpa in the video adds to this uniqueness I think!

I think the whole process of creating my e-tutorial for my e-SSC was about partnerships. Without the guidance of people who had produced tutorials before it would have been a very different process. This was particularly the case for issues such as copyright and computer expertise where I relied on other people's knowledge and experience to help me with my tutorial. As creator of the tutorial I wanted to ensure everything was correct, but working in partnership with staff at the faculty ensured that I could use their expertise and knowledge in the development process, making the whole process easier. The input of various different people to the tutorial ensured it was of an appropriate standard for teaching and also that it was of an appropriate format that other students would use and find beneficial for their learning.

Discussion

Partnerships
It was only when we began to write this paper that the extent of the various partnerships both existing and emerging became apparent. While the staff authors of this paper clearly acknowledge students as effective partners in the development of e-learning materials, and implicit in this as educators of current and future students, the multi-layered and complex nature of the partnership was unanticipated. In the following section, some of these complex relationships will be outlined briefly, using student quotes in

order to demonstrate different levels of engagement in the community of practice.

1. Student and supervisor

I felt a strong sense of partnership with my supervisor who [. . .] could offer the expertise and core knowledge, knowing that I was bringing an idea of what kind of information and learning experience we needed as students. I learnt how to take intricate concepts from [my supervisor] and present them in a logical, structured, student-friendly way.

Will Duffin

Here, both student and supervisor/consultant are mutually engaged in knowledge-building activities.

2. Student partners and peer support

The following year many students in the year below asked me for advice on creating an e-tutorial and so I became involved in a partnership with them, sharing ideas and offering advice.

Will Duffin

Using other people's knowledge from their previous e-tutorials and using people's technical expertise ensured my project continued to run smoothly.

Philippa King

3. Student and e-learning experts

It was essential that I had the support of the e-learning team behind me to guide me through and help me overcome these challenges.

Rachel O'Connell

I also enjoyed learning how to use software tools in order to make the films interactive with help from e-learning support officers.

Will Duffin

4. Student and medical programme/faculty

I felt a new partnership with the faculty. The faculty offered [. . .] an opportunity for others creating e-learning tools to meet and share problems and ideas. This created a healthy sense of community and helped prevent isolation.

Will Duffin

In the above categories, students are drawing on the learning and expertise of previous and current students, and e-learning professionals and their different roles through the joint enterprise, shared repertoire and history of the community.

5. Other partnerships emerged including that with publishers and other owners of media

We had always thought that clearing the materials for copyright would be fraught with difficulties and assumed requests for permission to reuse images would be denied. We have learnt that if you are honest, specific about where you found the material, and where and how you will reuse it, organizations are surprisingly generous. Some organizations expressed pleasure, wanting to learn more about the project and how their materials were benefiting medical education.

Staff authors

This represents an example of publishers adding to the enterprise of developing e-learning materials, and a widening participation in our community of practice ensuring it continues to evolve.

The partnerships above do not operate in isolation, with many coexisting; partnerships may be one-to-one, one-to-many or many-to-many. Neither will all of the above be experienced by every student nor be explicit.

I think the whole process of creating my e-tutorial for my e-SSC was a partnership between various different people.

Philippa King

The above brief analysis does appear to encapsulate Lave and Wenger's (2005) suggestion that a community of practice is '. . . a historically constructed, ongoing, conflicting, synergistic structuring of activity and relations among practitioners . . .' (p. 154) where they [communities] '. . . come together, they develop, they disperse, according to the timing, the logic, the rhythms, and the social energy of their learning' (Wenger 1998, p. 96).

Students educating us

An emerging outcome of this collaboration is that students have provided staff with considerable insights into how to best make use of online interactive material and its design. In a separate piece of work, an analysis was carried out of 31 reflective assignments (cohort 2007–08). The analysis has given us a rich picture of how students perceive interactive online learning materials, what they believe they contribute to their learning, how it compares to other forms of learning and how this kind of material is best designed and structured. Those of us (staff) working directly on the initiative also report on how students have informed our own e-learning materials development practice and support.

Our involvement with the initiative is immensely satisfying; in particular engaging with the diverse communities this involves: medicine, healthcare, education, art, business and publishing and of course our students. Their skills and enthusiasm for their subject area is infectious, and the creative, considered approach they take in presenting information for the benefit of peers is inspiring. They take ideas and materials from a variety of sources and produce something that is very different, and very much their own. For us this represents the creative process working at its best. Our students have provided us with a variety of inspirational and professional products and have incorporated many of their ideas into our own online learning material development.

Miranda Whinney

Models for e-learning development

Typically, e-learning materials are developed by subject experts together with e-learning experts by assembling knowledge and designing learning activities, selecting appropriate software packages to meet the learning outcomes, seeking any permissions, road testing with students and making final modifications before integrating into the curriculum by linking to core seminars or other modes of teaching. When developed by students, the process is altered. Students, like subject experts, follow a similar procedure but once the projects have been marked the materials go through a quality assurance procedure as outlined previously. At this stage, not all of the materials are deemed suitable for inclusion into the medical programme; content may be inaccurate, learning activities not suitable or materials are considered too poor to be included, with too much staff effort required to correct. As a result there have been concerns from some teachers querying whether students have the depth of knowledge or enough experience to achieve the right balance of coverage. Development of e-learning materials is time-consuming for over-committed teaching staff; involving students in their creation is attractive. For their part, students learn new skills, achieve their SSC project and in many cases produce a product worthy of being released into the curriculum. In our experience students spend a lot of time getting it right, working closely with their supervisors/teachers. In developing e-learning materials students have to review and clarify their own understanding in order to help others understand it.

> I felt an extra sense of responsibility that every detail of my tutorial had to be accurate if it were to be used [. . .] to teach [. . .] students.
>
> Rachel O'Connell

At Bristol, teachers tend to develop a suite of tutorials covering, for example, core clinical cases for a particular subject area. In contrast, students will develop single tutorials addressing specific aspects or topics relevant to what they perceive their learning needs to be. Students typically opt to do an e-learning SSC at the end of Year 3, concluding an intensive year of clinically based teaching. Their experiences of this year strongly influence the subject of their e-learning project. As reported earlier, learning opportunities may vary across academies, and on occasions, clinical priorities may mean that teaching is cancelled at short notice. Here the e-learning resource allows them an opportunity to cover the topic in more detail and strengthens the curriculum by 'plugging gaps'. It also enables all students, irrespective of where they are based, to have access.

> The structure of academy placements means that students are not subject to the same teaching experience, but if every student could access the e-tutorial this would provide a baseline teaching opportunity for all.
>
> Philippa King

Our students produce inspirational and creative materials in which they are not afraid to experiment with combinations of technologies and media to achieve high levels of interactivity. Furthermore, students go through a much more iterative cycle of development, reflecting on personal learning experiences and those of their peers, and testing out their assumptions in dialogue with each other.

> As a student I had completed various e-tutorials before, and knew what I liked and disliked in an e-tutorial, and to ensure my tutorial was going to be useful to other students I canvassed opinion about e-tutorials generally and also on the e-tutorial I was making. Feedback from both students and staff about what they liked and disliked in the e-tutorial contributed to the final product.
>
> Philippa King

Teachers, on the other hand, bring experience and knowledge that is both rich and current; they are an acknowledged source and within medicine often considered leading experts in their field.

Key factors for success
One of the aims in writing this chapter is to inspire others to involve students in the development of educational materials. We offer the following as key factors for success.

1. *Equality of partnership:* Treat students as equal partners in the development of educational materials. By doing so, students provide high levels of commitment to the task.

2. *Preparation:* Educate students in and prepare them for the practice of developing e-learning materials. This will ensure products of a higher quality as students will be forewarned of the challenges and pitfalls; products can be integrated into curricula quickly with little need for modifications.
3. *Support:* Establish a coherent support framework, defined by student need and informed by their creations. Provide a mix of face-to-face and online support, advice and information.
4. *Motivation:* Provide a means of encouraging students to get involved. Ensure materials are integrated into the curriculum quickly and used by their peers. Consider other forms of incentives. At Bristol we have established a student prize awarded annually for 'innovative use of technology in medical education'.
5. *Provide an educational framework:* Ground the initiative in learning and teaching theory and practice to support students as future educators.

Conclusion

In this paper we propose a mix of both student- and teacher-led development of e-learning materials: materials developed by subject specialists that provide a framework with core topics (breadth), augmented with materials developed by students focused on what they perceive as gaps (depth), thus strengthening and enriching our curriculum.

It is evident that some of our students clearly see themselves as partners in the delivery of medical education. For some it is not so explicit. For others, doing an e-SSC is simply a means to an end. Staff recognize the value of students as key contributors in helping shape and strengthen the curriculum not only by educating other students but in educating us as educators.

Brew (2006) talks about 'higher education institutions as places where academics work collaboratively in partnerships with students as members of inclusive scholarly knowledge-building communities' (p.3). She (Brew, 2007) invites us to consider who the scholars are in universities and how they might work in partnerships, where students are encouraged to be active learners, critical creative thinkers and lifelong learners.

> I was learning by interacting closely with the topic myself, following paths of intrigue and unanswered questions that could not have been generated through studying lecture slides or reading through a book. In this respect I developed as an adult learner much more than having spent that time studying topics selected for me by a dusty syllabus.
>
> Will Duffin

In summary, we set out to examine the notion of students as partners in the development of medical education. Using communities of practice as a framework, we have shown how their role as 'members of inclusive scholarly knowledge-building communities' has unfolded. Students have shown themselves to be active contributors, not passive consumers, engaging and participating in their learning and the learning of others not only as undergraduates but as future professional medical practitioners and educators.

References

Blackmore, P. and Cousin, G. (2003), 'Linking teaching and research through research-based learning', *Educational Developments*, 4, (4), 24–27.

Brew, A. (2003), 'Teaching and research: new relationships and their implications for inquiry-based teaching and learning in higher education', *Higher Education & Development*, 22, (1), 3–18.

Brew, A. (2006), *Research and Teaching: Beyond the Divide*. London: Palgrave Macmillan.

Brew, A. (2007), 'Research and teaching from the students' perspective'. International policies and practices for academy enquiry. An International Colloquium on Research and Teaching. Winchester, UK, 19–21 April. Retrieved 28 April 2010 from http://portallive.solent.ac.uk/university/rtconference/2007/resources/angela_brew.pdf

British Medical Association (BMA) (2006), *Doctors as Teachers*. Board of Medical Education. Retrieved 28 April 2010 from http://www.bma.org.uk/careers/training_trainers/doctorsasteachers.jsp

Eckoldt, S. M., Alder, D., Williams, P. J. and Smith, R. (2009), 'From lecture theatre to hospital – a case study: developing and delivering a new curriculum in clinical medicine', in *Proceedings of the Fourth International Blended Learning Conference*. Hatfield: University of Hertfordshire Press, pp. 160–168.

Garvin, A. and Carrington, S. (1997), 'Student-authored hypermedia in veterinary anatomy', *British Journal of Educational Technology*, 28, (3), 191–198.

General Medical Council (GMC) (2003), *Tomorrow's Doctors*. Retrieved 28 April 2010 from http://www.gmc-uk.org/education/undergraduate/tomorrows_doctors_2003.asp

Lave, J. and Wenger, E. (1991), *Situated Learning: Legitimate Peripheral Participation*. Cambridge: Cambridge University Press.

Lave, J. and Wenger, E. (2005), 'Practice, person, social world', in H. Daniels (ed.), *An Introduction to Vygotsky* (2nd edition). London: Routledge, pp. 149–156.

Mumford, D. B. (2007), 'Clinical academies: innovative school-health services partnerships to deliver clinical education', *Academic Medicine*, 82, (5), 435–40.

Nikolova, O, R. (2002), 'Effects of students' participation in authoring of multimedia materials on student acquisition of vocabulary', *Language Learning & Technology*, 6, (1), 100–122.

Seymour, E., Hunter, A. B., Laursen, S. L., and Deantoni, T. (2004), 'Establishing the benefits of research experiences for undergraduates in the sciences: first findings from a three-year study'. *Wiley InterScience*, DO1 10.1002/sce.1013.

Timmis, S., Williams, P. J. and Eckoldt, S. (2009), 'A co-operative inquiry model for researching practice and building interdisciplinary educational research and development capacity'. Society for Research into Higher Education Annual Conference, Challenging Higher Education: knowledge, policy and practice, 8–10 December, 2009. Retrieved 28 April 2010 from http://www.srhe.ac.uk/conference2009/abstracts/0206.pdf

Turner, S. V. and Dipinto, V. M. (1992), 'Students as hypermedia authors: themes emerging from a qualitative study', *Journal of Research on Computing in Education,* 25, (2), 187–199.

Wenger, E. (1998), *Communities of Practice. Learning, Meaning, Identity.* Cambridge: Cambridge University Press.

Chapter 7

Staff–Student Partnerships Can Drive Institutional Change: The Development of a Recognition Scheme for Postgraduate Students who Teach at an Irish University

Niamh Collins and Jacqueline Potter

This chapter illustrates the approach taken by postgraduate students and staff collaborating to catalyze institutional change at an Irish university, through the development of a scheme to support, recognize and reward postgraduate students involved in teaching activities.

Background

Teaching by postgraduate students in higher education and rewarding teaching

Postgraduate students are commonly involved in teaching at universities internationally (Hickson and Fishburne, 2007). In recent years postgraduate students have become essential to the provision of undergraduate teaching at universities (Park and Ramos, 2002).

Although there is a growing literature on best practice in teaching, such as rewarding excellence in teaching and encouraging development of teaching skills, empirical research into university teaching recognition and reward is limited (Taylor, 2007). Only two studies have been conducted at national level, one in the UK (Skelton, 2004), and one in Australia (Ramsden and Martin, 1996). Teaching is an important transferable skill for postgraduate students and their contribution to undergraduate education is substantial at many universities. The role of postgraduate students as teachers varies internationally, between universities, and between disciplines and departments. It is not known how postgraduates, across the diversity of their teaching roles, can be supported, recognized and rewarded to best promote student learning. Training and reward schemes have been introduced at many international institutions, for both staff and postgraduates, but there is little evidence of their effectiveness.

Teaching activities, support and awards at our university
Almost 60 per cent of postgraduates contribute to teaching at our university (Collins, 2009) in a range of formal, informal and ad hoc ways. Postgraduates can participate in voluntary preparation and generic teaching skills courses provided by the Centre for Academic Practice and Student Learning (CAPSL), (see Potter and Hanratty, 2008). In some departments, there are formal arrangements for postgraduates who teach, in the form of advertised 'teaching assistant' posts. Postgraduates may be employed on a part-time basis for teaching activities, and may be paid on an hourly basis. In some cases teaching commitments are built into postgraduate research scholarships. Postgraduate students commonly deliver elements of their supervisors' undergraduate courses, such as tutorials, lectures and supervision of laboratory activities. Their teaching contributions are most commonly between one and eight hours per week, excluding preparation time.

Genesis of the project
Positive developments to support teaching have occurred at our university over the last decade. A central academic enhancement unit, CAPSL, was established in October 2003, with the aim of developing a framework for supporting best academic practice and high-quality student learning. A teaching award scheme: the Provost's Teaching Award, was established for staff in 2000. Between 3–5 individual academic staff annually receive a €5000 award at a prestigious ceremony hosted by the College Provost, in acknowledgement of outstanding contribution to teaching excellence. In 2007, a proposal was developed by members of the Graduate Students' Union (GSU) suggesting extension of the Provost's Teaching Award scheme to include postgraduate students.

The GSU subsequently met with staff of CAPSL and provided CAPSL with seed funding intended to cover the start-up costs of such a scheme. This prompted the creation of a small group of staff and students (our 'staff–student partnership') working to research, develop and advocate a reward scheme for postgraduates who are involved in diverse teaching activities at our university. The group included three postgraduate students: the President and Vice-President of the GSU, and one of the faculty officers who was undertaking a Masters in medical education at the time (the student author). The group also included staff from CAPSL, including the Director, the Academic Development Manager and other staff with an interest in developing student learning. The two authors of this article were self-selected, and were the two members of the group with the greatest time commitment to the project.

An emergent view from early discussions among the staff–student group was that any reward proposal should be grounded in evidence from the literature regarding 'what works' in practice, should reflect the needs of postgraduates at our university, as well as the needs of the institution, and should promote good teaching. The ensuing debate within the group regarding the most appropriate form of teaching award scheme for our institution reflected the lack of international consensus on rewarding teaching. The group recognized that 'good' or 'excellent' teaching is 'situationally dependent' (Skelton, 2004), which motivated inductive data gathering with various stakeholders within our university, through focus groups and surveys regarding how best to support, recognize and reward teaching by postgraduate students. Following the initial discussions the student author was retained by the GSU–CAPSL group to work on the project (the resultant research formed the basis for the Masters research project undertaken by the student author), with CAPSL's Academic Development Manager as a research supervisor. The research project aimed to enable the staff–student partnership to present a well-researched case to the institution.

Our conception of 'staff–student partnership'

Our conception of 'staff–student partnership' is similar to McCulloch's (2009) metaphor of student as 'co-producer'. 'Co-production' is a concept taken from literature in public administration, and describes a process where authorities and the public engage in shared policymaking (Boviard, 2007). Co-production with students has three key requirements (Marschall, 2004): that students participate in a voluntary and meaningful way; that students are well informed, understand what is expected of them and communicate effectively; and that the institution fosters student engagement. Our partnership fulfilled these requirements, and indeed the staff within the partnership perceived the students' role as collaborators and colleagues throughout the project, with equal status in the definition and development of the project. This has been described as an important influence on student representatives' sense of efficacy and legitimacy (Lizzio and Wilson, 2009) and sits comfortably with the institution's conception of its staff and student body as a community of scholars.

Aims of this chapter

This chapter aims to explore the workings of our staff–student partnership, focusing on the process rather than outcomes of the project (it is intended to publish the outcomes and findings of the actual research project separately – they are not discussed in detail here). First, we discuss how the partnership developed. Second, we address the practical workings of the partnership: how we approached the challenges of leading academic change at a higher education institution. Third, we explore how the partnership functioned in terms of relationships, leadership, authority and decision-making within the partnership. The discussion is grounded in the educational and academic leadership literature.

How was our staff–student partnership fostered?

When the idea was first proposed within the GSU for an 'award' for post-graduates who teach, the GSU provided seed funding for CAPSL to set up such a scheme. The postgraduate students believed they could 'hand over' the issue to CAPSL, which would have the expertise to take it forward. However, the students were subsequently invited to meet with CAPSL to discuss how the project might work.

The student author's perspective on the initial discussions between the GSU and CAPSL was an expectation of paternalistic policymaking by staff:

> . . . I drafted a proposal outlining the rationale for an award, and how it might work, based on discussions among GSU committee members at meetings. At the GSU–CAPSL meeting it appeared that there was a clear interest in developing the idea, but also (surprisingly for me) that the views of the GSU were being sought on the issue, and that there was a lack of expertise within CAPSL regarding awards for postgraduates. I had assumed that CAPSL would step in and assume responsibility in a sort of paternalistic manner. The fact that I was being asked basic questions about award schemes at other institutions was genuinely surprising. It was a new experience, as a student, to have policymakers in college ask for your views and listen to your opinion . . . I feel the partnership grew from the first meeting, and there was a real sense that both GSU and CAPSL were valued partners in the process. Both parties contributed expertise and energy to the idea.

The staff author's perspective on the initial creation of the partnership shows an active engagement with the students to bring them into partnership on the project:

> The GSU offered CAPSL funding to develop something. The offer came to me and I had . . . very strong views about supporting postgraduates in teaching roles. I jumped at the money (banked it) knowing that doing so would instigate a process of serious consideration of the issue within CAPSL. I deliberately invited the Director and a student learning representative to work with me and the GSU on this, knowing I was a little 'out of my depth' in terms of protocol, but knowing I wanted the end result: improvement in the conditions and, indeed, the consideration given to postgraduates who teach as an integral part of how the college manages to function.

The concept of staff and students working in a motivated, equal partnership to bring academic change sounds like a robust catalyst for academic change. However, a cynic might surmise that the seed fund which the GSU gave CAPSL to develop the project was the main factor in driving the idea forward. Lack of resources and funding are key challenges in successful academic change (Lucas, 2000), and the seed fund may have removed some concerns regarding funding. In fact, the fund was not tapped during the course of developing the scheme, and it is still not clear in what way the fund will be used. Still the fund seemed to lend immediacy to the project. While staff within CAPSL were already considering ways to further develop support for postgraduates who teach, the seed fund undoubtedly demonstrated the conviction and commitment of the GSU and led to the establishment of the partnership. The combined GSU–CAPSL 'beyond consultation' approach that emerged comprised a useful pairing of resources and of mandates. The seed fund lent immediacy to the issue and brought the GSU and CAPSL together into a 'participative decision-making' process, key to an effective team (Lucas, 2000).

The practical workings of the partnership

The 'Adaptive' nature of the staff–student partnership's task

Heifetz (1994) used the term 'adaptive work' to describe a problem for which there is no established best practice, where the solution is not clear. The problem of developing a scheme to reward postgraduate students who teach was an adaptive one, given the lack of clear best practice or a clear concept of what would work in practice. Leadership is vital in addressing adaptive problems, and Heifetz states there is a need to look beyond authoritative solutions to such problems; rather the role of leaders in such situations is to engage all team members in facing the challenge. In engaging the GSU in a partnership process, CAPSL tacitly used a key principle of leadership (Heifetz, 1994): they shifted the locus of responsibility from those seen as being in 'authority' (CAPSL officers) to the primary stakeholders in the problem (the GSU as representatives of postgraduates themselves). This achieved a change in expectations of authority. The students no longer expected CAPSL to 'come up with the solution'. Instead, the students became engaged in trying to work out the problem, with the result that they gained a greater appreciation for the complexity of the issue, and had changed expectations of an 'ideal' or 'correct' solution.

Our collaborative approach to addressing the problem and leading institutional change

Higher education institutions, and particularly research universities, are anecdotally highly resistant to academic change. Lucas (2000) proposed an eight-step process to effectively launch academic change. Interestingly, in retrospect our staff–student partnership approach exhibited a number of the features of Lucas's eight-step process. Our partnership is discussed below with reference to each of Lucas's eight steps.

1. Establish a sense of urgency

A sense of urgency around a given problem is essential to circumvent the natural tendency to preserve the status quo, and resistance to change which is common at institutional level. There was a growing conviction within the GSU that staff rewards for teaching should be open to postgraduates who teach, and that postgraduates required greater support and recognition for their teaching activities. The staff within CAPSL were aware that greater support was needed for postgraduates who teach, and were considering ways of providing this; the seed fund brought together the two groups and provided a 'sense of urgency'.

2. Create a guiding coalition

An ideal 'coalition' or partnership requires commitment, time, energy and synergy. The staff–student partnership established between the GSU and CAPSL had many of these factors. Most participants were highly committed to the project, and the energy of members on both sides regarding the importance of the project was a key factor in its moving forward. The partnership worked synergistically, and viewpoints of both staff and students were freely shared during regular group discussions, which afforded both sides a greater understanding of the complexity and differing perspectives of the problem.

3. Develop a vision and a strategy

The partnership defined a vision and strategy, articulated these as a project proposal and submitted the proposal to the CAPSL advisory committee for approval. (The committee meets twice per year to discuss and approve proposals for developing teaching practice at the university.) Using feedback from the committee, the project proposal was revised and broadened: 'To investigate how best to enhance the general standard of postgraduate teaching, formally recognize and support postgraduate teaching across the full diversity of its roles, and reward excellent teaching among postgraduates who teach within the context of Trinity College Dublin.' The new vision represented a hugely complex 'adaptive' problem, and an opportunity to really benefit postgraduate students at Trinity College, as well as those they teach. Importantly, the ambition and scope of the new vision integrated the variations in perspective, priority and focus of the partnership members and allowed a way forward that all agreed would be of much wider benefit. The vision was translated into strategic goals to be delivered through a research project, consulting multiple stakeholders in teaching at Trinity, and investigating the research evidence and practices in other research intensive institutions internationally to provide evidence-based recommendations. The broadened perspective of the project increased the complexity of the task and aligned the process more closely with critical systems thinking and approaches: a method that has been advocated to manage quality improvement within higher education (Houston, 2007).

4. Communicate the change vision
The initial meeting between CAPSL staff and GSU students allowed the GSU to communicate their 'change vision', and the CAPSL staff were receptive to this. The 'change vision' was subsequently revised and expanded. Project progress reports and ongoing discussions maintained the momentum of the partnership, with institutional oversight provided through the formal reporting line to the advisory committee.

5. Empower broad-based action
'Broad-based action' should include multiple 'change agents' who have the authority to move change forwards (Lucas, 2000). While multiple stakeholders were engaged through consultation, the project's 'change agents' were very much contained within the staff–student partnership. How might a more broad-based action have been achieved in practice? Lucas (2000) suggests setting up subcommittees and informal meetings to empower individuals at ground level. However, it is doubtful the stakeholders would have agreed to spend additional time in subcommittees without prescribing a clear focus for their activities. Concurrent to the research project, CAPSL staff did undertake one-to-one interviews with school role holders concerning the institutional and school infrastructures and their aspirations of support for postgraduate teaching assistants with the intention of developing 'readiness' within the institution for any future change. Notably, it was not possible to engage undergraduate students during data gathering. The opinions of undergraduate students regarding how postgraduate students should be rewarded were considered to be of great importance in informing the project since undergraduates at the university are directly affected by the quality of postgraduate student teaching. Numerous attempts were made to engage undergraduates in the project, through the undergraduate Students' Union and via email. However, these attempts failed, and the partnership did not have sufficient time to attempt other means of data gathering from undergraduates.

6. Generate short-term wins

In the words of Rosabeth Moss Kanter (1999), 'everything can look like a failure in the middle' – this was certainly the case from the student author's point of view during this project:

> The data collection process was considerable and at some points gaining agreement among stakeholders seemed improbable. In addition, motivation within the partnership seemed to wane, and there was external pressure on the GSU to account for the seed fund money allocation, resulting in a growing negative view of the project.

However, considering each stage of the project as a 'win' was important to the student author:

> One 'short-term win' which motivated me was the favourable reception . . . at the second CAPSL advisory committee meeting at which the [revised] project was presented. I emerged from this meeting with a renewed belief that administrators and staff, that is, 'big people in college' really would listen to, respect and even act on what students had to say, if they presented a well-researched case.

7. Consolidate goals and produce more change

The challenge for the future is to consolidate the forward momentum and implement the project recommendations. This is a formidable task although the institutional readiness for change has been noted among members of the partnership across the institutional and school decision-making structures and personnel. A number of actions for the partnership were developed and these included opportunistic, short-term goals to tie change into the institutional strategic planning processes and within existing CAPSL work plans. More broadly and in the longer-term, the actions look across the institution, its structures and members to progress the change vision.

8. Anchor new approaches in the culture

It is vital that others outside the partnership recognize that the project and its recommendations for further action are effective and worthwhile. Unless 'anchored' within the concept of teaching at Trinity, the project and its recommendations risk falling by the wayside. To date, progress with the project and implementing early-stage recommendations are positive. However, remaining areas for action are more complex, difficult or still contentious. Into the future, a 'letting go' of the shared staff–student partnership vision as other actors take on the driving role is likely needed to embed new developments that anchor the changes within local contexts and at the heart of the institution's vision of its near-term future.

Navigation of the institutional political territories by the staff–student partnership

Navigation of the political territories of the institutional infrastructure in putting forward a proposal for change was difficult for the staff–student partnership. Traditional 'fixed' views regarding the roles of postgraduate students within the university posed a challenge for the partnership in terms of the actual project itself, as noted by the staff author:

> Beyond the working group, the political territories were, in the early days, pretty fixed in their views. [There is a view that] . . . postgraduate students don't really teach: they 'just do' tutorials, seminars and demonstrating, but lecturers manage their interaction and activities with undergraduate students. There was no consideration that teaching was good in terms of personal and professional development for postgraduates and there was no thinking around the implication of poorly prepared, poorly supported postgraduate teachers.

A significant challenge for the student author was the opaque nature of how change occurs at a university, and a lack of awareness of how to 'navigate' or 'negotiate' the system. This lack of understanding led to setbacks in the progress of the project, as commented on by the student author:

> Navigation of the institutional infrastructure within our university is still an enigma to me. The CAPSL advisory committee meeting was the first political landmine for our project . . . I think the partnership expected the project proposal to be summarily passed at the meeting. Surprisingly, at the meeting there was extensive debate of the merits of the project, and it was not approved, rather it was recommended to widen the remit of an 'award' to consider more broadly supporting teaching by postgraduate students 'across the full diversity of their roles'. This was a setback, the redefinition of the project would require a considerable amount of extra research . . . I felt daunted and deflated. The next meeting of the staff–student partnership was an uncomfortable one, and the project might have fallen apart. Motivation within the partnership was at a low ebb.

The staff author also described this setback in navigating the institutional infrastructure as a 'pivotal moment':

> I suppose, in the main, the critical path and process here was the CAPSL advisory committee meeting where there was such negativity around the award for postgraduates that teach . . . and I think this was a pivotal moment, particularly for the GSU, about marketing and pitch of ideas, and whether an award was feasible without an infrastructure of support for postgraduates' teaching.

This setback in navigating the institutional infrastructure brought the key skills and experience of the staff members of the partnership to the fore. Continuing the commentary from the student author:

> To the credit of the CAPSL Director, he showed great leadership at this 'crisis' point, by identifying the challenge that CAPSL advisory committee had presented, by providing a new structure to use to approach the problem, and to focus attention on relevant issues, rather than dwelling on the failure. In hindsight, I feel the CAPSL advisory meeting feedback did the project a great service, in that it led to the development of a well-researched case for the project, which would make it more likely to succeed at board level.

The staff author noted that further progress at institutional level was made, as a result of the actions of the staff fostering engagement between the students within the partnership and the pertinent college committee. This was progress in terms of an awareness of the role of postgraduates who teach, as well as the potential value of the proposed project to support and reward postgraduate students.

> [The Director of CAPSL] . . . got Niamh into a later meeting to present her work and I think this was the real beginning of the current research project within the political environment of an institution coming to realize the importance of postgraduates' teaching from the multifarious angles of vision possible on the topic. They were big moments in the process.

Relationships, leadership, authority and decision-making within the partnership

The locus of authority in the partnership, and how this evolved

Heifetz (1994) believes that in addressing complex, adaptive problems we need to look beyond authoritative solutions, to use instead authoritative provocation to mobilize work towards an adaptive solution. Taking this view, it was the authority of the GSU which provoked and mobilized the staff–student partnership. Despite this, the GSU initially felt that the authority to conduct the project rested with CAPSL. However, from these early expectations, through the gradual growth of the partnership, the locus of authority became more evenly shared. Both students and staff had influence on decisions. At some times it seemed most of the authority lay with those doing the research, having insight into some of the problems in detail. According to the staff author:

There was perhaps a shift when the research project was proposed and accepted as a way forward. In some ways, the authority was deferred until Niamh's (the student author's) research provided evidence for decision-making or next steps and there was a unanimous relaxation into having found a process for collaboration, deferred discussion and dealing with potential combat.

It is interesting that no real 'leader' emerged during the discussions. Handy's (1999) definition of a leader is 'someone who is able to develop and communicate a vision which gives meaning to the work of others' (Handy 1999, p. 117). The student author felt that members of the partnership often looked to the Director of CAPSL for approval, since his office held formal authority. Informal authority, the ability to 'influence attitudes and behaviour beyond compliance' (Heifetz, 1994, p. 101), is based on trust, respect and professional reputation. The commitment of some members of the staff–student partnership to the project afforded them this informal authority within the group. Starratt (2004) states that colleagues determine shared convictions, beliefs and values through dialogue and interaction, and Blackmore and Blackwell (2006) describe effective (academic development) leadership as inevitably values-based. It took time in discussion to share these, and was indeed a challenge to the partnership's initial proposal. However, the strong staff–student partnership that emerged was subsequently resilient both to institutional challenge and to the changeover in membership that occurred as new role holders in the GSU were elected.

Decision-making styles used during the project

An appropriate decision-making process within any team depends on the type of problem, the 'resilience' of the social system in the group and the time frame for action (Heifetz, 1994). The decision-making style among our staff–student partnership could be considered 'collaborative' (Lucas, 2000) or 'participative' (Heifetz, 1994); it was certainly 'beyond consultation'. However, participative decision-making is time-consuming, and can overwhelm a group with a limited history of working together. Therefore it is unsurprising that 'autocratic' action by the GSU and the GSU researcher was tacitly used to kick-start the process, in a way allowing the group to develop an adaptive capacity, and a more participative style, as trust was gradually built within the group.

A consultative decision-making style may be used to broaden perspectives into how different outcomes would affect other parties (Lucas, 2000). The consultative process among the various stakeholders in teaching and learning at our institution fulfilled this function. We gained specific feedback on the measures we were considering implementing as part of the project, as well as raw feedback on the general feelings of staff and postgraduates regarding wide-ranging aspects of teaching at Trinity. This afforded a useful overview of some contentious issues, and an insight into what it is like to teach at Trinity. It was a useful strategy to share the burden of decision-making during the project among the multiple stakeholders involved in teaching at Trinity. The researcher then collated the data and, with reflection on the research literature, summarized it into recommendations, rather than making a personal judgement on what might be most appropriate for the institution.

Challenges to the partnership

A key early resistance point, which was ultimately the reason for the extensive research project undertaken and the broader brief of the partnership, was the feedback from the CAPSL advisory committee meeting. The proposal for an award for postgraduates that teach was debated in depth and rejected; instead the remit redeveloped with a significant research component that incorporated wide consultation and data gathering of approaches that might work, based on theory and the practice of others. The outcome was a much stronger partnership and project. According to the staff author:

> I think the resistance [encountered during the CAPSL advisory meeting] strengthened our own resolve and consolidated our shared vision.

There was inevitably some resistance within the partnership itself. Such resistance is a natural part of team working. Any group has two key functions: accomplishing tasks and building relationships (Wilmot and Hocker, 1998). Relationships within the partnership were generally good, although there were inevitable differences in opinion. The 'task' function of the partnership was much easier to deal with than the 'relationship' function. As commented by the student author:

> I am not clear where the resistance of some team members originated from – possibly from a sense of responsibility and anxiety regarding the process, and perhaps accountability for the seed fund (accountability is a key challenge to academic change according to Lucas, 2000). This resistance . . . was a type of 'hidden agenda', unlike the open resistance encountered at the CAPSL advisory meeting, and therefore more difficult to address.

The influence of other institutional authority structures on the process

The main influence of institutional authority structures was through the CAPSL advisory committee. Membership included the college officer with responsibility for undergraduate education, the academic secretary, as well as members of academic staff and student services. The Dean of Graduate Studies was involved in facilitating some of the survey research. These comprised a formidable group of senior colleagues as well as representatives of the wider staff. It is perhaps inevitable that changes were made to the project brief given the breadth of their roles and experiences. Gibbs (2007) reflects that a consultative project to develop a teaching award scheme at the University of Oxford failed to reach consensus after two years of negotiation among the different disciplines. In hindsight, perhaps we did well to take and revise our vision to meet a wider body of senior colleagues' expectations.

The staff author commented that a major achievement of the partnership was to change the attitudes within institutional authority structures:

> I think quite possibly the major achievement of the project has been the awareness it has raised among senior role holders that postgraduates 'do' teach, that their involvement in teaching is critical to undergraduate student success and to the research-intensive focus of the institution, and that postgraduates' teaching is a positive feature of the graduate experience in terms of personal and professional development: but that needs careful management, or at least some guidance and infrastructure, at college and school level.

Key factors in the success of the staff–student partnership

Key factors in the success of the partnership included: a permanent core of members; fairly regular contact and discussions; the development of a shared vision and action steps; and the creation of a climate of trust and commitment to the project within the partnership. The discussions were important for keeping team members motivated, and these discussions were mostly honest and open. Differences of opinion were debated and the experience of both students and CAPSL were listened to, allowing a climate of trust to develop, and allowing students to become empowered and take risks with offering opinions. Conflicts were openly debated, rather than suppressed. There was an inspiring mix of creative thought and concerns as well as the sharing of ideas and a critical examination of those ideas. The partnership also provided affirmation and acknowledgement of the shared perception of value inherent in our work and the institutional change we hoped to engender, which was vital in sustaining the project through the long research phase.

Future trends

Nationally and internationally, graduate education practices have been the focus of reflective examination and research as nations have sought to increase the numbers of postgraduate students as part of the drive towards creating 'knowledge-based economies.' Like many other research-intensive institutions in the past decade, Trinity College has expanded its post-graduate student numbers and sought to retain the quality of education it provides. Over the period of this partnership project, the Irish Universities Association (IUA) has published a graduate skills statement and the Irish Universities Quality Board (IUQB) has revised its good practice guidelines for postgraduate education: both identify the need to support and develop teaching skills among the postgraduate population as important transferable skills. The project described in this chapter has occurred during a period of unprecedented growth in postgraduate numbers and 'adaptive' change at a national level.

The project has contributed to the development of an open acknowledge-ment within our institution of the many gains that result from close working with the postgraduate student body, viewed not only as researchers, but as teachers-in-training and as a collective, represented through the GSU. It is clear now, as the college lays down its plans for the near future, that there has been a shift in conceptualizing how the actual and the potential of the graduate student body can contribute to the university. This shift is partly a result of this project and the impact the project has had. The project's activity and recommendations, and importantly its structure, existence and persistence as an equal partnership of students and staff with a common goal of quality improvement for the benefit of the institution, have contributed to this shift in conceptions about the potential of student contribution.

Based on the gathered evidence of the student author's research project, 12 summary recommendations – regarding how best to support, recognize and reward postgraduate students who teach at our university – were pre-sented in a formal report. The recommendations include the provision of teaching opportunities, training, feedback, mentoring, accreditation, formal acknowledgement, payment and promotion recognition; the need for efforts to enhance the status of teaching at Trinity; and consideration of rewards for postgraduates who teach. At the time of writing, central, accredited training provision is now in place and is 'bought in' to the local graduate skills development structures within schools, and tailored to best fit their needs.

Conclusions

The experience of the collaborative process was overall a positive one. Co-production (McCulloch, 2009) was a challenging experience requiring active participation and engagement by staff and students in terms of time, resources and relationship building. The outcomes of the partnership were evident in terms of both product (a scheme to support and reward postgraduates who teach) and importantly, process. The 'process' outcomes were numerous; both staff and students gained greater perspective on the issues involved, gained insight into the workings of staff–student partnerships, and insight into negotiated policymaking in higher education.

The staff author commented:

> The project, one of few I've been involved in working directly with students, potentially the only one where I would view the interaction as genuinely collaborative (although I do believe the seed-funding contributed to that 'seriousness' of perspective and collaborative endeavour for both the students and staff) has demonstrated to me – that which I intuitively knew and certainly believed – that . . . [our university's] students are the most astonishingly focused collective of intelligence, capability and, within this context, of directed activism towards a broad goal capable of continuous refinement and reflection.

Students graduate through higher education institutions at a rate that is usually more rapid than the rate of academic change. Therefore, for the student in the staff–student author team, it was a positive realization to see real progress occur, even at a large academic institution, if a motivated core team of people are committed to a project. Further, the student author realized that students can actually take part in – and even instigate – academic change, if committed to a project. As concluded by the student author:

> I have a huge respect for the members of CAPSL who had the insight and trust to accept students as partners in this lengthy process . . . and I have a new-found optimism that students and staff in higher education can engage in shared decision-making to drive academic change through partnerships that extend far beyond consultation.

References

Blackmore, P. and Blackwell, R. (2006), 'Strategic leadership in academic development', *Studies In Higher Education*, 31, (3), 373–387.

Boviard, T. (2007), 'Beyond engagement and participation: user and community co-production of public services', *Public Administration Review*, 67, (5), 846–860.

Collins, N. (2009), *Supporting, Recognizing and Rewarding Postgraduate Students Who Teach at a Research University*. Unpublished thesis (MSc [MEd]), Queen's University Belfast.

Gibbs, G. (2007), 'Have we lost the plot with teaching awards?' *Academy Exchange, Journal of The Higher Education Academy*, 7, 40–42.

Handy, C. (1999), *Understanding Organizations*. London: Penguin.

Heifetz, R. A. (1994), *Leadership Without Easy Answers*. Cambridge, MA: Belknap Press.

Hickson, C. N. and Fishburne, G. J. (2007), *Can We Help? Mentoring Graduate Teaching Assistants*. Paper presented to the Australian Association for Research in Education. Adelaide. Retrieved 28 April 2010 from http://www.aare.edu. au/06pap/hic06205.pdf

Houston, D. (2007), 'Rethinking quality and improvement in higher education', *Quality Assurance in Education*, 16, (1), 61–79.

Kanter, R. M. (1999), *On the Frontiers of Management*. Boston, MA: Harvard Business Review.

Lizzio, A. and Wilson, K. (2009), 'Student participation in university governance: the role conceptions and sense of efficacy of student representatives on departmental committees', *Studies in Higher Education*, 34, (1), 69–84.

Lucas, A. F. (2000), 'A collaborative model for leading academic change', in A. F. Lucas and Associates (eds), *Leading Academic Change*. San Francisco: Jossey-Bass.

Marschall, M. (2004), 'Citizen participation and the neighborhood context: a new look at the co-production of local public goods', *Political Research Quarterly*, 57, (2), 231–244.

McCulloch, A. (2009), 'The student as co-producer: learning from public administration about the student-university relationship', *Studies in Higher Education*, 34, (2), 171–183.

Park, C. and Ramos, M. (2002), 'The donkey in the department? Insights into the Graduate Teaching Assistant (GTA) experience in the UK', *Journal of Graduate Education*, 3, (2), 47–53.

Potter, J. and Hanratty, O. (2008), 'Supporting graduate teaching assistants at Trinity College Dublin', in B. Higgs and M. McCarthy (eds), *Emerging Issues II: The Changing Roles and Identities of Teachers and Learners in Higher Education*. Cork: NAIRTL.

Ramsden, P. and Martin, E. (1996), 'Recognition of good university teaching: policies from an Australian study', *Studies in Higher Education*, 21, (3), 299–315.

Skelton, A. (2004), 'Understanding "teaching excellence" in higher education: a critical evaluation of the National Teaching Fellowship Scheme', *Studies in Higher Education*, 29, (4), 451–468.

Starratt, R. J. (2004), *Ethical Leadership*. San Francisco: Jossey-Bass.

Taylor, I. (2007), 'Pursued by excellence: rewards and the performance culture in higher education', *Social Work Education*, 26, (5), 504–519.

Wilmot, W. W. and Hocker, J. L. (1998), *Interpersonal Conflict* (5th edn). Boston, MA: McGraw-Hill.

Chapter 8

'What would happen if we treated the student as someone whose opinion mattered?':[1] Student Learning and Teaching Awards at Northumbria

Pat Gannon-Leary, Alan Dordoy, Sophie McGlinn,
Fiona Baldam and Gemma Charlton

Consultation of students at all levels of schooling is becoming a more normalized aspect of decision-making, through, for instance, representative student councils and the inclusion of student representatives on some governing bodies (Thomson and Holdsworth, 2003; Arnot et al., 2004). Frequently, however, student voice is confined to school management matters and opportunities for students to participate in more transformative action, such as issues of pedagogy, are less common. Cook-Sather (2006) called students 'the missing voice' in educational research (p. 5), while Levin (2000) has argued that education reform cannot succeed and should not proceed without much more direct involvement of students in all its aspects. Universities and academic staff may, then, need to change the ways in which they listen to students, including respecting the role students can play in relation to improving their own educational opportunities (Rudduck, 2007). Involving students more closely in educational decision-making and listening seriously to their stories of experiences as learners are essential first steps which, in turn, will reinforce students' commitment and academic progress. It was anticipated that the student learning and teaching awards would be a positive way to enable students to participate in transformative action and improve their own educational experience and opportunities.

Student learning and teaching award

Northumbria is a large modern university with a strong commitment to excellence in learning and teaching. Based in the North East of England, it has around 34,000 students including over 5,000 who study through distance learning or at partner institutions. In 2007 Northumbria introduced Student Learning and Teaching Awards, aimed at encouraging and rewarding practical suggestions and new ideas from students that could make an immediate difference to the student experience. These suggestions and ideas could be in any format including poster, booklet, CD or other such format. This competition, open to all Northumbria students with a first prize of £1,000, was launched in the spring of 2007 and run again in 2008.

Central to the Student Learning and Teaching Awards is the assumption that students have something worthwhile to say about learning and teaching coupled with an understanding that it is their choice to contribute (or not). At the outset we were seeking a relationship with students that relied significantly on the degree to which they were prepared to contribute. Bishop (2003) demonstrates that students have the capacity to provide well-articulated and theorized views on learning and the practices that support learning. Does analysis of our award entries also demonstrate this?

Student submissions

The staff authors were Alan Dordoy, Head of Learning and Teaching Support (LTS), Pat Gannon-Leary, Research Associate (LTS) and Sophie McGlinn, Education Caseworker, Northumbria Students' Union. They examined the submissions made by students in the two rounds of the awards in the context of constructivist pedagogy. In the light of constructive learning theories is it possible to predict the types of learning and teaching initiatives that students are likely to submit? The analysis was conducted to determine how far the student entrants wanted, as Dewey suggested, a more 'open-ended inquiry process rather than a teacher-dominated process of "handing down" knowledge as a finished product' (Gabelnick et al., 1990, p. 16). Constructivist epistemology recognizes that emphasis on performance and giving the 'right' answers is not conducive to long-term recall and argues that focus on learning and students' responsibility for their own learning facilitates long-term understanding and autonomous thinking, developing students' ability to use concepts and information outside the classroom. If this is the case, can we hypothesize that student submissions will indicate a desire on the students' part to be responsible for their own learning?

The authors hope that, as Bland and Atweh (2007) suggest, affording students an opportunity to engage in educational decision-making and listening seriously to the stories of their experiences as learners will contribute to their commitment and academic progress. What do the student submissions tell us about their experiences as learners and the progress they wish to make? We analyse their suggestions for promoting favourable conditions in which they may engage in the learning–teaching process and consider the extent to which these suggestions might change the nature of authority in the learning–teaching process, reshape practice and, in turn, impact upon the student experience at Northumbria.

Learning and teaching awards process

Students were required, along with their submission, to give a short summary on it along with a description of who would benefit from it. They were requested to include all relevant sections of the university community in describing recipients of benefits. Entries were judged by a panel of six comprising three members of staff and three students. The former tended to be drawn from staff employed as learning and teaching advisers or, for example, associate deans with responsibility for learning and teaching. The latter tended to be drawn from membership of the Students' Union (SU) or from school representatives who were keen to be involved in the project from the outset. Each panel member was given a scoring sheet which contained five criteria. They could assign up to four marks for each criteria so that the maximum score achievable was 20.

Scoring criteria were as follows:

- Usability
  - Is this idea practical? Can it be put directly into action to improve learning and teaching at Northumbria?
- Innovation
  - How original is this idea (in the context in which it is presented)?
- Impact (1)
  - Is this idea going to be relevant only to small numbers of students or can it be developed to have relevance to a wide student body?
- Impact (2)
  - How much difference could this idea make to the student experience?
- Presentation
  - How well produced is the booklet, poster or other product?

Relevance of recent studies

Much of the recent literature on the concept of giving students a voice focuses on school-based rather than higher education (Arnot et al., 2004; Fielding, 2004; Mitra, 2004; Cook-Sather, 2006; Rudduck, 2007) but still has relevance for higher education since it highlights that engaging students as authentic collaborators in learning and teaching is only achievable when students are partners in the process. As Martin (1999) says, 'Shared commitment, not imposition and mandate, brings about successful change' (p. 73). Students' willingness to contribute is likely to be based on the relevance of the initiative to them and the relationships they have established with their academic staff and those of us in the SU and in LTS.

Methodology

A modified grounded theory methodological approach was chosen as the nature of the undertaking fitted with Glaser and Strauss' (1967) argument that theory (consisting of conceptual categories, their properties and relationships) should be derived from, and illustrated by, data. Given the exploratory nature of the research and a desire to understand how students 'define the situation' (Thomas, in Marshall and Rossman, 1989, p. 46), a qualitative approach seemed more suitable than a quantitative one. In addition, as Walker (1985) comments, qualitative methods are flexible and opportunistic, thus allowing a great deal of data to be collected from a limited number of individuals. There were only 30 entries in total over the two years so this approach seemed appropriate.

In line with the grounded theory approach, joint collection, coding and analysis of data was the underlying operation. The generation of theory, coupled with the notion of theory as process, required that these operations be completed together as far as possible. The team of staff authors spent a day together working through all the student entries for 2007 and 2008, comparing instances from the data in the hope that tentative categories and their properties could be identified. It was anticipated that emergent elements of the theory would be modified and developed by comparison with instances from subsequent fieldwork, and further categories and properties might emerge. The subsequent fieldwork would involve interviews with the three second-prize-winning authors plus input from the first-prizewinners in their role as co-authors. Fiona Baldam and Gemma Charlton won the first prize for their 'Flying the Kite' submission and were invited to join the author team once the prize winners had been announced. Both Fiona and Gemma came from Northumbria's School of Health, Community and Education Studies and were on education-related courses so they were able to make valuable contributions to the theoretical aspects of this chapter as well as co-writing subsequent sections discussing the student entries. Throughout the initial process the staff team had written analytic memos, which served to guide and record the emergent theory. It was possible, subsequently, to reduce these categories to a smaller number of higher-order concepts (Glaser and Strauss, 1967).

The notes or 'analytic memos' written by the staff team while coding were used to construct the analysis. The original student entries along with scoring sheets were returned to frequently at this stage, to allow for clarification of the context of comments. Triangulation was also employed since the team examined the score sheets submitted with respect to all student award entrants. As the scoring panels comprised equal numbers of staff and students, it was felt that average scores from staff and from students could be used to provide some quantitative data which would enable the authors to identify differences in opinion between staff and students about the merits and demerits of suggestions for particular approaches to learning and teaching.

One limitation of this study is the low number of entries that the award attracted. There were only 13 in 2007 and only 17 in 2008. Given that the university has over 30,000 students, this is a disappointing response to the initiative, although this is not to detract from the entries that were contributed, many of which had clearly involved much hard work, effort and imagination. Clearly more thought needs to be given to marketing the award and this was indicated by some of our student entrants:

> It is a great opportunity but something that needs to be disseminated more and try to get as many students on board as possible. I am sure there are hundreds of students who all had bright ideas but these probably just resulted from a brief conversation with their friends and is then just forgotten about!

It is also apparent from this student's comment that more needs to be done in explaining to students what the criteria are and giving examples of the sort of suggestions that would be eligible:

> You kind of tell your friends [bright ideas]. People doubt their own ideas as well. I was not entirely sure if I was eligible because I had already had the idea and it was in development . . .

Results

Nine categories emerged from the initial data analysis conducted by the staff author team. These were as follows:

The staff author team gave a weighting of three stars to entries with a primary focus in a particular category. The number of entries awarded three stars is given in the final column of Table 8.1.

From this initial analysis it would appear that the two major learning and teaching themes emerging are traditional teaching and learner-centred education. These could be subdivided into traditional teaching – additional; traditional teaching – adjustment; learner-centred – group; and learner-centred – individual. Since the research question sought to explore the extent to which student entries demonstrated a desire for more student-centred rather than teacher-dominated learning, these four categories were the logical ones to explore further. Clearly entrants felt that other areas such as access, support and student representation were important but the main focus of the prize and of this chapter is on learning and teaching.

Table 8.1 Nine categories of ideas for improving learning and teaching

	Category	Description	Total submissions with a weighting of ***
1	Traditional teaching (Additional)	Ideas focusing on the traditional teacher/ student relationship, but suggested additional materials or ideas for teaching staff	3
2	Traditional teaching (Adjustment)	Ideas focusing on the traditional teacher/ student relationship, but suggested an adjustment to the methods or medium of teaching	7
3	Access	Ideas focusing on improving access to education for different groups	2
4	Service	Ideas focusing on improving customer service	4
5	Support	Ideas related to student support	2
6	Learner-centred (Group)	Ideas focusing on learner activity, aimed at enhancing learning and interaction by groups of learners	5
7	Learner-centred (Individual)	Ideas focusing on learner activity, aimed at enhancing individual experience, performance or employability	4
8	Student representation	Ideas related to increased or alternative participation by students in representation networks	3
9	Technical	Ideas related to technical support	0

Traditional teaching entries

Entries in this category were characterized by their focus on teaching staff using alternative methods of getting across the same information or new technology to deliver traditional methods. Entries in this group seemed to accept the premise of the teacher–student dynamic being one of active–passive.

Additional

The student prize panel and judges had expected some entries focusing on expanding traditional teaching but had anticipated a higher number of entries related to student participation. Examples of entries that the team categorized as 'traditional teaching – additional' included 'Web Class' which comprised video or webcasting of lectures and an associated query box feature which would act as a forum for frequently asked questions or FAQs. This entry advocated the use of information and communication technologies to improve traditional teaching and there was an element of learner-centredness in it in that content would be led (but not created by) students. The judging panel felt that this idea was in existence already to some extent in the use of podcasts, video lectures and the university's version of Blackboard. Also some judges highlighted technical issues and the need for staff willingness for this suggestion to be practicable.

Entries such as this involve facilities which already exist and/or have been implemented by some teachers. They that be subject to discussion by learners, for example, 'Why doesn't my lecturer put more material on Blackboard?' or 'Why doesn't my lecturer provide podcasts?' but are less likely to facilitate greater learner involvement in syllabi, delivery, etc. However, since these entries concentrated on expanding traditional teaching, the motivating factor for student entrants may have been their perception that they could be easily implemented (although with concomitant resource implications) and this could be indicative of students' 'testing the water' to see how receptive and committed to student ideas the university really is. Such ideas could be seen as a 'quick win' for the university in that they are relatively straightforward to implement while also appearing demonstrative of its commitment to taking student suggestions on board.

Adjustment

Entries in this category were concerned with adjusting traditional methods so that they might be used in new or different ways while still retaining the concept of the teacher delivering 'the answer' to students. Some imaginative suggestions were offered in terms of content and methods but these did not challenge the basic premise that the 'teacher knows best' and that the student's responsibility is limited to receiving this information. One example from this category, which was one of the 2008 runners-up, was 'Business News: one week in one hour' which suggested one or two one-hour optional sessions every week for students to learn about the latest developments in the business world. If online sessions were offered, these could be developed as a discussion forum. This last-mentioned facet has an element of learner-centredness about it since it would broaden out to include student engagement. The second prize was awarded to this entry since it took the traditional lecture format but opted to use it in a way that not only had the potential to develop knowledge and skills but also to build on a sense of school community, since implementation could involve a staff–student partnership. It was an idea that was transferable to other schools but lecturer workload had to be taken into consideration as did the question of whether or not students would actually give optional time to this.

Another entry in this category – 'Catalogue of assessment essentials for higher education' – was the first-prizewinner in 2007. This was a catalogue-style guide through which staff could browse to help them choose innovative assessment methods. It gave insight into the depth of learning each method could provide, how and why it was important. It included some innovative assessment methods and some learner-centred approaches. This entry was subsequently developed into a *Red Guide*, a university publication addressing educational and staff development issues.

The themes in the above categories were modification of methods to try to make sessions more 'fun', interesting or relevant. The organizers expected some entries of this type but perhaps not so many in which delivery is explicitly aimed at making e-learning more enjoyable or 'student-friendly', fitting in with student lifestyles but not necessarily promoting student engagement. However, the projects are clearly relevant to the students who indicate a requirement for alternative means of delivery and adjustments to topics to spark their interest and enable them to participate on their own terms. Perhaps these should be viewed as prerequisites for greater engagement? This may be indicative of 'groundwork' on behalf of the entrants, which may prepare the way for more learner-centred entries in further stages of the learning and teaching awards process.

Learner-centred entries

This category of entries was deemed of particular importance by the authors and the judges because they challenged the notion of the teacher as expert and focused on personal development and learning through others, that is, removing the teacher from the equation and creating the idea of the 'expert learner', students as the main part of the learning process. It had been expected that more entries would fit into this category because it resonated with the constructivist notions of students taking responsibility for their own learning.

These ideas represented a change in delivery and also in focus of teaching; learning from others is seen as key rather than from one expert individual, increasing the confidence of students in group situations and concentrating on fostering a learning community, either within course or whole university, as a vital part of successful learning. These entries were particularly interesting since they were indicative of a move from some entrants beyond the traditional teacher–student dynamic and were considering holistic learning. These are the types of ideas that should be promoted to encourage students to 'think outside the box' and two prize-winners were drawn from this category.

Group

Entries in this category focused on group situations and learning through, or with, others. Ideas concentrated on increasing learner interaction and getting the most out of each other rather than from the teacher. One of the 2008 runners-up was 'Virtual Learning Centre Northumbria', a 3D virtual learning environment created within Second Life software. This contained a diverse range of media technologies accompanied by various forms of formative assessment that could be modified and cross-applied to any learning module or group within the university with links to various academic resources within the university.

The first-prizewinner for 2008 also came from this category. This was 'Flying the Kite: how to encourage effective group work for positive learning experiences in relation to assessment – a student's perspective'. This was an easy-to-use aid in the form of a poster, which gave students and staff the opportunity to reflect on their group work practice. An attachment to this was a flyer, which was designed in tandem with the poster, and gave students a chance to record verbal and written feedback with regard to their group work. This was in tune with Northumbria's drive on providing feedback and being easily adaptable to all courses.

Individual

In 2008 a second-prize-winning entry came from the 'learner-centred – individual' category. 'Personal portfolio website tutorials' offered students the opportunity to develop their own online portfolio through a series of tutorials available on university computers. This idea was seen as improving students' CVs and employability after they finished their degree.

The authors and judges felt that entries such as this challenged the idea of specific knowledge as the central part of learning, focusing instead on more general skills, attitudes learned and the value of education for personal development. There was a strong focus on employability and transferable skills as well as generally helpful attitudes for students to adopt. These entries were indicative of students really engaging with their learning, not just as a passive receptacle but taking control of their own personal development and attitudes to learning. They demonstrate a move beyond what the teacher can do to what the students can do to maximize the value of the experience to them.

Marker preferences

There was an almost equal balance between entries focusing on student-centred learning and those focusing on teacher-dominated learning. The marks awarded by the judges were analysed to determine whether there was any preference among student judges. In fact, there was no bias towards learner-centred teaching among the student judges and the marks they awarded were similar to those of the staff who gave similar weighting to traditional teaching and learner-centred approaches. So neither student entries nor student judges demonstrated a strong desire for more student-centred rather than teacher-dominated learning.

Student motivation

So what motivated those students who *did* enter, to do so? Can we learn from them? These are some of the comments they made when asked about motivation:

> I thought what I had done as part of my dissertation would help people and . . . I might as well bring it out into the open. After all you are at uni to learn and build on things . . .
>
> I . . . decided just to put it out there to see what happened because I thought it was quite a good one . . . It was something that I found was lacking from my time at Northumbria . . .
>
> Students have a lot to say and it is often the case they don't always say what they want to happen . . . I thought this would be worth telling the rest of the uni about.

Another important motivator for potential entrants would be proof that the university takes students' ideas seriously and actually takes them forward. We were learning in 2007 when the award was launched and did not really do enough to take suggestions forward. We may have let the students down in this respect if they were 'testing the water' to see if the institution was prepared to respond actively and positively to suggestions. Student entrants indicated how they would like their ideas to be taken forward, indicating that they had done prior research for their entries and they anticipated further research being undertaken by the institution during the development process:

> It does have the potential to be used more . . . it kind of exploded on me. I started looking at one thing and then before I knew it was building . . . maybe if people just try to get more of an understanding of it because it is relatively new . . .
>
> More of a study should be conducted on how other unis are using it . . . if people look at how it has been used in that sort of context they might see how it could have more use here . . .
>
> Focus groups with students to see how they would like it . . . Also discussions with the lecturers who have an involvement in it . . . See how it goes . . . and then possibly expand it to other areas . . .
>
> I talked with quite a lot of people from a range of subjects . . . to get some feedback on how it would apply. I was building a bigger picture of how different people would use it and what kind of things would be involved in it . . .

With respect to 2008 prize-winners, at least two lecturing staff are looking to take forward the suggestions made by entrants. This fact can be used in future marketing of the award as it is the kind of practice we would like to encourage around the university. Once ideas are implemented rather than just received, the awards should be more relevant to students and will afford an opportunity to build productive teacher–student relationships across the university, as staff support is a major motivating factor.

However, from the above comments, there is some indication that students are relatively happy with the idea of 'handing over the reins' to another person within the university once their idea is raised and don't necessarily want to be involved beyond having generated the idea. This would seem to endorse a more traditional view of teaching-learning, although university resource and time commitments impact on their involvement, as does the time lag between the announcement of the prize and the implementation of the idea. How far do we want students to be more involved in not only coming up with an idea but actually rolling it out if it is adopted? How far is this practicable? If ownership is transferred from the student to the teacher is this reasserting the power relationship?

Tuning in to the student voice

It has become clear from discussions with students about their entries that they desire more active involvement in learning and teaching development. There were differences apparent to the extent of which they felt their opinions mattered and were taken into consideration. Students commented on the lack of attention they feel is given to their viewpoints, with some reporting:

> There are other things where students get the chance to give feedback but I don't think they are general enough. I don't think they interest enough students, only a selected group.
>
> There is a tick box but I don't think they really take that on board. It is best not to try to pressure people into answering stuff. There should be more encouragement on the students' part.
>
> Some things I see in the uni where I think, 'that could be better'; I am not asked about what could be improved or how it could be improved. The award was the only chance I have had so far, I feel, to put forward.
>
> I know they do the questionnaires at the end of the year – but that just gives a tiny aspect of what the students are thinking.

Northumbria's active approach to student involvement with learning and teaching indicates a positive step in overcoming such feelings like those listed above. Strong emphasis is given to the appreciation of students' ideas and suggestions for future teaching innovations. Engagement in producing a teaching innovation for this award was found to be affected by conflicting pressures such as personal course workloads and time management.

There is always a flood of information from the uni to the students. It is easy to brush it off or think 'this is the wrong time for me, I have too much work on, I have this thing I need to do' . . . difficult to promote.

Most students should have involvement. It is difficult because so many have so many things going on in their lives outside the uni and within the uni but it is important this network of feeding back and feeding in is strong. That is where these ideas spring from.

When asked about the students' role in learning and teaching in comparison to that of a lecturer, several of the entrants displayed a tendency to see these in a traditional light. One student used non-verbal communication to indicate the gap he felt existed between 'them and us', stretching his hands apart and saying:

You tend to think, teachers are like there and you are here . . .

On the other hand, one student spoke of a member of staff to whom he felt he could express his opinion:

If you feel [the lecturer] is trying to help you, you feel happier to talk to him about things. If you are given an overall sense that they are trying to help, that promotes that.

This is indicative of a more equal relationship between lecturer and student, which entrants believe contributes to a more well-rounded student experience. This highlights the importance of the staff–student relationship and perhaps suggests that we should aim to influence staff attitudes and behaviours as much as those of students.

Entrants were asked in what ways they feel the lecturer–student roles should change. One student felt that it was not until he entered third year of university that he was able to be more free in terms of what he was doing and in giving opinions:

Listen more, adapt to the students more. From my experience it is like when you are at secondary school. There is a rigid structure. When I came here, the first two years, I did not get much out of it. Third year, when I could do things my way as well as the way dictated by the teacher . . .

This student was asked whether he thought students needed the maturity that comes with being a third-year before they can input more and he said that, while first-year students were somewhat fazed by their transition and were still adapting, he felt that, by second year, students should be given more freedom of expression.

Try to get the school together and get people talking a bit more and . . . actively promote ideas.

I think students have to give as well as receive . . .

These comments indicate the value that these students ascribe to being treated as important in the learning process and able to participate on a more equal footing as well as the benefits that this brought to them in terms of confidence, skills and their ability to take control of their learning experience. Northumbria University Learning and Teaching Awards signify a great example of ways in which the student's voice can be tuned in to.

Concluding remarks

Constructive learning theory would predict that submissions would include a high number of learner-centred proposals, indicative of a desire for more student-centred rather than teacher-dominated learning. However, this proved not to be the case although we have posited some suggestions as to why this might be and anticipate an increase in learner-centred entries as the awards progress.

It had also been anticipated that students would provide well-articulated and theorized views on learning and the practices that support it. Again, this proved generally not to be the case as they have tended not to provide a theoretical underpinning to their entries. However, maybe we should ask if we need them to do this for their ideas to have value. If the awards are accessible we might expect a greater emphasis on the idea itself and the ability to explain the benefits likely to be derived from it, rather than being able to locate it in theory.

However, it is notable that the winning entry in each year came from students based in the School of Health, Community and Education Studies. A range of factors might account for this but one prize-winning student perspective was that:

Traditionally a student's role at university would be to listen, learn and absorb: the lecturer knows more than the student and so they 'teach' them. However, this is not the process that I have experienced . . . students are given a lot more respect and encouragement to learn from each other . . . staff are open to learning from the experience of students: a two-way process is appreciated . . .

These prize-winners from this school felt that they and their ideas were valued. This is in marked contrast to a prize-winner from another school, who was also a student rep, who commented that even in that role, he was

not seen as massively influential or what I have to say as that important
. . . unless it is backed up by a member of staff or the Dean or something
like that . . .

Comments such as this are indicative of the notion of student participation
as 'tokenism'. If this is a common student experience, how can we expect
students to engage in activities such as the Learning and Teaching Awards? Is
there a wider issue that needs to be addressed before learning and teaching
awards can achieve the number and type of entries we are hoping for? The
dearth of submissions may in itself tell us something about our students'
experiences as learners and in examining the entries, talking to entrants
and members of the student body, we have been afforded an opportunity
to address the issues raised and look forward to the future potential of the
awards scheme.

One message that emerged from the study is how few students were
motivated to enter the award and that other approaches may be necessary
if we are truly to tap into the student voice. Ideas under consideration now
are embedding the awards in existing courses; encouraging teaching staff
to promote the awards in sessions to students with projects or ideas focusing
on teaching and learning. The authors speculate that this embedding might
improve the student perception of the award and increase their likelihood
of applying for it since relevance and relationship are motivating factors.
Another consideration is that pre-entry advice and/or support is offered
to students, for example, a workshop to discuss ideas with others or with
a staff member. The authors posit whether the awards might seem more
valued within the university or more student-friendly if these facilities were
available.

The authors remain optimistic that students' suggestions can reshape
learning and teaching and impact on the student experience. The 2007
and 2008 Learning and Teaching Awards have provided valuable data in
respect of what worked and what did not work. Not enough was done with
the prize-winning entries from the first round and this has been rectified
in the second round, with prize-winning suggestions being followed up.
Prize-winners from 2008 are being involved in marketing the next award,
providing more in-depth information as students who have actually entered
and experienced the process. This is a major step forward, indicating not
only commitment from and to students but also the quality of ideas that
enable students to participate on a truly equal footing.

Overall, the author team feels that the whole collaborative writing process has been really rewarding, involving them in something beyond their
normal range of work and increasing their confidence. It has been a positive experience for us all and serves to emphasize the value of staff–student
partnerships.

Acknowledgements

The authors would also like to acknowledge contributions from Tom Gyr, Matthew Hunter and Daryl Johnson.

Note

[1] Fullan, M. G. (1991) *The New Meaning of Educational Change.* London: Cassell, p.70.

References

Arnot, M., McIntyre, D., Pedder, D. and Reay, D. (2004), *Consultation in the Classroom: Developing Dialogue about Teaching and Learning.* Cambridge: Pearson.

Bishop, R. (2003), 'Changing power relations in education: Kaupapa Maori messages for 'mainstream' education in Aotearoa/New Zealand', *Comparative Education*, 39, (2), 221–238.

Bland, D. and Atweh, B. (2007), 'Students as researchers: engaging students' voices in PAR, *Educational Action Research*, 15, (3), 337–349.

Cook-Sather, A. (2006), 'Change based on what students say: preparing teachers for a more paradoxical model of leadership', *International Journal of Leadership in Education*, 9, (4), 345–358.

Fielding, M. (2004), 'Transformative approaches to student voice: theoretical underpinnings, recalcitrant realities', *British Educational Research Journal*, 30, (2), 295–311.

Gabelnick, F., MacGregor, J., Matthews, R. S. and Smith, B. L. (1990), *Learning Communities: Creating Connections among Students, Faculty, and Disciplines – New Directions for Teaching and Learning – No. 41.* San Francisco: Jossey-Bass.

Glaser, B. and Strauss, A. (1967), *The Discovery of Grounded Theory: Strategies for Qualitative Research.* Chicago: Aldine Transaction.

Levin, B. (2000), 'Putting students at the centre in education reform', *Journal of Educational Change*, 1, (2), 155–172.

Marshall, C. and Rossman, G. B. (1989), *Designing Qualitative Research.* Newbury Park, CA: Sage Publications.

Martin, E. (1999), *Changing Academic Work: Developing the Learning University.* Buckingham: Society for Research into Higher Education/Open University.

Mitra, D. (2004), 'The significance of students: can increasing student voice in schools lead to gains in youth development?' *Teachers College Record*, 106, (4), 651–688.

Rudduck, J. (2007), 'Student voice, student engagement, and school reform', in D. Thiessen and A. Cook-Sather (eds), *International Handbook of Student Experience in Elementary and Secondary School.* Dordrecht: Springer, pp. 587–610.

Thomson, P. and Holdsworth, R. (2003), 'Theorising change in the education "field": re-readings of "student participation" projects', *International Journal of Leadership in Education*, 6, (4), 371–391.

Walker, R. (1985), *Applied Qualitative Research.* Aldershot: Gower.

Chapter 9

Communication as Performance: A Cross-Disciplinary Approach to Staff–Student Partnership

Elena Zaitseva, Elizabeth Clifford, Sarah Nixon,
Elizabeth Deja and Andrew Murphy

The recent economic recession aside, contemporary UK Higher Education (HE) is being challenged to produce graduates who can support the continued growth of the economy. A series of UK Government-commissioned reports from Dearing (1997) to Leitch (2006) and the *Higher Education at Work – High Skills: High Value* consultation report (DIUS, 2008) have urged universities to do more to enable students to develop the skills, knowledge and attributes required by employers.

Findings from graduate and employer surveys (Morgan, 1997; Ennis-Reynolds, 2001; Sleap and Read, 2006; Shah et al., 2004; CBI, 2009) indicate that presentation and communication skills (in all their various forms) are among the most important skills a student must develop and possess in order to succeed, whether that be in academic, personal or employment-related spheres. The challenge facing academics and other related staff is how best to support these aspects of student development.

While opportunities for developing and assessing communication and presentation skills do exist within and outside of the HE curriculum (see, for example, Pulko and Parikh, 2003; Langan et al., 2005; Callow and Roberts, 2008), there are significant limitations on the extent to which students' individual needs can be specifically addressed. In a busy academic schedule, students have only limited opportunities to reflect on their communication and presentation experience, identify gaps in their own ability to present, and learn strategies for improvement. Staff may feel that they lack the expertise or time to provide individual coaching in an already crowded curriculum, while the assessment environment may add additional unwelcome anxiety to students already concerned about speaking in front of others.

This situation led Sport Development staff (later referred to as Sport staff) at Liverpool John Moores University (LJMU) to consider what other mechanisms could be employed for providing direct support to students identified as struggling with presentation/communication skills. Being one of 74 government-funded Centres for Excellence in Teaching and Learning

(CETL) with a specific focus on enhancing student employability, leadership and enterprise-related skills and attributes, gave LJMU an added impetus, with available resources, to investigate and pilot potential solutions.

Staff concerns were related specifically to verbal communication in both professional and semi-professional situations. Sport Development students (later referred to as Sport students), in preparation for future careers, are expected to lead coaching sessions, deliver formal presentations or use persuasion/negotiation skills to encourage others in the wider community to participate in physical activity. Students must, therefore, learn to feel comfortable with communicating in a range of scenarios and to varying group sizes.

It was decided to take a peer tutoring approach whereby performing arts students, believed to have specific expertise to offer in terms of communicating in a range of styles, and to know techniques for overcoming nerves associated with presenting to unfamiliar audiences, would act as the peer-tutors. The model developed involved Sport staff working in partnership with Drama students to address the needs of the individual Sport students.

Emerging from the 'story' of the formation of this cross-disciplinary collaboration as well as drawing upon theoretical and empirical perspectives on skills acquisition, peer-tutoring, peer-coaching and staff–student partnerships, this chapter explores the outcomes of the project from the perspectives of both student groups. It also reflects on the model of staff–student partnership created, identifying factors that may have limited its transformative potential.

Building partnerships: a story in three parts

The project took shape in three stages and involved four different groups of staff and students. Outlined in Figure 9.1 are the various interrelationships and partnerships (the stronger partnerships denoted by solid lines) that emerged as the initiative progressed.

Stage 1 – Identifying the problem and finding a solution
To verify the initial anecdotal concerns of staff and to obtain, first-hand, Sport students' opinions on their perceived strengths and weaknesses related to communication, the students were asked to complete a self-assessment questionnaire. Findings from the questionnaire suggested that these first-year students experienced anxiety and lacked confidence in many communication and presentation situations, leading to poorer performance (perceived or actual). The following factors were mentioned by respondents as having significant impact on their ability to communicate:

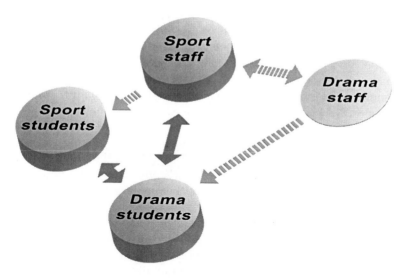

FIGURE 9.1 Interconnections facilitated by the project

Status of the group and familiarity with the audience
Some students indicated that they found it easier to deal with groups of children than adults, particularly if those adults were in positions of authority, such as tutors.

Perceived importance of situation
Assessed presentations or situations with a degree of formality led some students to feel less able to make a good impression or perform well.

Personal factors
A number of students identified their accent as providing a source for personal concern. One mentioned sounding 'a bit scouse' (colloquial term for a Liverpool accent), whereas another described the effect of others' comments: '. . . sometimes my peers take the mick out of [tease me about] my accent'.

Audience behaviour
Dealing with difficult or distracting audience behaviour was also a cause of anxiety. Students might feel confident with their material but if the audience appeared not to be listening or were disruptive then this affected their performance.

The multiplicity of factors influencing students' ability to communicate was clearly seen in the student responses and echoed Cohen and Cohen's (1998) findings that communication proficiency is dependent on many variables, including individual, cultural and contextual influences. Skills acquisition theorists (e.g. Schmidt, 1991; Tomlinson, 1995; Schön, 1987) emphasize the complexity of the skills learning process and its iterative nature, which includes observing more experienced individuals, and 'perhaps, attempting to mimic them' (Blunden, 1996, p. 178), followed by practice and receiving further feedback. Each subsequent cycle of the process involves the individual in cementing the constituents of that improved performance in their communication behaviour as well as developing them further.

Schön (1987) highlights the pivotal role of a coach in supporting individuals through that practical learning process. The coach is one who is responsible for guiding the learner by 'the right kind of telling' (Dewey, 1974, p. 151, as cited in Schön, 1987, p. 17), demonstrating how to solve certain types of problems, giving feedback and helping to establish priorities for further attention. While the decision of Sport staff to develop a model utilizing coaching was intuitive, rather than grounded in the literature, upon reflection it was the best approach to address the students' needs.

Peer-tutoring was chosen as a means of diminishing the perceived student–staff boundaries highlighted in the questionnaire responses, encouraging learning and development in a less 'power-oriented' environment. A pragmatic reason for choosing peer-tutoring, mentioned by Topping (1996) and Boud et al. (2001), was the cost-effectiveness of this form of learning.

The peer-tutoring approach involving 'more skilled or experienced individuals tutoring younger or less experienced tutees' (Falchikov, 2001, p. 8) is widely explored in the literature (e.g. Falchikov, 2001; Topping, 2005; Boud, 2001; Ladyshewsky, 2006). Our particular case, being a more specific type of peer-tutoring, will be referred to as 'peer-coaching', since it had a particular intention to help students improve their performance in relation to internal thoughts, behaviours or skills (Ladyshewsky, 2006) as opposed to mastering course concepts (e.g. Rittschof and Griffin, 2001) or understanding curriculum content (Topping, 2005) – outcomes more usually associated with the term 'peer-tutoring'. Aspiring to achieve the freedom to 'learn by doing' in a setting relatively low in risk (Schön, 1987), it was decided that it should be a non-assessed activity, with Sport students participating voluntarily in this pilot.

Stage 2 – Creating the staff–student partnership
Having previously identified performing arts students as potential student coaches, Sport staff approached colleagues in the Drama department. Final-year students were seen to be the ideal candidates for this project, given their levels of development and maturity. During initial discussions between the two groups of staff, possibilities for accrediting the work of the Drama students were discussed should the pilot project be continued for future cohorts. Suggestions included giving academic credit via an Independent Study module.

The next phase involved direct negotiation between the Sport staff and four selected Drama students to secure them as partners and develop a project action plan. Both parties met together to share ideas and, through open discussions, agreed how the project would be enacted. Having undertaken their own research on the topic of developing communication skills, the Drama students developed a six-week coaching programme. A member of the Drama staff was consulted by the students for generic guidance and approval of their ideas; however, the programme that emerged was principally the students'own work.

Exploring the concept of partnership

The notion of partnership is defined variously in different knowledge domains (e.g. Furlong et al., 1996; Lee, 2001; Charles et al., 1999) and, as Guest and Peccei (2001) point out, there is no agreed definition or conceptualization of partnership in the academic literature. However, irrespective of the area where the concept is applied (e.g. business, human resource management, education, health etc.), it seems rooted in principles of relative independence of the parties who are bringing their knowledge, expertise or other resources into the partnership; reciprocity of interests (could be individual pragmatic motivations); shared responsibility; and a willingness to achieve desired aims and objectives.

The partnership outlined here features some of the core elements mentioned in the various definitions, such as mutuality – 'shared interests of two or more interdependent parties while recognizing that they have other potentially differing interests' (Guest and Peccei, 2001, p. 211); willingness 'to solve a problem or create an opportunity that neither can address individually' (Selin and Chavez, 1995, p. 192); and 'clear objectives and strong commitment, and statements [verbal in our case] of the respective partners' responsibilities' (Rowley, 2005, p. 13).

Drama students had the knowledge, skills and time available to deliver the training which the Sport staff did not possess; they were fully independent in terms of their academic status (Sport staff had no assessment jurisdiction over them) and willing to achieve the goals set up for them. They perceived the project as an opportunity for their own development, particularly in terms of building up their CV just prior to graduation and seeking employment. As well as the shared benefits to be gained should the initiative prove to be successful, there were risks involved, but these are a distinctive feature of any partnership (Lee, 2001).

The specific feature of this partnership model, discussed in more detail later, is that it was formed to address the needs of a 'third party' and, although the staff and student collaboration was absolutely critical to the success of the initiative, the closer 'working' relationship or partnership to emerge was that between the two sets of students.

Overview of staff–student partnership literature

Research on staff–student partnerships (sometimes referred to as 'staff–student collaboration') is rather limited, with just a handful of papers exploring this concept in the HE context. The partnerships cited are predominantly associated with a learning environment where staff and students openly share and negotiate their understanding of the teaching and learning aims and where responsibility for the learning process is largely placed on students themselves (e.g. Stefani, 1998; Lizzio et al., 2007; Bosch et al., 2008).

Stefani, for example, introduces the term 'staff–student partnership' in the context of assessment, reflecting on a project where students formulated assessment criteria for a team project. Stefani argues that 'teaching and learning are not unilateral activities but rather depend upon the development of partnerships between the teachers and learners' (Stefani, 1998, p. 340). In Lizzio et al. (2007), the term 'staff–students respectful partnership' is enlisted to present an 'ideal' mode of 'fairness' within the learning environment where student voice and opinions are heard and sought after. The authors believe that 'respectful partnership' does exist in a learning environment that 'evidences both consistent and fair procedures' (p. 203).

While we agree that giving students a voice and responsibility for setting aims and outcomes of their learning process are important characteristics of partnership, it could be argued that there are obvious limitations to the models mentioned above. Inequality in the partners' status clearly exists in these models and, even if the power balance is shifting, assuming more active student engagement and their 'voice' being heard, the students' role in the partnerships described is still rather limited. It also must not be forgotten that where assessment exists there will always be some power play in operation between staff and students.

Specific cases of research-driven staff–student partnerships or collaborations were considered in Nagda et al. (1998) and Perrier (2006). Nagda et al., for example, suggested that integrating students into the core academic mission of the university via research-driven staff–student partnerships is an effective means of improving student retention, especially those from higher-risk groups. Perrier (2006), aiming to 'reinvent the spaces in which learning takes place' introduced a multidisciplinary research project where staff, undergraduate and postgraduate students all equally contributed to the research design, data gathering and analysis of the materials and produced a collaborative research paper, where the traditional practice of putting the leading researcher's name first was challenged. These are, perhaps, examples of more equal relationships, particularly the case of Perrier, where the cross-disciplinary nature of the initiative capitalized on everyone's unique input. But we could still argue that staff here are the more experienced and knowledgeable partners, setting standards and helping to develop students' expertise.

Stage 3 – Implementation of the peer-coaching project

The Drama students initially met 20 Sport students, identified as ones who could benefit from additional assistance in the development of communication skills, in a sports practical session. Here they had a chance to observe their future tutees communicating in a 'professional' setting and to identify individual problems and needs. As Blunden (1996) pointed out, skills are 'taught within a cultural matrix in which the cast of mind required is shaped by the norms which characterize a discipline' (p. 175). Getting to know the disciplinary context and being able to make relevant links while delivering training was important for the future communication skills coaches. The Sport staff were present in this first session, to introduce Drama students and give some background information, but subsequent training sessions were conducted by Drama students independently.

From an organizational standpoint these peer-coaching sessions were incorporated into the Sport Development curriculum through an existing Leadership module, the premise being that improved ability to communicate should enhance students' potential in presenting to and leading others. Via interactive, practice-based sessions Sport students were developing 'technical' skills – such as breathing, voice projection and tone; improvization and leadership skills – persuasive speaking and role playing; confidence in speaking in front of others; body language; and generally how to create a connection with a diverse audience and in various environments. Work undertaken during the peer-coaching sessions culminated in the Sport students delivering an individual presentation on a topic of their choice to the rest of the group. This gave the Drama students an opportunity to provide feedback to the students on their progress through the course and performance during the presentation.

Outcomes of the peer-coaching project

To allow the students time to reflect on the experience and to put into practice the skills they had started to master, evaluative data was collected two months after the completion of the sessions. Both sets of students completed a questionnaire, and separately took part in in-depth focus groups facilitated by independent researchers.

Sport development students' perspectives

When asked about the benefits of being involved in this project, 45 per cent of students thought it was beneficial for them, with 33 per cent being neutral and 22 per cent deriving no benefit. Having rated perceived skills development on a 4-point Likert-type scale (from not developed at all to substantially developed), students indicated that self-confidence, verbal/presentation skills, collaborative work and self-efficacy (beliefs about own effectiveness in a particular domain or situation) (Bandura, 1982) were the skills and attributes that had been most developed by the project. Commenting on the experience, they highlighted the specific skills gained: 'better understanding of breathing, improved body language, better voice projection', as well as more generic learning outcomes: 'it encouraged me to think on the spot which will be useful in placements'; 'got more confidence in public speaking'.

The feedback from the Drama students further substantiated the Sport students' perceptions. Reflecting on the Sport students' learning outcomes, they commented that the most noticeable difference between the first and last sessions was in students' self-confidence, with some remarkable trans-formations having occurred:

> In the first week there was one boy who didn't even look, he could not speak loud enough, just really under-confident . . . Then, at the end, you could not stop him talking, he was making jokes, he was confident, really made such a difference when he was giving a presentation.

The peer-coaching approach, it seemed, worked well for creating a 'power-free', liberating learning environment – the training was perceived by more than half of the Sport students as an enjoyable experience: '. . . it was fun to participate; . . . it was more relaxed [than usual learning environment]'; 'you could do a lot more, you were not afraid to get up and do silly things like the games'.

Those with a neutral or negative attitude based their comments either on the lack of direct links with their course of study or on the type of exercises used: 'it was not very beneficial to me – I did not know why I was doing it; . . . not directly related to the course; sometimes we played too many games and they were a bit repetitive'.

While staff had been careful to choose students for the peer-coaching role with particular expertise in communication, the lack of mutual subject knowledge was not appreciated by some Sport students. These students ques-tioned the interdisciplinary nature of the project, stating that they might have benefited more if the coaches had a sports background so as to make the session content more relevant: 'People on sports courses surely would respond to successful people within their own or desired field . . .'. They also cast doubts on the Drama students' abilities to transfer their skills into a specific sports-related environment: 'The drama students may be really confident and good at acting in front of large groups of people but . . . what do they know about presenting in a real life [sport-related] situation?' One of the factors mentioned as limiting their engagement was the 'theatrical' behaviour of the coaches: '. . . drama students tend to be theatrical, over the top and even eccentric'. It is likely that some of these factors led to certain students withdrawing from the project.

Drama students' perspectives

Establishing a proper peer learning environment was not an easy task for the Drama students since, as soon as they started the first session, they realized that the type of activities they were asking Sport students to do were outside of their tutees' 'comfort zone'. The Drama students understood the need to quickly establish the 'peer atmosphere', trying to put themselves on equal footing and emphasizing that they were not lecturers or tutors but peers with a different set of skills.

Balancing the peer-coach identities proved to be challenging for the Drama students. Initial lack of power meant that they were often confronted with scepticism: 'Well, you are still students . . . I'm not going to look silly just because you tell me to . . .'. Positioning themselves as equals, beneficial in some senses, meant they felt they lacked authority to comment on such things as attendance, as illustrated by the following quote: 'Because you are working with your peers you don't feel that you have the authority really to say – right, you have to be there or you are not going to learn anything'.

To quickly address this problem Drama students had to reconsider and introduce the notion of authority and mutual responsibility into the peer-coaching relationship: 'We were just like . . . we are lecturers, we know what we are doing . . . and this is what we have to do'. As one of the Drama students pointed out: 'I think it took a while to get there . . .'.

The learning outcomes gained by Drama students were multiple, including practical experience of coaching: 'It was beneficial to find your feet as an adviser, as I don't think any of us had done that before – actually have to plan and research and follow through with everything', and the realization of how much they already knew:

> I think we learnt about how much we did know; we went in not thinking we knew that much about leading groups . . . We were just taking things from our realm of drama and seeing how it applies to a different setting . . .

They also gained a lot of personal satisfaction observing improvements in some of the students, and highlighted the trust developed during the project: 'I think it is more about our own attitudes toward the people we were working with, like learning to try and get the best out of them, as well as them getting the best out of us'.

Students' recommendations

The project was successful in achieving its goals, given that 70 per cent of the Sport students said they would recommend this activity to future student cohorts. Both groups of students suggested two main areas for improvements. In terms of organization, students recommended a smaller group size; more intense regime (have two one-hour sessions rather than one per week) over a longer period of time; having it as a timetabled activity for everybody on the course; as well as using a more suitable room.

From a pedagogic perspective, Sport students suggested that the next cohort of students should be made aware of the benefits as well as responsibilities of being involved in the training from the very beginning. Clearer links with the subject content and better integration of the sessions with the rest of the course was perceived by students as important conditions for success.

Reflections on the staff–student partnership formed

At the outset our primary intention was not to form a staff–student partnership but, in retrospect, that is what happened. Probably this is the nature of most initiatives – the need drives the innovation. To consider how this approach differs from others and what its strengths and limitations are, a comparison has been made with the models of staff–student partnership referred to in the literature. Table 9.1 summarizes the similarities and differences of the two models of staff–student partnership: one within the course (e.g. as presented in Lizzio et al., 2007) and a cross-disciplinary model of partnership (our case).

Table 9.1   Comparison of cross-disciplinary and in-course staff–student partnerships

Feature	Cross-disciplinary (staff-external students) partnership	In-course (staff-own students) partnership
Knowledge, expertise or resources brought into the partnership	Staff – limited, students – having a specific, expert knowledge	Staff – main expertise holder, students – developing the expertise and having an opportunity to contribute
Standards (acceptable level of outcomes)	Defined by students (some initial advice could be sought from staff in their disciplinary area)	Defined by lecturer, guidance for students
Power balance	Equal: staff refrain from interfering in order to create a pure peer-learning environment. Lack of assessment reduces power imbalances	There is still some power imbalance since students are assessed (in various forms) upon results of the exercise
Motivation to participate/engage in partnership	Staff-driven, but individual/specific motivation for both sides	Staff-driven, more explicit for staff than for students
Involvement of staff external to programme	Required to some extent (stronger staff–staff relationship would help to preserve/sustain partnerships)	Not required

The student voice is clearly heard through our model of partnership since this was where the expertise lay. Our partnership was based on a deficit/ surplus model where staff helped with structuring and timing issues but the content was created and delivered by Drama students. Given that there was no prior relationship or connection between the Sport staff and the Drama students, issues that might arise from the traditional staff–student collaboration model and power imbalances were avoided. Using the words of Perrier (2006), it 'successfully challenged the hierarchies of academia': while staff initiated the partnership, the power distribution was shifted toward students, who took control of project delivery.

Disciplinary differences between partners contributed positively to achieving the main aim of the partnership, but also presented a challenge. While communication and presentation are often used as generic or 'catch-all' terms, they conceal a multitude of interpretations and manifestations of practice in different subject areas. The theatrical nature of Drama students' communication expertise – specific to their disciplinary environment, but alien for Sport students – was too prominent for some and sometimes caused tensions in those being coached.

At the same time, the freedom and trust given by the Sport staff to the Drama students led to a certain level of anxiety and a steep learning curve, especially at the initial stage of the project. It is an unusual and possibly disconcerting situation for students to find themselves in. Some may struggle with the role reversal but these Drama students, despite some initial uncertainty, thrived in this environment.

As Lee (2001) pointed out, partnership is a dynamic process, evolving over time 'as the actors mutually and sequentially demonstrate their trustworthiness . . .' (p. 327). However, the short-term nature of this partnership (over the course of one semester in total) imposed certain limitations and there was little time for growth and the development of relationships between the staff and students.

Rowley (2005) regards successful partnership working as requiring 'persistence in managing' (p. 10). This is what was lacking in our case. Despite initial intentions to replicate this exercise the following year with the possibility of creating more sustainable, curriculum-based opportunities for Drama students to engage in the activity, this was never implemented. Students are, by their nature, transient partners, therefore attention needs to be paid to how an ethos of partnership is achieved even when individuals in that partnership will change. Drama students expressed keenness to develop materials used into a resource pack for future use – funding was agreed, but eagerness to remain involved with the project was lost once students had graduated and moved ahead with individual aspirations.

Conclusions and future trends

Having reflected on our experiences, we find ourselves concurring with Perrier's (2006) comments that 'collaborative work between students and teachers is an empowering' but at the same time 'difficult exercise'. Despite many beneficial outcomes to the partnership, its sustainability would require the following adjustments to the model:

1. Benefits for both parties need to be more clearly articulated and discussed from outset.
2. When using students from outside of staff jurisdiction, equal attention needs to be paid to developing a partnership with staff from that area to assist with identifying benefits for students.
3. Sport staff could perhaps have had more direct involvement in supporting the peer learning aspects of the partnership to promote Sport student participation and attendance. Staff had a clear aim to demonstrate to both groups of students that they were trusted and that this undertaking was about individual development rather than an assessed part of the course for which they would be judged or measured. It is possible that both groups of students found this too far removed from their usual experience of education.
4. If student coaches are from a different subject background from tutees, care should be taken to use more authentic training scenarios.

On reflection, a paradoxical situation emerged where, in a reversal of the normal staff–student power balance, staff were more reliant on the expertise of the Drama students than could be sustained by the commitment of the Drama students to remain involved. Guest and Peccei (2001) reinforce the importance of 'building trust and sustaining partnership through appropriate institutional arrangements' (p. 215). For the staff–student partnership to be sustainable in our case it would need to be forged with something that sits above individual students, that is, through programme, module or programme leader structures and channels.

It appears there is little information in the literature about how effectively communication skills are being taught and how well students are learning these skills. The majority of authors agreed, however, that it would take a long time for the effects of training to be seen (see, for example, Nerdum, 1997). The cyclical nature of skills acquisition, cited above, also reinforces the need to have a longer-term partnership, with a possibility to follow up the progress of students who took part in the training.

Logistical issues notwithstanding, we feel that cross-disciplinary partnerships provide significant potential for development and further research, for all parties involved: staff–staff and staff–student and student–student. Real life requires interprofessional communication and connection for workplace projects to come to fruition and universities should pursue such connections as part of a rich and varied teaching and learning environment (Knight, 2007).

Thoughts on collaborative writing
The collaborative writing process was an enriching and beneficial experience for all authors involved, but we have to admit that it has not happened to the extent we would have liked. Both groups of students involved in the initiative had graduated and moved on by the time actual writing started. Despite our efforts it was not possible to get hold of the student partners. However, their voice is strongly represented through the evaluative data. With the added perspective of the Sport student co-author, their experiences were interpreted and situated in the context of what happened during the project. Our co-author, a mature student with a critical approach, has added 'validity' to the story, so that the voice of the three central parties is heard.

Note: The project benefited from funding made available through LJMU's Centre for Excellence in Teaching and Learning

References

Bandura, A. (1982), 'Self-efficacy mechanism in human agency', *American Psychologist*, 37, (2), 122–147.

Blunden, R. (1996), 'The mind dependency of vocational skills', *Journal of Vocational Education & Training*, 48, (2), 167–188.

Bosch, W. C., Hester, J. L., MacEntee, V. M., MacKenzie, J. A., Morey, T. M., Nichols, J. T., Pacitti, P. A., Shaffer, B. A., Tomascak, P. B., Weber, S. P. and Young, R. (2008), 'Beyond lip-service: an operational definition of "Learning-Centered College"', *Innovative Higher Education*, 33, (2), 83–98.

Boud, D. (2001), 'Introduction: making the move to peer learning', in D. Boud, R. Cohen and J. Sampson (eds), *Peer Learning in Higher Education: Learning From & With Each Other*. London: Kogan Page, pp. 1–17.

Boud, D., Cohen, R. and Sampson J. (2001), 'Peer learning and assessment', in D. Boud, R. Cohen and J. Sampson (eds), *Peer Learning in Higher Education: Learning From & With Each Other*. London: Kogan Page, pp. 67–81.

Callow, N. and Roberts, R. (2008), *Effects of an Imagery Intervention on Students' Verbal Presentation Performance*. Retrieved 28 April 2010 from http://www.heacademy.ac.uk/hlst/projects/detail/ourwork/pedagogic_projects/r8_effects_imagery_intervention

Charles, C., Whelan, T. and Gafni, A. (1999), 'What do we mean by partnership in making decisions about treatment?' *British Medical Journal*, 319, 780–782. Retrieved 28 April 2010 from http://www.bmj.com/cgi/reprint/319/7212/780

Cohen, J. and Cohen, B. Z. (1998), 'Graduating social work students' communication competencies and motivations: their effects on satisfaction with social work', *International Social Work*, 41, (3), 357–70.

Confederation of British Industry (CBI) (2009), *Emerging Stronger: The Value of Education and Skills in Turbulent Times. Education and Skills Survey.* Retrieved 28 April 2010 from http://www.cbi.org.uk/pdf/20090406-cbi-education-and-skills-survey-2009.pdf

Dearing, R. (1997), *Higher Education in the Learning Society,* Report of the National Committee of Inquiry into Higher Education, London: HMSO. Retrieved 28 April 2010 from https://bei.leeds.ac.uk/Partners/NCIHE/

Department of Innovation, Universities and Skills (DIUS) (2008), *Higher Education at Work – High Skills: High Value.* Consultation report prepared for the Department of Innovation, Universities and Skills by the Central Office of Information (COI). Available at: http://www.dius.gov.uk/consultations/high_skills, [accessed 30 May 2008].

Dewey, J. (1974), *John Dewey on Education: Selected Writings* (ed. R. D. Archambault). University of Chicago Press: Chicago.

Ennis-Reynolds, G. (2001), 'Are leisure degrees out of touch with employability?' *Link, Newsletter of the LTSN Hospitality, Leisure, Sport & Tourism,* 1, (5), 6–7.

Falchikov, N. (2001), *Learning Together: Peer Tutoring in Higher Education.* London, UK: RoutledgeFalmer.

Furlong, J., Whitty, G., Whiting, C., Miles, S., Barton, L. and Barrett, E. (1996), 'Re-defining partnership: revolution or reform in initial teacher education?' *Journal of Education for Teaching,* 22, (1), 39–55.

Guest, D. E. and Peccei, R. (2001), 'Partnership at work: mutuality and the balance of advantage', *British Journal of Industrial Relations,* 39, (2), 207–236.

Knight, P. (2007), 'Grading, classifying and future learning', in D. Boud and N. Falchikov (eds), *Rethinking Assessment in Higher Education: Learning for the Longer Term.* London: Routledge, pp.72–86.

Ladyshewsky, R. K. (2006), 'Peer coaching: a constructivist methodology for enhancing critical thinking in postgraduate business education', *Higher Education Research & Development,* 25, (1), 67–84.

Langan, A. M., Wheater, C. P., Shaw, E. M., Haines, B. J., Cullen, R. C., Boyle, J. C., Penney, D., Oldekop, J. A., Ashcroft, C., Lockey, L. and Preziosi, R. F. (2005), 'Peer assessment of oral presentations: effects of student gender, university affiliation and participation in the development of assessment criteria', *Assessment & Evaluation in Higher Education,* 30, (1), 21–34.

Lee J.-N. (2001), 'The impact of knowledge sharing, organizational capability and partnership quality on IS outsourcing success', *Information & Management,* 38, (5), 323–335.

Leitch (2006), *Review of Skills.* London: HM Treasury. Retrieved 30 May 2008 from http://www.hm-Treasury.gov.uk/independent_reviews/leitch_review/review_leitch_index.cfm

Lizzio, A., Wilson, K. and Hadaway, V. (2007), 'University students' perceptions of a fair learning environment: a social justice perspective', *Assessment & Evaluation in Higher Education,* 32, (2), 195–213.

Morgan, G. J. (1997), 'Communication skills required by accounting graduates: practitioner and academic perceptions', *Accounting Education,* 6, (2), 93–107.

Nagda, B. A., Greggerman, S. R., Jonides, J., von Hippel, W. and Lerner, J. S. (1998), 'Undergraduate student-faculty research partnerships affect student retention', *Review of Higher Education,* 22, (1), 55–72.

Nerdum, P. (1997), 'Maintenance of the effect of training in communication skills: a controlled follow-up study of level of communicated empathy', *British Journal of Social Work*, 27, (5), 705–722.

Perrier, M. (2006), 'Reflections on practicing student-staff collaboration in academic research: a transformative strategy for change', *M/C Journal*, 9, (2). Retrieved 28 April 2010 from http://journal.media-culture.org.au/0605/08-perrier

Pulko, S. H. and Parikh, S. (2003), 'Teaching "soft" skills to engineers', *International Journal of Electrical Engineering Education*, 40, (4), 243–254.

Rittschof, K. A. and Griffin, B. W. (2001), 'Reciprocal peer tutoring: re-examining the value of a co-operative learning technique to college students and instructors', *Educational Psychology*', 21, (3), 313–331.

Rowley, J. (2005), 'Foundation degrees: a risky business', *Quality Assurance in Education*, 13, (1), 7–16.

Schmidt, R. A. (1991), *Motor Learning and Performance*. Champaign, IL: Human Kinetics Books.

Schön, D. (1987), *Educating the Reflective Practitioner: Toward a New Design for Teaching and Learning in the Professions*. San Francisco: Jossey-Bass.

Selin, S. and Chavez, D. (1995), 'Developing a collaborative model for environmental planning and management', *Environmental Management*, 19, (2), 189–195.

Shah, A., Pell, K. and Brooke, P. (2004), 'Beyond first destinations: graduate employability survey', *Active Learning in Higher Education*, 5, (1), 9–26.

Sleap, M. and Read, H. (2006), 'Views of sport science graduates regarding work skills developed at university', *Teaching in Higher Education*, 11, (1), 47–61.

Stefani, L. A. J. (1998), 'Assessment in partnership with learners', *Assessment & Evaluation in Higher Education*, 23, (4), 339–350.

Tomlinson, P. (1995), *Understanding Mentoring: Reflective Strategies for School-Based Teacher Preparation*. Philadelphia: Open University Press.

Topping, K. J. (1996), 'The effectiveness of peer tutoring in further and higher education: a typology and review of the literature', *Higher Education*, 32, (3), 321–345.

Topping, K. (2005), 'Trends in peer learning', *Educational Psychology*, 25, (6), 631–645.

Chapter 10

Performance Matters When You're Playing the Professional: Co-authored Research and Relational Pedagogy

Rebekka Kill, Keeley McDonnell and Michael Thorne

Prologue

This is the tale of a very unusual series of collaborations between a member of staff and two MA students. It's 'unusual' in that all three change their roles throughout: shifting from student to professional, from lecturer to performer; sometimes the participants were in multiple roles simultaneously, other times they travelled between them. It's important to state that this is the story of collaborative 'practice as research' in performing arts. There is a distinction to be made here between the (often used interchangeably) terms of 'practice as research' and 'practice-based research'. For Kershaw practice-based research is 'research into performance practice, to determine how and what it may be contributing in the way of new knowledge or insights', while practice as research is thought of as 'research through performance practice, to determine how that practice may be developing new insights into or knowledge about the forms, genres, uses, etc. of performance' (Kershaw, 2000).

Rebekka Kill is a Senior Lecturer in the performing arts subject area at Leeds Metropolitan University. She has been engaged with both practice-based research and practice as research for the majority of her teaching career. She also has expertise in pedagogic and interdisciplinary research. This story is about how her practice as research collided with the MA Performance Works at Leeds Metropolitan University, and about how she worked together with two students to produce research, performances and some unexpected outcomes.

Keeley McDonnell and Michael Thorne have both recently completed two courses at Leeds Metropolitan University. The first was Contemporary Performance Practices, a one year 'top-up' degree aimed at students who had previously completed a two-year (often vocationally focused) foundation degree. This course functions like a conversion course; it is an intensive, one-year programme that has at its core an intention to instil in students an understanding of research and higher-level protocols in performance practice. Both Michael and Keeley subsequently progressed onto the MA Performance Works. These two courses constituted a two-year period of study during which they became progressively involved in a series of staff–student 'practice as research' collaborations. The bulk of this chapter is a transcript of a discussion between the three of us: Michael, Keeley and Rebekka. We chose this approach, first because of the way that it echoes a script (playing with the idea of plays) and also as a mechanism to provide parity, or a level playing field between us all.

The narrator within the script functions as a mechanism for academic clarity. In this instance not only does the narrator reveal subtext but also reveals the collaborators' tacit knowledge made explicit for you, the reader, to revel in the academic interruption.

As we tell the story of our collaborations there are three central ideas that have been really important during our time working together. The first big idea, for us, that runs through all of these projects, is Bourriaud's notion of 'relational aesthetics' (Bourriaud, 2002); second, we are interested in issues around co-authorship in 'practice as research'; and third, we'd like to dig down and explore the notion of collaboration into issues of co-authorship – where does collaboration start and stop? and can any project be truly collaborative? – taking into consideration the context in which these works were situated.

Narrator: Consider the possibility as you read this text of reading the script aloud. Breathe life into the characters and become a fourth collaborator. View this text as a creative act and feel free to add voices, gestures, facial expression, sound effects and all the essential components of a great piece of performance. Relax, have fun; we hope you enjoy the show.

Act I

[Interior. Typical university office. Michael, Keeley and Rebekka sit around a table with a dictaphone in the centre. Michael presses record.]

Keeley: I would like to talk about relational aesthetics; I think that's a good place to start. *[takes a deep breath]* Nicolas Bourriaud in his influential text, *Relational Aesthetics*, proposes relational art that is 'an art taking as its theoretical horizon the realm of human interactions and its social context, rather than the assertion of an independent and private symbolic space' (Bourriaud, 2002, p. 14). This type of art is immediate and requires presence, it is essentially urban, 'art as a state of encounter' (Bourriaud, 2002, p. 18). The content and ideals of this text resonate within our practice. We are interested in performances that are activated by audience members. For example, we created relational vignettes where the outcome of the performance was changed or altered depending on who was witnessing, or participating in, our performance.

Rebekka: The second idea we need to discuss is authorship and co-authorship. My background is in fine art; my first degree is fine art and my second degree is in art history. One of the traditions of fine art is a solo practice; practising alone. Making work, making research with solo authorship. As part of the performing arts team at Leeds Met, I became more interested in collaboration. I have collaborated with students on both practice-based creative projects and on written projects. I've also collaborated with staff to produce research papers and research projects both in practice and written outcomes. *[turns and makes eye contact with Michael]* And finally, Michael, do you need to say a little bit about collaboration?

Michael: Well, put simplistically, collaboration is a way of working where everyone potentially has equal status. With teams people tend to be organized with specific duties, but the beauty of collaboration is that you can allow participants much more freedom to contribute to the particular work that you're doing. By collaborating you put everything into the mixing pot and come up with something which is much bigger than each of the collaborators might have come up with individually. Collaboration, in many ways, can be far more meaningful and far deeper than pure teamwork. Deirdre Heddon and Jane Milling said of collaboration:

Widespread mistrust of narratives was appropriately taken up by contemporary performance makers, who used the processes of collaborative devising to create works which were complex, multi-layered, multi-vocal and multi-visioned, resisting the imposition of any single perspective, answer, or 'truth'.

(Heddon and Milling, 2006, p. 218)

Act II: From assistant to collaborator

Rebekka: I did a piece of practice as research called *24/7* in an empty shop (now a gallery performance space), in the centre of Leeds. I played '7 inch' records for 24 hours; 446 in total, in alphabetical order. I started at 9 a.m. on the Saturday and finished at 9 a.m. on the Sunday. I was exploring music and music nostalgia as a kind of cultural commons and as identity construction. Michael and Keeley participated in the work as assistants and tour guides, and helped develop the performance by working alongside me. They produced a mosaic of record sleeves, documented audience response and facilitated public access to the work as it progressed. The three of us had worked together previously at a nightclub in Leeds, where performances were co-devised initially through tutor-led discussion and then through the making process. *24/7* cemented this collaborative relationship.

Michael: I was the first assistant in *24/7* doing the 9 a.m. to 1 p.m. slot, and in many ways *24/7* was the least collaborative of the projects that we worked on together. Although we were working together as a team, it was very much Rebekka's project and that was clear from the word go. Having said that, the early slot involved me unexpectedly taking responsibility for a part of the project; I had to lay down the record sleeves to start making a mosaic *[pushes an A4 printout of the record sleeve mosaic towards Rebekka and Keeley]*. Early in the morning there weren't that many people visiting the performance, so Rebekka and I started to talk about the music that was being played and the resulting mosaic. Our collaboration started to evolve at that point, but not necessarily in any way that either of us had thought about when the project was being considered. We developed our collaboration by talking about our favourite bands and the way our musical interests had evolved.

Keeley: I started as the assistant at 10 o'clock in the evening and I finished at 3 o'clock in the morning. I had the busiest slot; I needed to manage the public, most of whom had been drinking. They were enjoying the performance immensely and were keen to share their stories and experience of the songs with me. Bourriard states, 'art is a dot on a line' (Bourriard, 2002, p. 16), and this line extends in many directions; it weaves its way through our homes, our social spaces, our conversations, our thoughts; it slices through geography and history. According to Bourriard, this dot might be an object like a painting or a sculpture found in a gallery, but equally it might be found in 'meetings, encounters, events, various types of collaboration between people, games, festivals and places of conviviality' (Bourriard, 2002, p. 28). Rebekka's role within the performance meant she could only play records; she was trapped behind the decks changing the record every three minutes. You could argue that my role was much more 'relational' than Rebekka's; this hadn't previously been imagined or expected.

Narrator: In the previous scene we can see the anticipated role of assistant within the performance increased significantly into collaborator. Through this process, trust was developed and also a professional working relationship that was above and beyond the requirements of the MA. When the characters collaborated, creative electricity was generated. Andrew Northedge discusses: 'by designing carefully plotted narrative excursions into expert discourse teachers can help students to accumulate a working knowledge of the characteristics of the discourse, so that they can make their way around it for themselves. [. . .] [T]hrough dialogue, teachers can "coach" students in speaking the discourse, so that they can come to function as competent members of the knowledge community' (Northedge, 2003, p. 179). Michael and Keeley grew in confidence and Rebekka was able to envisage how her teaching might best function to suit the requirements of the students.

Act III: A different type of collaboration and co-authorship

Keeley: Leeds Metropolitan University has a cultural partnership with Festival Republic. This allows students and staff to be volunteers and interns at both Leeds and Latitude festivals. Michael and I worked as performers at Leeds Festival in the summer of 2007. Rebekka was involved with the project in a managerial position. We were given a brief to perform to people as they entered the arena gates. We were collaborating with different performers with a range of skills, and authorship was firmly located with us as performers. On the first day of the festival our pre-planned performance was particularly successful; the festival was busy and the audience were very receptive to our material. However, on the second day we experienced a problem: there were no people queuing up to enter the arena because people were entering at different times. Day two of the festival and we didn't have anybody to perform to . . .! *[laughs]*

Rebekka: Through telephone conversations and a brief meeting I was aware of the problem. However, I was managing various people and projects at once and this was their project and I knew they had the skill and ability to fix it. Michael, can you talk about the process you went through in order to solve the problem?

Michael: We thought about what we'd done before and that was to involve the audience in a series of challenges. We realized that to generate an audience we needed to do something relational where small audience numbers could be used to great effect. So we came up with the concept of blindfolded line dancing. Effectively this was our first unsupervised practice as research performance. So we devised a very simple dance that we could perform near the arena entrance where people could see what we were doing. People were interested, not vast numbers, but they engaged with our performance. My task was looking after the security of the performers and also trying to draw in members of the audience, getting them to join in so that they could learn the dance and become collaborators in our performance. Over the period of time that we were doing it we got quite a few people to join in. *[pauses, thinking]*

Collaboration in performance allows the opportunity for people to invent their own narrative. The group can then decide how that narrative is used, or not, in the performance event. This echoes Heddon and Milling's (2006, p. 218) notion of reworking an existing idea in collaborative performance.

Keeley: The performance was something which the audience didn't necessarily understand. We were performing at a music festival, but we weren't singers or musicians and there were no other performances of this type. This was, at times, a difficult concept for the audience to grasp.

Michael: One of the things that we experienced was the difference between being in a safe, student zone where we were told what to do and how to do it and being in what was really our first self-authored professional gig. Rebekka gave us the opportunity to take control, the space and the time to do it, and then it was very much up to us to make it work. We were responsible for our performance and so the importance of the group collaborating became very significant. Keeley and I drew on our experience of *24/7* and as a result we were better able to understand and use the power of collaboration, trust and relational performance. This gave us a collective working method with which we could generate our performance material. I think at the end of it we all felt that it was a real achievement, being professional performers in a very exposed position.

Narrator: Keeley and Michael discovered during this event – although they would not have realized it at that point – the difference between collaboration and co-authorship. The work that they did in preparation for the performances – entertaining the crowd at Leeds Fest – the thinking and idea generation, assigning roles and deciding on the actual location, was the 'collaboration'. What happened during the performances – a result of the site specificity and the audience – was co-authorship; it was about the research project – actually performing at Leeds Fest – producing outcomes.

Act IV: Performing tangier

Re-framing our academic identities

Rebekka: By this point Michael and Keeley were on their MA and I was teaching them on a module called Performance Matters 2.

This module functions as the equivalent of the dissertation in this pedagogically progressive course. It is the module where students explore academic protocols in performance. The central assessment of Performance Matters 2 is a conference paper. I had also decided that this particular module would be the core case study for my PhD. My PhD was in its final stages; it's about academic identity construction and authorship within, and throughout, the space of the university. I'm particularly interested in academic identity as a site of change. I'm interested in the way in which change is identified, described and, perhaps most importantly, the implications of the way this change is spoken about. The vocabulary that is used to describe and analyse this change has important implications for the way in which that change is perceived. There are complex power relations and hierarchies in play here.

Keeley: As part of the Performance Matters 2 module, we needed to explore an environment that stimulated a high level of debate and encouraged us to extend our critical perspectives. Rebekka found a conference that sounded particularly exciting. It was in Morocco, and was encouraging performative papers.

Rebekka: It was a traditional academic conference in many ways, but it was unusual in that it was accepting these performative responses as well as more mainstream academic papers.

Michael: The conference *Performing Tangier 2008: Borders, Beats and Beyond* was held in Tangier, Morocco. So we entitled our performative paper 'A Tale of Tangier; Conversations with Ghosts'. We stated that 'We'll take you on a journey; in groups of three or four, we'll walk you through Tangier where you'll encounter three charismatic characters; they are ghosts from the past but they exist in the present and have something to say about Tangier reinventing itself in the twenty-first century.' *[Looks to Keeley]*

Keeley: We used the term 'research-informed invention' to explain our exploration of three mythical characters who could have lived in Tangier. A woman, a Westerner, a famous painter and a spy, or pirate, we hadn't decided yet. We promised 'tales of adventure, treasure, self destruction, unpleasant guiding and, maybe, the odd tangerine lying around.' We created a very playful, imaginative site-specific performance from the research we had done in and around the themes of the conference.

Rebekka: Michael, can you discuss site-specific performance for a moment?

Michael: Site-specific performance can most simply be defined as a performance that is devised to be performed in a specific location. Such a performance is usually the result of finding a location and wanting to make a performance around that place, such as the old town in Tangier. That means that the performance could not be repeated anywhere else. The impetus for creating a site-specific work is explained well by Johannes Birringer who says:

. . . I discovered that the stage holds less interest to me than dysfunctional industrial architectures and other locations we tend to call 'site-specific', for no particular reason other than their apparent inadequacy as functional (useful) places holding commercial or exploitable interest or cultural value. Vacant, abandoned and crumbling buildings caught my fantasy, and inspired performances that could only be devised in such environments that smelled and tasted of a bygone history, showed wounds or proudly held on to the engineering feats of a nineteenth-century era when such buildings provided work and livelihood for many people.

(Birringer, 2006, p. 86)

Rebekka: I think it's interesting to explore our roles as part of this project. I'm a lecturer and Michael and Keeley are students. By asking them to write and submit we made it deliberately unclear to the conference organizers that these were students as opposed to lecturers or researchers applying to the conference.

Keeley: Any contact that was made between us and the organizers in Morocco was done by either Michael or me.

Rebekka: We half-wrote the performative paper before we went to Tangier. It was interesting that we read guide books, we read websites, we read beat poets, we read novels, we looked at pictures, we tried to get as much information as possible but none of us had been to Tangier before, and I think none of us expected how it would affect us when we got there. In terms of my role, I can identify points in this project where I was working as an artist, as a performer, as a lecturer, as a project manager, as a PhD student and probably some other roles too.

Keeley: I think when we arrived in Tangier we were over-researched and under-experienced. The problem, of course, being that it is difficult to create a site-specific performance without having visited the site previously.

Rebekka: During the four days before the conference we devised a 45-minute performance. We each played a character, and we took small groups of conference delegates on a walk through Tangier. It was part ghost walk and part conference paper. We were interested both in the responses of the conference delegates/participants and in the responses of the people in the streets.

Keeley: We didn't anticipate the number of people who would become involved with the project. When we were walking the streets planning our route, practising our characters, we already started to attract a big

Moroccan audience. Shopkeepers and café-goers saw us every day. They witnessed the eccentric English people who were wandering the streets bizarrely dressed in orange clothes. These witnesses became an essential part of our performance. Every day Michael bought some oranges to give to our participants, and every day the shop owner would be waiting for his big moment where he would have an international captive audience watching his every move. On reflection, I suppose he was a collaborator, but didn't realize it.

Rebekka: When we arrived, we were introduced to our guide provided by the organizers, a Moroccan MA student called Abdelilah, and in many ways he became a fourth collaborator.

Michael: But I think there were different levels of collaboration. Abdelilah's part in the performance was interesting. It became very clear that Rebekka, Keeley and I had got very clear views about what we were trying to achieve. Up to then a lot of tacit development had taken place; unsaid, we just knew what we wanted. When Abdelilah started to accompany us he was trying to understand what we were doing. But he had no frame of reference of this type of performance work, nor the depth of relationship that we'd built up over the previous projects. For instance, we were looking for 'typical' parts of Tangier to walk through, whereas he wanted us to find 'the best bits'; if we wanted to go to a typical restaurant he'd take us to a 5-star restaurant. But we wanted something far more representative of everyday Tangier. Another instance of us not communicating our ideas to him clearly enough was when we wanted to abandon our participants halfway through the performance. Abdelilah insisted that it was rude for us to walk off and leave our guests behind; however, this was an important part of our performance (relating to our research on 'bad guiding'), and something that the three of us tacitly understood. This flagged up for us the complexity, and history, of our collaborative relationship. Initially, we treated Abdelilah as our guide and failed to recognize that his role was developing into that of a collaborator, but that began to change as the performance process developed.

Rebekka: One of the really interesting things is that in some ways we were all students on this project. I was a PhD student, and Michael and Keeley were MA students. However, I think there's something quite interesting that happened here, where it far exceeded our expectations and shifted outside of just doing what we needed to do to get credit or to get closer to finishing a PhD.

Michael: I think the performance became everything for us; far more important than just a part of our MA. We were enjoying developing the performative paper and learning a great deal from our collaboration; and we were appreciating Abdelilah's role as a non-performing collaborator.

[Keeley, Rebekka and Michael simultaneously nod. It seems so choreographed, almost fake. They all laugh.]

Act V: Homeward bound

Rebekka: When we got back to the UK, Michael and Keeley presented their experiences as a seminar paper for assessment, so it was a peculiar reversion to the student/lecturer roles, but one of the things that we all felt was that we'd experienced something extremely important and so much beyond the assessment process. What was that 'beyondness' to you, Keeley?

Keeley: When I got back, initially I found it incredibly difficult to reflect upon the experience. It's really difficult to be critical about a situation that means so much to you. How do you judge the success of this research project? What questions should you be asking in relation to a complex, personal progressive journey such as this? I began thinking about reading art and decoding pictures and images. Our complex journey needed judging on its own terms, I needed to take in its elements and begin a process of decoding. This was an effective mechanism for understanding the performance and its cultural position in a critical manner. For me it was about framing my professional practice in an academic environment. The cultural exchange was also a really valuable tool for self-reflectivity. I also cannot ignore the relationship between Michael, Rebekka and me; this is something that the Moroccan students were fascinated with. They found the lack of hierarchy in our relationship really interesting. It was outside of their frame of reference; it was an atypical construction of academic identity.

Rebekka: They didn't understand the flattening off of the power relationship, did they?

Keeley: No, and this was particularly strange to the Moroccan MA student, Abdelilah, who said that although he enjoyed working alongside us, he had never experienced performance like this and was surprised at the relationship between us as lecturer and students. He said, 'We believe in the relationship – that is, between our professors and we are students. It is like a tradition and I think it is a good practice, because there should be a difference between students and their professors' (Mchichou, 2008).

Michael: I think that one of the successes of our performance was the fact that we were able to present a paper in a very different way to how everyone else was presenting at that conference. We got people out on the street, we had done our research; we were broadening the knowledge of people who were specialists in the fields of beat poets and Tangier itself. Our research and the way that we had interpreted it enabled the three of us to engage on the same level as these experts, not only with the conference delegates but also with people on the streets of Tangier.

Keeley: While we were at the conference, there were lots of questions from the academics about how Tangier could reinvent itself. I believe our 'research-informed invention' was successful in pushing forward new ideas, breaking boundaries, entertaining people and encouraging ownership. Our performance engaged an international audience of academics in creative imagination and, together, we were able to envisage new realities within an old ideology. This 'state of encounter' re-emphasized the concept of relational aesthetics.

Epilogue: pedagogy

Rebekka: I'm really interested in how education can instigate paradigmatic shift and I wrote a short Assessment, Learning and Teaching reflection for our university website on this idea in relation to masters-level study. Let me read it to you. *[holds a printout of the page at arm's length and squints at it]* 'There are lots of people in the university interested in masters-level education but what is it actually for? Why do we, as a university, want and need to provide it? I recently described the aim of masters education as paradigmatic shift. Imagine all your information, ideas and experiences have been parked in a multi-storey car park. Paradigmatic shift is an earthquake, everything shifts, and for a while your car park/ brain looks like the leaning tower of Pisa. Everything is different; everything needs to be reconsidered. The benefits to staff are equally monumental. Academics function in a community of practice. Within this ecology, whether we are experienced academics or new researchers, we need to nurture and support the academics of the future and we need to ensure that industry is populated by advanced practitioners, or our ecology will die. Masters-level education needs to be responsive, flexible and honest; it also needs to provide us with doctoral candidates and new lecturers. These two aims aren't always concurrent and a balance needs to be found. Masters-level education is absolutely pivotal; it's in a delicate position but it is one of our most important areas of activity.' *[Pause]*

The project in Morocco certainly represented a paradigmatic shift for me. After this conference I reconsidered my approach to collaboration, I reframed my own performance practice and I also constantly refer back to the many experiences on this project. So, it's as though the experiences that come after this are viewed through the lens of this project and it seems the experience was similarly monumental for Michael and Keeley. How did Morocco affect you, Keeley?

> *Keeley:* I was able to frame my practice and I developed advanced subject-specific knowledge that is crucial for me in my role as a teacher. I regularly draw upon the experience of Morocco. I trust in my own ability to meet the curriculum and the requirements of individual learners. I encourage the pupils to get involved, to take ownership and aim daily to inspire. I thrive on the collaboration that happens between me and other staff members. I'm constantly on the lookout for how we can exchange knowledge, how can I get involved to create something new and exciting.

> *Michael:* One of the things that I've taken forward into my work as a business mentor is this: by becoming collaborators exploring an issue you can come up with very unique solutions, more so than by pure teamwork. For example, I had a group of people who were all concerned about networking and talking to strangers. They weren't particularly outgoing people but wanted some experience of how they could network, so we talked about the sort of things they wanted to be able to do and the solution that evolved from all of us was, 'OK, why don't we go to the pub after work and we'll try talking to strangers? We'll try and talk to people in a way that we've never talked to them before and just see what happens'. So we moved a concept out of the classroom environment into a completely different environment, something the group would never even have dreamt of doing before. I think the Morocco performance gave me another way of reframing the way I approached issues and the confidence to involve people in a more collaborative way. Perhaps breaking with convention sometimes and working in a more collaborative environment helps people to develop more, because they are able to draw from other areas of their life experience to see and explore things in a different way.

> *Keeley:* As a collective, Michael, Rebekka and I understand each other. That's not to suggest that we are better or more knowledgeable than others. But as a collective, because of our relationship building over a period of time, we have a deeper understanding of each other. We all have different levels of expertise, we are comfortable in our own skin and we understand the working methods and mechanics of our group.

Rebekka: It's about valuing each other's experience, valuing each other's skills and looking at that without seeing it through a hierarchical lens. That, I think, is something that has come through for all of us. For me, when I was thinking as a fine artist, co-authorship – particularly co-authored research – was an anathema; it wasn't something that was usual, or common, in the field I was in. After Tangier, I have been involved in lots of co-authored projects, and I think I'm becoming a better co-author as a result of the paradigmatic shift that I experienced. I think I am more able to listen to other people's ideas and more able to get away from seeing that as some kind of compromise or some kind of dilution of my own practice or my own concepts. That is extremely important in terms of thinking about the benefits of co-authored research. As a final point, issues around co-authorship and co-authored research have become embedded into research-informed teaching for me so I'm more and more working in a co-authored, collaborative way with students and building that into the various curricula that I've been working in.

Keeley: *[Suddenly sits up, back straight, eyes wide]* I want to come back to the idea of 'relational aesthetics'. This idea has informed all of these practices as research projects, but by doing them, we have also reshaped the pedagogical relationship between Rebekka, and us as students. We need to remember that all of our outcomes have been influenced by teaching, learning and collaborating together. Do you think we have experienced something that could be called a 'relational pedagogy'? Perhaps this is pedagogy as a 'state of encounter'?

Rebekka: Keeley, that's amazing. *[Rummages through a pile of papers]* That's a term I've heard before but not used in exactly the same way. Here we go, this is quite an old text but it sums it up nicely. For Paul Ramsden, writing in 1987, 'a relational approach encourages teachers to test ideas about learning as a means of professional development . . . They also have the potential to connect the apparently unconnectable; staff research interests and undergraduate education' (Ramsden, 1987, p. 284).

[Unprompted, Michael leans forwards and switches the dictaphone off. In silence they gather up the images and papers strewn all over the table and pack them into their bags. Rebekka switches off the light in the office. They leave.]

Narrator: After recording the interview, Michael, Keeley and Rebekka did a lot of thinking and a lot of reading and even more talking. They realized they had gone through a process that they, in subject-specific language, would have called co-devising but that they had begun to call this collaboration. They also realized that the perfect environment for this collaboration was a different, or radical, kind of pedagogy. This type of pedagogy has been referred to as dialogic pedagogy; drawing on the work of Bakhtinian and Marxist theorists. It also has some resonance with the work of Paulo Freire (1970). However, these three had explored Nicholas Bourriaud's relational aesthetics and some writing about relational pedagogy and it was this that they were beginning to understand as the environment, or context, that had provided the perfect conditions for this work to happen.

Co-authorship was a much more tricky term for them to grasp. In contemporary performance practice, solo authorship is unusual. It is also common for staff and students in higher education to co-devise work, to collaborate, if you like, and to publicly perform these works. But Michael, Keeley and Rebekka were all aware of two important differences. One was about the particular type of collaborative processes that they had used that weren't the same as those commonly used in a contemporary performance teaching space. There was no sense of 'lecturer as theatre director'. The devising, writing and collaborative processes were absolutely non-hierarchical. Somehow relational pedagogy had facilitated, no, catalysed this. The second was something about context. This work was presented at an academic conference. That can be viewed as its first 'published outcome' – the first moment where the product of co-authorship could be viewed. The second co-authored outcome is this document, in its various incarnations.

It's worth noting that the space in between these two outcomes is where this notion of collaboration as process came into being. Over the weeks that they were writing and revising and editing they began to understand their skills and roles and what these would bring to this second co-authored outcome. They realized that Rebekka's enthusiastic conceptualism was sometimes very distracting, that Michael's attention to detail, project management skills and deep understanding of context was often the thing that kept them going and that Keeley was often the one who kept them on track because she was the one who understood the Bourriard text best. These realizations, among others, were what finally evolved the lecturer/student relationship into a truly collaborative and collegiate one.

Finally, they considered co-authorship as outcome or product. The literature in this area mainly comes from science where issues around co-authorship for postgraduate or research students are paramount. In these contexts co-authorship is super-hierarchical. The most important name first, professor or head of department, and often the research student, who may have done most of the work, might be fourth or fifth on the author list. In contemporary performance a solution is often to create a performance company, with a company name. Often, however, the senior academic becomes Creative Director or similar. This, also, didn't seem right to these three research colleagues.

After beginning to understand collaboration as process, and co-authorship as outcome, after understanding that they had been through a three-year process – undergraduate assistant, postgraduate playing the professional, and now co-author, colleague and collaborator – they were all determined to continue. But how? There wasn't a model for this!

On Saturday, 21 December 2009, Rebekka sent Michael and Keeley the following email message:

> Dear both,
>
> I'm so pleased that you both want to carry on with this collaboration and I've been trying to think of ways of making that happen. I had a conversation a few months ago with the people at Palatine [HEA subject centre] about the possibility of a research project on collaborations with postgraduate students in our subject area and they were very interested. I realize that funding and time are issues for all of us and as I'm writing up my PhD now, I was wondering if you could do me a favour? I think we should go for some research funding but I also think that you guys should draft the bid. What do you think?
>
> R
>
> **Rebekka Kill**

Note

Lone Twin produced a piece of work, *Ghost Dance*, that involved two blindfolded cowboys line dancing in silence, with no music, for 12 hours. They were to try to keep in step using only the sound of their boots. We saw a video of this performance and created our own two-hour version from memory with six performers and guests dancing in silence, blindfolded and on grass.

References

Birringer, J. (2006), 'FutureHouse, blind city: a life', in L. Hill and H. Paris (eds), *Performance and Place*. Basingstoke: Palgrave Macmillan, pp. 93–94.

Bourriaud, N. (2002), *Relational Aesthetics*. Dijon: Les Presses du Réel.

Freire, P. (1970), *Pedagogy of the Oppressed*. London, UK: Penguin.

Heddon, D. and Milling, J. (2006), *Devising Performance: A Critical History*. Basingstoke: Palgrave Macmillan.

Kershaw, B. (2000), *Performance, Memory, Heritage, History, Spectacle – The Iron Ship*. Paper given to American Society for Theatre Research Conference, New York.

Lone Twin. (2007), *Ghost Dance* [Performance].

Mchichou, A. (2008), *Conversation* [Private video].

Northedge, A. (2003), 'Enabling participation in academic discourse', *Teaching in Higher Education*, 8, (2), 169–180.

Ramsden, P. (1987), 'Improving teaching and learning in higher education: the case for a relational perspective', *Studies in Higher Education*, 12, (3), 275–286.

Chapter 11

Problem-Based Learning and the Teaching–Research Nexus: Stimulating Research for Both Staff and Students

Mark L. Manning, Lesley Willcoxson, Katrina
Gething and Natasha Johnston

This chapter presents the case study of the transformation of an undergraduate research methods course from one focused on statistics and the underlying mathematics of statistical analysis to a course in which students actively participated in research. Students actively engaged with teaching staff in both design and execution of a research project conducted in an area novel to both students and instructor. The approach taken throughout this process was one of problem-based learning (PBL) which itself is a product of constructivist learning philosophy. This process provided positive outcomes for both staff and students. This chapter was written by the instructor, another academic involved in the initiation of the project, and two students of the cohort described. The initial draft of the literature review and background theory was produced by the student authors and initial draft of the case study was produced by the academic authors. The conclusions and reflections section was developed by all authors and all authors revised and edited drafts of the manuscript.

Background

Constructivist learning philosophy has its foundations in cognitive learning psychology (Dewey, 1916; Piaget, 1954; Vygotsky, 1978). From the constructivist position, learners construct knowledge through their own experiences rather than from an external source. Constructivism emphasizes social and collaborative process in learning and stresses the importance of problem-solving of realistic and authentic tasks (Draper, 2002). PBL represents a teaching method arising from this philosophy.

Barrows and Tamblyn define PBL as 'learning that results from the process of working towards the understanding or resolution of a problem' (1980, as cited in Ertmer and Simons, 2006, p. 40). It is a student-centred teaching approach and contrasts to instructor-directed approaches where students are passive recipients of factual knowledge (Gijselaers, 1996). Hung (2006, p. 55) argues that PBL constitutes 'an effective instructional pedagogy that inherently engages students in active, meaningful learning, resulting in deeper understanding and longer retention'.

Although it may be argued PBL has a history stretching back at least to the time of Socrates, in its modern manifestation it emerged in the medical faculty of McMaster University in Canada in the late 1960s (Savery, 2006; Ball and Pelco, 2006). This initiative came in response to a regimen of lectures regarded in the faculty as unproductive and 'inhumane' and manifestly failing to transfer knowledge and prepare students for clinical practice.

Features of PBL include learner autonomy, cooperation and collaboration, and authentic activities (Barrell, 2007). Student work is organized around a complex, ill-structured problem that may not necessarily have any one correct solution. PBL is more effective when combined with some traditional approaches (Barraket, 2005) and the problem is ideally presented before course content and tools are made available. Students collaboratively strive toward solutions and to locate relevant information required to solve the problem. PBL takes advantage of social aspects of learning including discussion and peer interaction (Hmelo-Silver, 2004). Instructors take on a facilitating approach rather than a transfer mode of instruction, often providing guidance and information on a just-in-time basis. In order to facilitate the construction of knowledge, instructors need to create opportunities for constructive discourse (Hmelo-Silver and Barrows, 2008). In a modern university environment of large classes, these may mean including technological support, such as Blackboard, to facilitate the required collaboration and communication among students (Hunt and Tyrell, 2000; Van Rooij, 2007).

There is a wealth of evidence supporting the notion that PBL is a particularly effective method of learning (Mergendoller et al., 2006; Johnson and Dasgupta, 2005), particularly in courses where a lack of student interest and motivation has been a serious issue (Mykytyn et al., 2008).

Perhaps unsurprisingly, problem development is a key to the success of PBL (Lee, 1999, as cited in Hung, 2006). The problem itself functions as 'a content and knowledge organizer, learning environment contextualizer, thinking/ reasoning stimulator, and learning motivator' (Hung, 2006, p. 56). Weiss (2003) notes that a poorly designed problem, far from inspiring learning, may well only act as the catalyst for 'a scavenger hunt for information' (p. 25). A problem needs to be interesting and relevant, but there are other, less immediately apparent, requirements. Most significant among these are complexity and lack of structure (Weiss, 2003) or what might be thought of as 'messy' problems (Torp and Sage, 2002, as cited in Savery, 2006). Easily solved problems excite limited interest as students perceive the subject area as lacking in worth and credibility (Trafton and Midgett, 2001) whereas ill-structured problems inherently have 'multiple reasoning paths and multiple solutions', causing students to pursue a range of valid solutions and to engage with the problem at greater depth (Jonassen, 1997).

Instructors may experience frustration with the time the implementation, management and assessment of PBL entails (Simons et al., 2004). These are genuine concerns, but by and large they may be alleviated by support and guidance both for instructor and learner. Technology also has its role to play in making PBL possible across a wide range of contexts. Ball and Pelco (2006) state unequivocally that the use of PBL in research methods, which is the focus of their own research, would not be possible were it not for the internet and in particular, online literature search engines.

PBL is not unguided, or minimally guided, instruction (Kirschner et al., 2006) as it is highly 'scaffolded' (Hmelo-Silver et al., 2007; Savery, 2006). This scaffolding often incorporates substantial direct instruction (Schwartz and Bransford, 1998, as cited in Hmelo-Silver et al., 2007).

It is also noteworthy that learners often prefer PBL to more traditional approaches and benefit from its use. As Barraket (2005) reports from a study of masters-level social research students, while value was still placed on 'more formal teaching methods,' (p. 1) the very positive overall response to the 'student-centredness' (p. 10) that was a feature of the reoriented course was undeniable. Johnson and Dasgupta (2005) report that around two-thirds of students in their sample preferred student-centred learning over more traditional forms of learning, and measures of student satisfaction and motivation from a study of students in a computer applications course endorse such findings (Mykytyn et al., 2008). The enhanced involvement in task creation and resolution inherent to PBL also has a very positive impact on commitment and student attrition rates (Nuutila et al., 2005).

The application of PBL in the case study described here is presented in the context of the 'teaching–research nexus'. The teaching–research nexus refers to the 'notion of a symbiotic relationship between research and teaching' and is a concept that 'constitutes the very core of higher education' (Robertson, 2007, p. 542). Put simply, learning is enhanced when the instructor is a productive and enthusiastic scholar of the relevant discipline and involvement of students, even at undergraduate level, may contribute meaningfully to departmental research initiatives (Baldwin, 2005, p.8). This nexus may be constructed via approaches including: drawing on personal research in designing and teaching courses; placing the latest research in its historical context; designing learning activities around contemporary research issues; teaching research methods, techniques and skills explicitly within subjects; building small-scale research activities into undergraduate assignments; involving students in departmental research projects; encouraging students to feel part of the research culture of departments; infusing teaching with the values of researchers; and researching student learning to make evidence-based decisions about teaching (Baldwin 2005).

Healey proposes a four-quadrant schema to represent variation in application of the research–teaching nexus (Healey and Jenkins, 2006, see Figure 11.1). Healey and Jenkins propose 'often the most effective learning experiences involve a combination of all four approaches, but . . . emphasis should be placed on the student-centered approaches in the top half' (p. 48).

A case study

Advanced Research Methods is a compulsory course for undergraduate third-year marketing students, and an optional course for other undergraduate students, at a regional Australian university. The course takes place in semester 1 each year. Its long-term goal is to provide marketing students with the skills to conduct research in the business world. Its short-term goal is to provide marketing students with skills necessary to work in small groups and conduct a research consultancy in the following semester when they undertake a placement in an organization. Advanced Research Methods comprises 25 per cent of a full-time student load. It is the second, and final, undergraduate research methods course provided by the faculty. Each week students attend a two-hour lecture, a one-hour tutorial and a one-hour computer laboratory.

In its original form, prior to the revisions described here, instruction was heavily concentrated upon the mathematics of statistics. Three textbooks were used comprising a univariate statistics textbook, a multivariate statistics

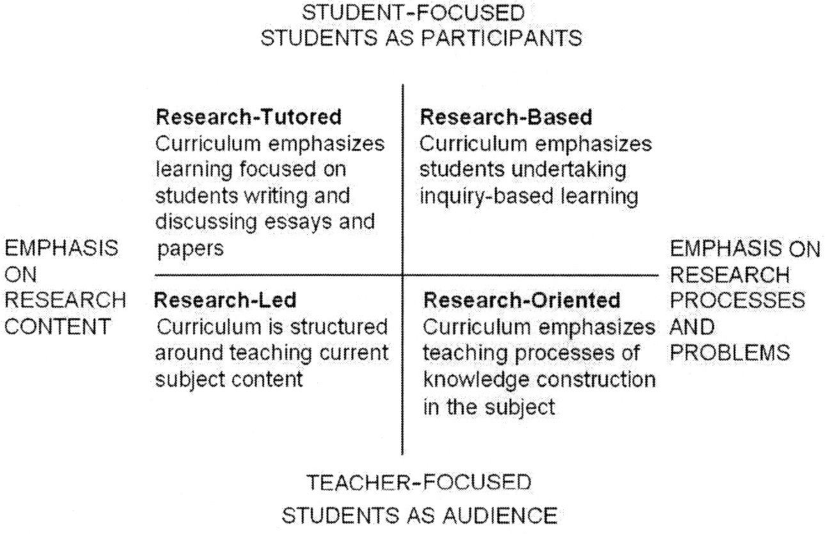

STUDENT-FOCUSED
STUDENTS AS PARTICIPANTS

	Research-Tutored	Research-Based	
	Curriculum emphasizes learning focused on students writing and discussing essays and	Curriculum emphasizes students undertaking inquiry-based learning	
EMPHASIS ON	papers		EMPHASIS ON RESEARCH
RESEARCH CONTENT	Research-Led	Research-Oriented	PROCESSES AND
	Curriculum is structured around teaching current subject content	Curriculum emphasizes teaching processes of knowledge construction in the subject	PROBLEMS

TEACHER-FOCUSED
STUDENTS AS AUDIENCE

FIGURE 11.1   Curriculum design and the research–teaching nexus (Healey and Jenkins, 2006)

textbook, and a guide to the SPSS statistical software package. A 416-page book of selected readings was also prescribed. Assessment comprised mid-semester (15%) and final (50%) exams and two assignments (15% and 20%) in which students were provided with 'dummy' data sets and were required to conduct and write up appropriate statistical analyses.

To gain entry into Advanced Research Methods students were required to perform at least at the credit level (65% or higher) in their first-year introductory research methods course. Despite being a demanding course, many students performed very well. In its last year of traditional presentation, for example, 38.96 per cent of students achieved a final grade of credit or higher. At the same time, however, a large proportion (37.66%) of students failed. This figure includes 18.42 per cent of students who, although still formally enrolled, dropped out and did not attempt the final exam.

Plan of revised course

There were several goals underlying the revision of Advanced Research Methods. First, increased engagement of students, particularly the less able students, was desired in an effort to reduce both dropout and failure rates. Second, the revision aimed to provide students with more practical research skills. Although at the end of the course the students were well prepared with the skills to analyse quantitative data, when conducting their small-group research placement in the following semester they often made many naïve mistakes in research project design and execution. Common mistakes would, for example, include: overestimating potential participants' interest and willingness to participate; poor choice of variables representing concepts they hoped to measure; and poor choice of measurement scales making analysis of data difficult. So it was hoped revision of the course would bring forward many of the mistakes they tended to make in their 'real world' research placements in semester 2 into their first semester course.

Changes in the course were substantial. First, assessment no longer included a mid-semester exam, as poor performance in this early piece of assessment might serve to demotivate and discourage students struggling with the material. Second, following a PBL model, a research question was to be presented which would provide the focus for two assignments (worth 20% and 30%, respectively). Third, the nexus between teaching and research was to be strongly reinforced with their instructor's research integrated into the course in two ways. Relevant examples from the instructor's own research in the area of 'organizational climate' were to be included in lectures. The two statistics textbooks and the SPSS guide for this course were replaced by a single textbook co-written by the instructor. This text *The Survey Researcher's SPSS Cookbook* (Manning and Munro, 2006) provided both a guide to statistical analysis of survey data and a guide to the use of SPSS. Examples used in the textbook were also drawn from the instructor's organizational climate research. A 446-page book of readings was also to be used which included several reprints of the instructor's papers serving to illustrate the application of different statistical techniques.

The research question providing the problem and focus of the students' work across the course was planned to be presented at the end of the first lecture of the course. The ultimate task for the students would be to provide an answer to this question. To achieve this, students were to act as a single group, but to write up their results individually. The project was to encompass two stages. Stage 1 would comprise the design of the study. The constraints to be placed on the students were that the study must use a questionnaire survey and the sample must comprise undergraduate students of their university. Stage 1 would require both literature searches and focus groups (using themselves as focus-group members). The outcome of this stage would be a report, written individually, presenting: a set of concepts relevant to the study; a conceptual framework graphically illustrating proposed relationships between the concepts; a brief questionnaire that would serve to operationalize each of the concepts as measurable variables (which might include items from existing scales, modified items from existing scales, or new items where no existing scale was identified); a theoretical framework graphically illustrating proposed relationships between variables; and the set of hypotheses (predictions) that logically arise from the theoretical framework.

Data gathering for Stage 1 was to take place within tutorials. In each of the five tutorial classes students were to be divided into two focus groups each comprising around nine students. One student from each group was to act as moderator, and a second would record the results. Communication between the instructor and each of the 91 student members of the group was to be conducted online via Blackboard. On Blackboard students were able to post themes or concepts identified in the focus groups, concepts identified in the academic literature, details of relevant articles, and details of possible instruments that were available to measure the concepts so identified. Blackboard would provide students with the opportunity to present competing models to describe how different concepts might relate to one another.

Tutorials and Blackboard were to provide environments within which possibilities could be explored. In Stage 1, the last 30 minutes of the lecture was to be devoted to providing a forum for both discussion and democratic resolution of all issues relating to the design of the project. These issues would include concepts to be measured, the model to be tested, instrument/items to be used to measure each of the concepts, the population from which the sample would be selected, and the logistics of data collection.

Stage 2 was to comprise quantitative data gathering and data analysis. The outcome of this stage was to be a report providing descriptive statistics describing their sample and inferential statistics testing their hypotheses.

Execution of revised course

When attempting to generate an appropriate topic for the students' research, another faculty staff member, not involved with the teaching of the course, suggested the research question 'What factors influence students' decisions to drop out of university?' This question was presented, at the end of the first lecture, to the 91 students enrolled. This represented a new research area for both students and instructor.

In Stage 1, each week, the instructor specified which issues needed to be resolved by the end of that lecture. One of the earliest sets of issues resolved related to the concepts to be measured and the model describing the relationships between concepts. Two models, both with strong support, had been posted onto Blackboard. In the lecture, arguments were presented to support both. The issue was resolved via a show of hands among the students. The outcome was viewed as 'less than satisfactory' by some who had supported the alternative position and at least one student commented to the instructor that they would withdraw from the course due to the model chosen (they didn't). The conceptual framework agreed upon by the students is presented in Figure 11.2.

The conceptual framework provided an interesting mix of concepts. The concept of *self efficacy*, for example, could be measured using a pre-existing scale, with known reliabilities, which provided a single sensitive variable representing the concept. The concept of *academic workload* could be measured with a single item, designed by the students, measuring the number of courses in which a student was currently enrolled. Although having the advantage of representing the concept with a single score, the measure was relatively insensitive with possible integer values ranging from 1 to 5 – with almost all of the sample (81.6%) responding that they were undertaking the usual full-time load of four courses (serving to effectively make the scale even coarser). Other concepts, like *reasons for attendance* or *external factors*, were much more 'fuzzy' and represented concepts that were less easy to tie down and less able to be, ultimately, represented by a single variable. The difficulty in representing *external factors* by a set of multiple items that could not be aggregated was not appreciated by many students until they had gathered their data and attempted to test their hypotheses.

Throughout the process, students made both good and poor decisions. For example, in the lecture, when the group finalized how each concept would be measured, the group agreed upon the concepts and agreed upon the questionnaire items that were to be used to represent the variables, and were satisfied this part of the design process was completed. It was not until it was brought to their attention by their instructor that anyone in the group realized they hadn't worked out how to measure their most important concept and the focus of the whole study – *student retention*. That is, they didn't have a dependent variable. The group collectively realized if they collected data from undergraduate students on campus, their entire sample would, obviously, still be at university and so every student would be in the same category – there would be no variation for that 'variable'. The instructor commented he had used *employee turnover intention*, measured by a single item on a Likert-type scale, to represent the concept of *employee turnover* in large organizations. The group considered whether, similarly, *student retention* could be operationalized as *student turnover intention*. It was decided that students' perceived likelihood of leaving university would be measured on a 7-point scale with the item 'I am likely to leave this university within the next twelve months'.

In another example, students voted that data would be collected within the lectures for 'core' courses (compulsory undergraduate introductory courses). Unfortunately, no student had bothered to ask for permission from the staff members teaching these courses. At the time, no comment was made by the instructor regarding this decision. In Stage 2 of the project, it was found that such permission would not be forthcoming and alternative arrangements were hurriedly made.

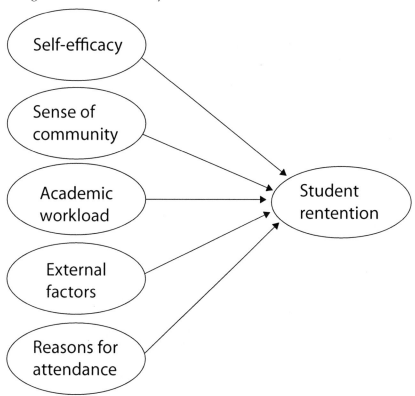

Figure 11.2   Research project conceptual framework agreed upon by students of Advanced Research Methods

Once the list of questionnaire items was finalized, the instructor prepared the questionnaire and arranged for the printing of 500 hard copies. These were left outside his office door and students collected them as needed. Completed questionnaires were brought to their computer labs and entered into SPSS files in class time and emailed to the instructor. The instructor aggregated data into a single SPSS file which was posted on Blackboard. Students then individually decided upon the appropriate analyses to be conducted, conducted the analyses and wrote up the results of their analysis as their second assignment.

Student feedback on the course

At this institution, each year in each course, students evaluate their instructor's teaching on a set of ten items. The summary of the results for Advanced Research Methods for the year prior to the introduction of the PBL model and the year the PBL model was first implemented are provided in Table 11.1.

Table 11.1   Student feedback on teaching for MKG301 Advanced Research Methods, in original and PBL form. Responses were on 5-point Likert-type scales.

Survey item	Original	PBL
1. The lecturer makes clear what I need to do to be successful in this unit.[1]	4.50	4.20
2 The lecturer is skilled at developing a class atmosphere conducive to learning.[1]	4.40	4.30
3 The lecturer has a good manner (e.g. friendly, helpful, enthusiastic).[1]	4.60	4.80
4 The lecturer shows appropriate concern for student progress and needs.[1]	4.00	4.10
5. The lecturer provides feedback that is constructive and helpful.[1]	3.90	4.00
6. The lecturer helps me to improve my understanding of concepts and principles.[1]	4.30	4.10
7. The lecturer structures and presents the unit in ways that help me to understand.[1]	4.30	4.10
8. The lecturer is knowledgeable in their subject area.[1]	4.70	4.70
9. The lecturer sets tasks that are useful as learning experiences.[1]	4.10	4.30
10. Overall, how would you rate the teaching of this lecturer in this unit?[2]	4.60	4.60

[1] = 'strongly disagree', 2 = 'disagree', 3 = 'neutral', 4 = 'agree', 5 = 'strongly agree'.
[2] = 'very poor', 2 = 'poor', 3 = 'satisfactory', 4 = 'good', 5 = 'very good'.

No dramatic changes were observed in response to any item. Responses were stable for 'Overall, how would you rate the teaching of this lecturer in this unit' and 'The lecturer is knowledgeable in their subject area'. Slight improvements were shown in response to 'The lecturer has a good manner (e.g. friendly, helpful, enthusiastic)', 'The lecturer shows appropriate concern for student progress and needs', 'The lecturer provides feedback that is constructive and helpful', and 'The lecturer sets tasks that are useful as learning experiences'. However, slight reductions were found in responses to items 'The lecturer makes clear what I need to do to be successful in this unit', 'The lecturer structures and presents the unit in ways that help me to understand', 'The lecturer is skilled at developing a class atmosphere conducive to learning', and 'The lecturer helps me to improve my understanding of concepts and principles'. This suggests that the uncertainty introduced by the change in the course may have both minor positive and minor negative outcomes for student evaluation of teaching.

Student outcomes

Although little change was observed in the student evaluations of Advanced Research Methods, dramatic changes were observed in student grades (Table 11.2) with: a significant reduction in the proportion of students failing from 37.66 per cent to 18.68 per cent; and a significant reduction in the proportion of students 'dropping out' and failing to sit the final exam from 18.18 per cent to 8.79 per cent. However, there was no increase in the number of students receiving high distinctions (proportionally 1.30% to 1.10%) or distinctions (15.58% to 12.09%). In fact, the proportion of students receiving a grade of credit, or higher, was relatively stable from

Table 11.2 Student results for MKG301 Advanced Research Methods, 2005 and 2006

	2005 (n=77)		2006 (n=91)	
	Frequency	**%**	**Frequency**	**%**
Grades				
High distinction (85–100%)	1	1.30%	1	1.10%
Distinction (75–84%)	12	15.58%	11	12.09%
Credit (65–74%)	17	22.08%	26	28.57%
Pass (50–64%)	18	23.38%	36	39.56%
Fail (<50%)	29	37.66%	17	18.68%
Breakdown of fails				
Didn't sit final exam	14	18.18%	8	8.79%
Completed all assessment	14	18.18%	5	5.49%

pre- to post-implementation of the PBL model, with 38.96 per cent, and 41.76 per cent, respectively, falling into this range.

It may be argued that this pattern of results serves to show the changes implemented made the course less intimidating (as evidenced by lower drop-out rate) and more comprehensible (as evidenced by the lower failure rate) for the struggling students, without compromising academic standards by simply making the course easier (as there was no accompanying increase in the proportion of students receiving a credit or higher).

Staff outcomes

The transformation of Advanced Research Methods from a traditional statistics course to a PBL research methods course had significant positive research outcomes for individual staff members, the Faculty of Business, the university, and several of the students involved. With respect to the individual academic staff members, in parallel to this activity, the academic staff member who proposed the research question and the instructor invited anyone who was interested to join a group wishing to study the factors leading to undergraduate student attrition. The work of the Advanced Research Methods students fed into this process. The results of their focus groups and literature searches were made available to the members of this new research group as was the outcome of the quantitative study conducted by the students. An application by the group for a small internal university grant to conduct a pilot study (Willcoxson, Manning and Wynder, *The Whole of University Experience: Exploring the Experience Beyond First Year – A Pilot Study*), received modest financial support ($4,974) from the university. This was followed by an application for external support from the Australian Learning and Teaching Council (ALTC) for the project. The ALTC, funded by the Australian Government, is the premier funding body for learning and teaching grants within Australia. In that funding round, the project was one of only 17 successful applications of 154 in that round, and the largest grant awarded ($219,877). It was also the first ALTC grant received by the Faculty of Business, or by the university. The input of Advanced Research Methods students is acknowledged in papers emanating from the project and the nature and extent of student input will also be fully described in the final report to the ALTC when completed.

Conclusion and reflections

Healey (2005, as cited in Healey and Jenkins, 2006) proposed a four-quadrant framework (Figure 11.1) for the research–teaching nexus, and Healey and Jenkins (2006) propose that the most effective learning experiences may involve a combination of all four, with the emphasis on the student-focused approaches where students act as participants. The case study reported here clearly places its emphasis on students acting as participants and, in particular, the curriculum may be placed within Healey's research-based quadrant in which the curriculum emphasizes students 'undertaking inquiry-based learning' (as cited in Healy and Jenkins, 2006, p. 48).

The research collaboration between staff and students continues. The two student authors of this chapter subsequently enrolled in fourth-year honours degrees co-supervised by their Advanced Research Methods instructor. This represented all of the students enrolling in honours in the business faculty in that year, and the first honours students of this faculty supervised by that staff member. Although neither student elected to study student retention and attrition for their dissertation, both elected to investigate organizational climate – the research area used in Advanced Research Methods to illustrate many of the research issues described. The subjective views of both student authors and instructor are presented below.

Student author perspectives

From one student perspective, this course was both disconcerting and rewarding. The class decision-making process seemed, at first, time-consuming and frustrating. Rather than debating with my fellow students on the concepts to be included in the study, there were many times that I just wanted to be able to get on with the required assessments. Yet the collaborative exercises – during lectures and tutorials and the online communication system – helped me to invest deeply in the subject. Rather than passively receiving information, I found myself questioning and exploring. Instead of sequestering myself and learning by rote, I tended to seek the opinion of others in my cohort. Although challenging, I unexpectedly found the course to be enjoyable.

That satisfaction was further heightened by the subject matter and the support materials. The knowledge that the class was contributing to an actual study gave the course relevance, while the examples and articles in the book of readings provided some sort of context within which I could place qualitative and quantitative research. Ultimately, I feel that the overall positive experience was instrumental in my decision to embark on a research career.

From a second student perspective, I initially approached Advanced Research Methods with a great deal of trepidation; its difficulty was legendary. However, the structure of the course and the support received from the instructor made it clear to me fairly quickly that I would be able to manage its requirements. The confidence I gained from this experience and the support I received were primary considerations in my decision to undertake honours in the field that I did, with that instructor.

Instructor perspective

PBL involved a much closer engagement with students than did the traditional presentation of Advanced Research Methods. Students interacted more with me, both in terms of asking questions in face-to-face situations and also in terms of emails and postings on Blackboard. This additional interaction served to enable me to better understand where the students were in their progress in the course and provided a better appreciation that students may well have gained knowledge, without having yet gained the capacity to apply that knowledge.

One of the important aspects of a feeling of 'partnership', from my perspective, was that the research area of the project was as new to me as it was for the students. This meant, for example, that they led me with regard to relevant literature and concepts, whereas I could guide them (as opposed to leading them) with regard to the 'brass tacks' of the design and execution of the project.

The question arises as to the degree of partnership and relationship of the teaching–research nexus to the new ALTC project. I really hadn't thought about this until writing this chapter, and the simple answer is that there isn't any. The research project that evolved from this experience became entirely a project planned and conducted by academic staff (many of them senior) across six Australian universities.

As an instructor, the experience is not all positive. As noted by Simons et al. (2004), instructors experience frustration with the amount of time the implementation, management and assessment of PBL entails, and the additional interaction had a cost in terms of instructor workload. The slow progress of the students through the process (particularly in Stage 1) is also emotionally taxing for an instructor. Each year it seems that the students will never arrive at a conclusion about anything – the most recent cohort took five weeks to agree upon the first item to be included in their questionnaire. Although PBL is not unguided teaching (Kirschner et al., 2006), this is not always appreciated by students, one of which recently wrote on Blackboard that 'unless we get more help, many students will fail assignment 1'. Despite these negatives, and the mixed results on formal student feedback (taken very seriously by the university when promotions are considered), the teaching of Advanced Research Methods continues to follow a PBL model as, when all things are considered, for this particular course it feels like the right thing to do.

References

Baldwin, G. (2005), *The Research Teaching Nexus: How Research Informs and Enhances Learning and Teaching in the University of Melbourne*. Retrieved 28 April 2010 from http://www.cshe.unimelb.edu.au/pdfs/TR_Nexus.pdf

Ball, C. T. and Pelco, L. E. (2006), 'Teaching research methods to undergraduate psychology students using an active cooperative learning approach', *International Journal of Teaching and Learning in Higher Education*, 17, (2), 147–154.

Barrell, J. (2007), *Problem-Based Learning: An Inquiry Approach*. London: Sage Publications.

Barraket, J. (2005), 'Teaching research methods using a student-centred approach? Critical reflections on practice', *Journal of University Teaching and Learning Practice*, 2, (2), 64–74.

Barrows, H. S. and Tamblyn, R. M. (1980), *Problem-Based Learning: An Approach to Medical Education*. New York: Springer.

Dewey, J. (1916/1966), *Democracy and Education: An Introduction to the Philosophy of Education* (1966 edn). New York: Free Press.

Draper, R. J. (2002), 'School mathematics reform, constructivism, and literacy: a case for literacy instruction in the reform-oriented classroom', *Journal of Adolescent and Adult Literacy*, 45, (6), 520–529.

Ertmer, P. A. and Simons, K. D. (2006), 'Jumping the PBL implementation hurdle: supporting the efforts of K-12 teachers', *The Interdisciplinary Journal of Problem-based Learning*, 1, (1), 40–54.

Gijselaers, W. H. (1996), 'Connecting problem-based practices with educational theory', *New Directions for Teaching and Learning*, 68, 13–21.

Healey, M. (2005), 'Linking research and teaching: exploring disciplinary spaces and the role of inquiry-based learning', in R. Barnett (ed.), *Reshaping the University: New Relationships Between Research, Scholarship and Teaching*. Maidenhead, UK: Open University Press.

Healey, M. and Jenkins, A. (2006), 'Strengthening the teaching-research linkage in undergraduate courses and programs', *New Directions for Teaching and Learning*, 107, 43–53.

Hmelo-Silver, C. E. (2004), 'Problem-based learning: what and how do students learn?', *Educational Psychology Review*, 16, (3), 235–266.

Hmelo-Silver, C. E. and Barrows, H. S. (2008), 'Facilitating collaborative knowledge building', *Cognition and Instruction*, 26, (1), 48–94.

Hmelo-Silver, C. E., Duncan, R. G. and Chinn, C. A. (2007), 'Scaffolding and achievement in problem-based and inquiry learning: a response to Kirschner, Sweller and Clark (2006)', *Educational Psychologist*, 42, (2), 99–107.

Hung, W. (2006), 'The 3C3R model: a conceptual framework for designing problems in PBL', *The Interdisciplinary Journal of Problem-based Learning*, 1, (1), 55–77.

Hunt, N. and Tyrell, S. (2000), 'Learning statistics on the web: DISCUSS', *Teaching Statistics*, 22, (3), 85–90.

Johnson, H. D. and Dasgupta, N. (2005), 'Traditional versus non-traditional teaching: perspectives of students in introductory statistics classes', *Journal of Statistics Education*, 13, (2). Retrieved 28 April 2010 from http://www.amstat.org/publications/jse/v13n2/johnson.html

Jonassen, D. H. (1997), 'Instructional design models for well-structured and ill-structured problem-solving learning outcomes', *Educational Technology Research and Development*, 45, (1), 65–95.

Kirschner, P. A., Sweller, J. and Clark, R. E. (2006), 'Why minimal guidance during instruction does not work: an analysis of the failure of constructivist, discovery, problem-based, experiential, and inquiry-based teaching', *Educational Psychologist*, 41, (2), 75–86.

Lee, J. (1999), 'Problem-based learning: a decision model for problem selection', in *Proceedings of Selected Research and Development Papers Presented at the National Convention of the Association for Educational Communications and Technology*. Houston, TX.

Manning, M. L. and Munro, D. (2006), *The Survey Researcher's SPSS Cookbook*. Frenchs Forest, Australia: Pearson Education.

Mergendoller, J. R., Maxwell, N. L. and Bellisimo, Y. (2006), 'The effectiveness of problem-based instruction: a comparative study of instructional methods and student characteristics', *The Interdisciplinary Journal of Problem-based Learning*, 1, (2), 49–69.

Mykytyn, K., Pearson, A., Paul, S. and Mykytyn Jr, P. P. (2008), 'The use of problem-based learning to enhance MIS education', *Decision Sciences Journal of Innovative Education*, 6, (1), 89–113.

Nuutila, E., Torma, S. and Malmi, L. (2005), 'PBL and computer programming – the seven steps method with adaptations', *Computer Science Education*, 15, (2), 123–142.

Piaget, J. (1954), *The Construction of Reality in the Child* (translated by Margaret Cook). London: Routledge and Kegan Paul.

Robertson, J. (2007), 'Beyond the "research/teaching" nexus: exploring the complexity of academic experience', *Studies in Higher Education*, 32, (5), 541–556.

Savery, J. R. (2006), 'Overview of problem-based learning: definitions and distinctions', *The Interdisciplinary Journal of Problem-based Learning*, 1, (1), 9–20.

Schwartz, D. L. and Bransford, J. D. (1998), 'A time for telling', *Cognition & Instruction*, 16, (4), 475–522.

Simons, K. D., Klein, J. D. and Brush, T. R. (2004), 'Instructional strategies utilized during the implementation of a hypermedia, problem-based learning environment: a case study', *Journal of Interactive Learning Research*, 15, (3), 213–235.

Torp, L. and Sage, S. (2002), *Problems and Possibilities: Problem-Based Learning for K-16 Education* (2nd edn). Alexandria, VA: Association of Supervision and Curriculum Development.

Trafton, P. R. and Midgett, C. (2001), 'Learning through problems: a powerful approach to teaching mathematics'. *Teaching Children Mathematics*, 7, (9), 532–536.

Van Rooij, S. (2007), 'WebMail vs WebApp: comparing problem-based learning methods in a business research methods course', *Journal of Interactive Learning Research*, 18, (4), 555–569.

Vygotsky, L. (1978), *Mind in Society: The Development of Higher Psychological Processes*. Cambridge, MA: Harvard University Press.

Weiss, R. E. (2003), 'Designing problems to promote higher order thinking', *New Directions for Teaching and Learning*, 95, 25–31.

Chapter 12

A Collaborative Foray into Undergraduate Publishing

David Metcalfe, Caroline Gibson and Cath Lambert

The development of undergraduate research

Undergraduate participation in research is not a new phenomenon (Robbins, 1988; Boyer Commission, 1998). In medicine alone, undergraduates were fundamentally involved in the discovery of insulin, characterization of the pancreas, and in understanding nerve transmission (Metcalfe, 2008). However, undergraduate research has attracted increased attention and resources in recent years. Its importance within the UK higher education (HE) community was highlighted in two recent reports commissioned by John Denham, Secretary of State for the (then) Department for Innovation, Universities and Skills (DIUS), to structure a higher education policy framework for the next 10–15 years. In the first, Professor Paul Ramsden, Chief Executive of the Higher Education Academy, advised that the HE curriculum should include research-based study at undergraduate level, with students treated as partners rather than customers (Ramsden, 2008). In the second, Professor Nigel Thrift of the University of Warwick proposed that '[r]esearch councils should work with universities, research institutes, charities and industry to develop a national Research Experiences Programme for undergraduate students' (Thrift, 2008). These reports follow increasing involvement of undergraduate students in research within the UK. A number of universities have successfully established schemes to sponsor research scholarships for undergraduates, and the Centre for Excellence in Teaching and Learning (CETL) initiative[1] has helped raise the profile of enquiry- and research-based methods of teaching and learning[2]. While these projects encompass a diverse range of approaches and activities, they share a commitment to enabling students to become active producers of ideas and knowledge rather than passive learners or consumers.

This chapter draws on our work as students and academics within the Reinvention Centre for Undergraduate Research[3] and, in particular, our collaboration on the creation of an undergraduate research journal, *Reinvention: a Journal of Undergraduate Research*. The primary aim of the Reinvention

Centre is to integrate research-based learning into the undergraduate curriculum. The goal is not simply to teach undergraduates research skills but to enable them to become actively involved in research and integrated into the research cultures of their disciplines, departments and institutions. To this end, staff–student collaboration has been central to the work of the Reinvention Centre. In practical terms, this has involved a range of activities including the collaborative writing of academic papers (WASS Collective, 2007), the production of documentary films (FKUC, 2005; Reinvention Centre, 2009), and presentations at academic conferences. Other activities have included the creation of collaborative spaces (Lambert, 2007; Neary and Thody, 2009), the establishment of a 'collaboration fund' to promote creative collaborative practice, and the launch of *Reinvention: a Journal of Undergraduate Research.*

The Reinvention Centre launched *Reinvention* in September 2007 as an outlet for high-quality undergraduate research being undertaken in its two host institutions, Oxford Brookes and the University of Warwick, and beyond in the wider HE community. The journal represents a collaboration between staff and students from a range of academic disciplines. It is led by an editorial and management team composed of undergraduate students as well as academic, administrative and technical staff, with individual disciplines represented by student/academic co-editor teams. The Editor is an undergraduate student. In the course of this chapter we draw on our experiences as Editor (DM), Managing Editor (CG) and Academic Advisor (CL). We reflect critically on these experiences alongside evaluation data from authors, board members, reviewers, and students undertaking training to write for publication. In doing so, we also consider the potential and challenges of collaboration in undergraduate publishing.

While the discussion draws primarily on our work on *Reinvention: a Journal of Undergraduate Research,* our ideas are informed by ongoing and diverse experiences of collaborative intellectual practice. Through these projects we have struggled over and contested what it means to collaborate within contemporary higher education. In the UK, as elsewhere, rapid changes in HE are having a significant impact on the roles and identities of those who work and study in universities (Henkel, 2000). In particular, the changing political and economic landscape has influenced what it means to be 'a student' or 'a lecturer' (Slaughter and Leslie, 1997). This has created an unequal division between research and teaching, and reconfigured students as consumers (and lecturers as providers) of an educational product (Naidoo and Jamieson, 2005; Boden and Epstein, 2006). In response to these developments, the Reinvention Centre is committed to re/creating an inclusive academic community in which all members of the university are seen as scholars in the common pursuit of knowledge. In 1990, Ernest Boyer urged universities to 'break out of the tired old teaching versus research debate and define in more creative ways what it means to be a scholar' (1990, xii).

Working with the theoretical resources provided by Boyer (1990) and the Boyer Commission (1998) and others (in particular Freire, 1970; Benjamin, 1973), we developed the concept of the 'student as producer' (e.g. Neary and Winn, 2009); connecting research and teaching in ways that enable students and teachers to become productive collaborators. These ideas underpin the work of *Reinvention: a Journal of Undergraduate Research* and provide an intellectual framework for evaluating and understanding the issues raised by the production and publication of undergraduate research.

Having established the broader issues around undergraduate research, we now consider the field of undergraduate publishing. We locate *Reinvention* within this field, particularly attentive to its commitment to collaboration. We then consider both the benefits and challenges of collaborative practice before raising critical questions about the future of undergraduate research and publication.

Undergraduate publishing: the bigger picture

It is unsurprising that increased undergraduate involvement with research has been accompanied by a growth in the number of undergraduate journals. Outside of the United Kingdom there have been many successes. The Canadian *McGill Journal of Medicine*, a student-founded and student-run publication launched in 1994 is now indexed as a scholarly publication by leading research databases. It was described by one academic as a 'thoroughly professional entry into the world of medical publishing' (Schwartz, 1997). The US *Journal of Young Investigators*, a student-led initiative which publishes undergraduate research in mathematics, science and engineering has won a number of awards and sends representatives every year to the Annual American Association for the Advancement of Sciences (AAAS) Conference.

Undergraduate journals are now becoming established in the UK. *Bioscience Horizons*, one of the first undergraduate journals to be launched in Britain, surveyed students and academics, finding their publication was being regularly accessed at 'very respectable levels' and that 84 universities had so far 'engaged with the journal' (*Bioscience Horizons*, 2009). The journal is supported by Oxford University Press and addresses the challenge of sustainability and, in 2008, the journal was awarded a Highly Commended Certificate by the Association of Learned and Professional Society Publishers (ALPSP) for publishing innovation.

Although united in publishing undergraduate research, these journals differ in a number of ways. *Bioscience Horizons* is managed and edited by academics. The *McGill Journal of Medicine* and *Journal of Young Investigators* are both organized by undergraduate and postgraduate students. *Reinvention* is, by contrast, a collaborative project between undergraduates and academic staff members. The journals also differ in the *types* of research published.

The *McGill Journal of Medicine* encourages collaborative submissions, as long as an undergraduate legitimately claims lead authorship. *Bioscience Horizons*, however, requires undergraduates to have sole authorship, with academic supervisors being credited by an acknowledgement alongside the published paper. As will be discussed later in the chapter, the issue of whether to publish collaborative submissions has generated much discussion when formulating our own editorial policy.

Reinventing the undergraduate journal

Reinvention: a Journal of Undergraduate Research was first launched at the 'Student as Producer' Conference at the University of Warwick in 2007. However, the journal was conceptualized some years before as a linchpin of the Reinvention Centre's commitment to providing meaningful outlets for disseminating undergraduate research. Students and staff from a number of institutions worked together to establish the principles and policies underpinning the journal. It was agreed it would aim to raise the profile of undergraduate research activity across disciplines and provide a realistic but supportive environment in which undergraduates could experience publication. Unlike most journals, *Reinvention* is multidisciplinary; a move facilitated by the decision to publish the journal in an online, open-access format. It is published biannually, in April and October, and accepts submissions from undergraduate students anywhere in the world. All submissions are subject to double blind peer review. This distinguishes the journal from other undergraduate publications (e.g. newspapers and magazines) and provides an important measure of research quality. During the development of the journal the reviewing process has proved one of the most contentious and complex challenges. It has raised issues of accessibility and inclusion, and the tricky question of who – in the hierarchical world of academia – counts as a 'peer'. These are issues considered in the following section.

The benefits of collaboration in undergraduate publishing

The benefits to undergraduates of publishing their research have been widely documented. These include giving students an outlet for their efforts, helping them develop and refine their research, and developing their ability to reflect on and be critical of their own work (Banks, 2008; Metcalfe, 2008). Others benefit from having a publication on their CV, particularly those pursuing careers that emphasize the importance of research (Ellis, 2009). One academic reviewer described the *Reinvention* journal as an 'exciting initiative' as 'in [her] own undergraduate days [she] only discovered journals just before graduating at bachelor's level, and resented the way these rich storehouses of knowledge were kept from [her] in [her] earlier undergraduate years.' Similarly, an undergraduate described the experience of understanding the publication process as getting a key to 'the secret garden' of research and publishing. For some students, the process of undergraduate publication is considered a step towards an academic career; for others it is a chance to take risks with their research, which they know will not be formally assessed and a chance to choose a topic they *want* to research. Almost all published authors in *Reinvention* claim to have experienced increased confidence and pride in their academic work. Some authors' comments are illustrative:

> I think it is a good way of highlighting the quality of undergraduate work. It is useful for developing confidence in students, enhancing academic writing and the ability to take on board constructive criticism.

> I think undergraduate publishing can make an important contribution to the student experience; even if the work produced is not cited by professional academics, its real value lies in the confidence and inspiration it can give to undergraduates.

> Ultimately the experience has given me a greater level of confidence in my abilities and helped me to realize that even as a student I might still have something important to contribute the production of knowledge.

This sense of making a contribution was echoed by another author whose comments illustrate the importance of 'producing':

> It made me engage with the topic in far greater depth than is usual with undergraduate study; the extra motivation existed because of the promise of a tangible end product, and a sense of actively creating something, rather than the usual undergraduate activities of writing essays simply to 'make a grade'.

This view illustrates the value of reconfiguring the student as an active producer. It also shows that undergraduate publication has potential far beyond initiating students into academia. Undergraduates are increasingly defined in terms of their consumer status and their work conceptualized solely in terms of assessment and preparation for the paid labour market (McCulloch, 2009). This is a critical reminder that students have creative potential – and a strong desire to realize that potential – when appropriate mechanisms are available. Compared to the 'intangible' production of essays that exist only to be marked, a publication is a real 'thing', to be read and responded to by other people. As another author commented, 'it was nice to know that some of the undergraduate students at Warwick were using my article in the masculinities module in the week where they learn about gender and work'. A sense of freedom to investigate and research a topic of their choosing has also been highlighted as a benefit of independent research and undergraduate publishing opportunities. Students attending Writing for Publication training sessions run by the Reinvention Centre have spoken of being able to take more 'risks' in writing up research for publication as compared to writing an assessed essay. The feeling that students are doing more than just answering a set question and regurgitating facts has been strongly expressed and students speak of excitement and pride in undertaking independent research. We argue these brief examples not only demonstrate genuine advantages to individual authors but also raise the more radical possibility of reinventing the undergraduate experience to foreground creativity in the pedagogic process. These comments not only reinforce the benefits of undergraduate publication but issue a challenge to the current educational system which often constructs students as passive learners whose work has little, if any, value beyond the currency of assessment.

Clearly these benefits are factors unaffected by the organization of the journal. They would still pertain even if the journal were managed in a traditional hierarchical format. However, there are additional advantages to running the journal as a collaborative venture. We have found that collaboration encourages a different working relationship between students and staff, with students gaining in confidence and experience, and all members learning from one another. For student Subject Editors in particular, the experience of working directly in an academic and administrative role with staff has been productive. One commented that 'many students pass through university without ever having had the opportunity to work with non-academic members of staff', while another explained that a positive outcome of their work on the journal had been 'working *with* academic staff instead of *for* them' because 'moving between student and staff roles has to be the ultimate collaborative experience!' The role of Subject Editor also requires students to work with other students, possibly in different cohorts or departments, as they advise potential authors on submissions. As one student Subject Editor explained, 'encouraging submissions to the journal has put me in closer contact with the rest of the student body, especially outside of my year and course.' This serves as a reminder that undergraduate students are traditionally limited by work within highly regulated cohorts based on subject options and year of study. Collaboration, then, is not limited to students and staff working closely together – it also necessitates a range of shared working practices among students themselves.

The collaborative nature of the journal has raised a number of challenges but fundamentally informs its philosophy and approach to collaborative research itself. Indeed, one of the most important – and difficult – aspects of collaboration involves the co-production of research with associated implications for hierarchy and shared authorship. This chapter will now explore the advantages and challenges of collaboration in the context of academic publishing.

Challenges of staff–student collaboration

There are a number of obstacles to involving undergraduates in publishing research. Many of these are logistical. Undergraduates often remain at an institution for only three years, resulting in a high turnover of those taking an active part in running any collaborative venture. Similarly, undergraduates are unsalaried and lack resources (such as office space) with which to run a successful publication. However, in most cases, these obstacles can be overcome with appropriate institutional support. The Managing Editor of *Reinvention* is, for example, a member of staff, so providing continuity and experience for new student editors.

However, there are also *fundamental* challenges to collaborative publication. The first is the compelling argument that undergraduate research should not be sequestered away in 'undergraduate-only' journals. According to this view, research worthy of publication should be published in established journals, regardless of whether the author is an undergraduate or faculty member (Gilbert, 2004). However, our experience is that a number of barriers exist between undergraduates and publication in the scholarly literature. First, undergraduates do not perceive themselves as potential contributors to knowledge. Second, they lack exposure to, and practice of, submitting their work for peer review. Finally, undergraduates often lack the resources and support that academics can draw upon when approaching the publication process. Undergraduate journals respond to these barriers by providing a supportive environment in which students can *develop* their work for publication. As noted in our first editorial: 'experience gained by authors will encourage them to produce papers for high-impact journals within their own areas of interest . . . chang[e] the undergraduate experience . . . [and potentially] have a greater impact on academia than any of its proponents might now hope or imagine' (Metcalfe, 2007). Although a bold ambition, this has not proven unachievable. Since the launch in September 2007, at least two authors have published again, as undergraduates, in established journals within their own fields.

The second obstacle has been achieving recognition as a 'genuine' scholarly journal. Although outright opposition has rarely been encountered, a number of responses from peer reviewers indicated they do not view *Reinvention* as equal to other established journals in their field. Reviewers often comment that, while a submission has failings, it is of a good enough standard for an undergraduate publication. For example one reviewer wrote 'I have reviewed the article with the consideration that this is an undergraduate essay for an undergraduate journal and have made allowances accordingly'. Similarly, a survey of 382 academics found that many would not recommend publication in, or use of, undergraduate research journals (Ferrari and Davis, 2001). However, we recognize that undergraduate publications are not alone in struggling against elitism. Each discipline has its own hierarchy of eminent journals and it is perhaps natural for undergraduate publications to be placed somewhere along this spectrum. We also acknowledge that some reviewers are, necessarily, making allowances for students' restricted access to resources and depth of knowledge, rather than automatically assuming that work will be of a lesser standard.

The perception of undergraduate journals occupying a lower tier of publications is inextricably linked to perceived quality. For one critic, there remains 'a question of quality control that might worry others about citing the article or using the data in their own research' (Gilbert, 2004). Indeed, the issue of quality has raised considerable discussion among stakeholders in our journal. Many have seen as mutually exclusive the desire to publish high-quality research *and* the aim of making research more accessible to a general undergraduate audience. According to one professor, the journal must either be 'for a limited elite set of students embarked on an academic journey to be the next Research Professor' *or* 'a more inclusive form of knowledge development and sharing'. Another academic asked:

> I am probably missing a trick here, but why would I suggest to my students that they publish their research in your journal rather than the existing and well-recognized professional literature?

Student authors, however, have made their views clear on the issue of quality: '[Undergraduate publishing is a] brilliant idea as long as the standard expected is the same as normal academic publishing' and 'I remain concerned that, in some quarters, undergraduate research is labelled as inferior . . . What rubbish! Good research is good research, period'.

Reinventing the 'peer' in peer review

In academic publishing, quality is traditionally guaranteed by peer review. Although *Reinvention* uses a process of double-blind peer review, this has itself raised challenges. For example, a number of commentators have suggested that, since undergraduates and faculty members are not 'peers', the latter should not 'peer review' undergraduate manuscripts. The feeling that staff should not peer review undergraduate work belies an important prejudice. It assumes that undergraduate researchers are somehow – almost by definition – different to 'real' academics. According to one academic approached as a potential reviewer, 'peer reviewers for a journal devoted to publishing undergraduate essays must be undergraduates . . . not being an undergraduate, I am in no position to [review] . . . nor am I able to suggest an undergraduate who might be competent to . . . review [the manuscript]'.

Our response is that *Reinvention* considers its authors to be researchers first and foremost, regardless of their substantive status as undergraduates. The point raised did, however, contribute to an ongoing discussion regarding peer review. Although we felt academics could be considered 'peers' when reviewing undergraduate work – in the same way as an eminent professor might 'peer review' the work of a junior academic – we agreed that undergraduates could gain from reviewing each other's work. As a result, the journal supports a mentoring system to train undergraduates in peer review. This has led to a further collaborative dimension: undergraduates may now peer review manuscripts with the support of an established academic peer reviewer.

It is nevertheless important to address the 'question of quality control' (Gilbert, 2004) which is one barrier to the acceptance of undergraduate research. Undergraduates do – perhaps by definition – have limited experience and access to resources. There is therefore a compelling argument that undergraduate journals should accept substandard work because 'genuine' research is beyond the capability of most undergraduates. As noted previously, some peer reviewers indicate this attitude when appraising undergraduate manuscripts. The *Reinvention* editorial team has responded to this challenge in two ways. The first is to recognize that undergraduates *can* conduct legitimate academic research. Although undergraduates may not have access to travel budgets and teams of research assistants, neither do many established researchers. Undergraduates do, however, have access to the same library facilities and stimulating intellectual environment as their lecturers. As we noted in an editorial, 'students do not have to run a . . . [large-scale study] to learn about the research process . . . undergraduates might be involved in critically appraising literature for a review article, or preparing . . . case reports for publication' (Metcalfe, 2008). The outcomes of these often-manageable projects are legitimate candidates for publication. Furthermore, imaginative undergraduates can organize the resources to conduct primary research. This is illustrated by the publication of original data in our own journal (Hodgkiss and Handy, 2007; Moore, 2008; Wilding, 2008). Such projects are often facilitated by scholarships aimed specifically at undergraduate researchers. However, resources *are* a limiting factor in undergraduate research; to claim otherwise would do both undergraduates and the research community a disservice. For this reason, it is perhaps unreasonable for undergraduate journals to expect research on the same scale as found in established publications. In cases where reviewers have reported adequate methods and analysis but limited scale we have treated such manuscripts sympathetically.

When does undergraduate research stop being undergraduate research?

One possible response to the 'question of quality control' is to encourage submissions written by undergraduates collaboratively with faculty members. However, there are potential pitfalls to collaborative research and authorship. For this reason, some undergraduate journals (e.g. *Bioscience Horizons*) do not consider collaborative manuscripts. The dangers of publishing collaborative work are threefold. First, some academic researchers may see undergraduate journals as a way to publish small-scale studies that they do not have the resources or inclination to expand to meet the requirements of established journals. Such projects could have an undergraduate appended to the author list for the sole purpose of ensuring its consideration by an undergraduate journal. This risk is heightened by increasing pressure to publish as a result of initiatives such as the Research Assessment Exercise (RAE)/Research Excellence Framework (REF), the mechanism for assessing the quality of UK research and informing the distribution of research funding (HEFCE, 2010). Intellectual dishonesty of this type should be discouraged and is of little benefit either to undergraduates or to the academic community as a whole.

The second danger of publishing collaborative work including undergraduate authors is inherent in the first. Although 'collaboration' implies a flattening of traditional hierarchies, these may still underlie collaborative research projects. In particular, there is a risk that the balance of workload may be inequitable. According to one student, 'my supervisor sent me away and, over two months, I completed the literature review he asked for . . . when I sent it to him he added one line at the end . . . and even that wasn't grammatically correct'. Another reported writing a paper which was 'checked by two academics who, between them, added a table and changed the font . . . before adding their names to the author list'. These examples of 'collaboration', resulting – as they did – in multi-authored publications seem both unfair and potentially dishonest. However, this problem is not limited to undergraduate research. For this reason, many journals have moved towards a model of 'contributorship' in which authors explicitly describe their individual roles within the published project.

The final risk of collaborative publishing is that students working with staff members may have an advantage over those working alone. This is because staff bring greater resources and – perhaps – expertise to any given project. Nevertheless, collaboration is an important part of all research projects; even among senior academics. It is not necessarily a disadvantage for undergraduates to learn that collaborators at all levels provide different sets of resources and skills.

After much discussion, the *Reinvention* editorial team resolved to consider collaborative submissions on the same basis as those written solely by undergraduates. Despite the dangers highlighted above, the decision was reached on a number of grounds. Collaboration is an important element of research which should be appreciated by any researcher-in-training. When included as an author, staff may feel more 'invested' in the project outcome and provide a greater level of support to undergraduate researchers as a consequence. Many projects – by their very nature – require academic input. This is particularly true of those requiring laboratory facilities, which are almost universally 'owned' by academic staff. In addition, safety concerns and expensive resources are likely to prevent undergraduates pursuing independent research in the natural sciences.

To discourage collaborative research by limiting papers to undergraduate authors could threaten an apprenticeship from which both undergraduates and faculty members might benefit. Such collaborations have potential to transcend traditional hierarchies in higher education and reinvent the undergraduate experience to include a greater level of research-based learning. Finally, it is inevitable that some undergraduates will involve faculty members in one or more aspects of their research. These may include advice, direction, resolving specific problems and/or accessing resources. In some cases, the staff contribution may be great enough to justify authorship. It soon became apparent that restrictive editorial policies result in staff contributions being confined inappropriately to brief acknowledgements. It is clearly incorrect for journals to encourage undergraduates to publish work alone when another party has a justified claim to co-authorship.

On the basis of these arguments, *Reinvention* does now consider collaborative submissions for publication. However, such manuscripts are closely monitored to ensure an undergraduate is the lead author. *Reinvention* is also committed to ensuring that any academic involvement in collaborative research is supportive and that student participation is not exploitative. Where suspicion exists, the editorial team will ask the authors to submit explicit statements of contributorship. We have observed clear benefits of encouraging such collaborative partnerships. One student reflection shows how collaborative work can change working relationships between academics and students: 'Being able to discuss articles and the peer review process with my academic supervisor has provided me with the opportunity to interact with the professors of my department on a more personal level'.

Conclusion: future trends

With central HEFCE funding for the CETL initiative coming to an end in 2010, the Reinvention Centre and *Reinvention* are at an important point in their development. Sustainability beyond the initial funding period is vital to continue the work that has been started, and a central component of that sustainability involves further engagement with the HE community, not only around undergraduate research but around collaborative practice in all aspects of scholarship. Sustainability is a major issue for most undergraduate publications and, in order for undergraduate publishing to contribute in the long-term to the research culture of universities, journals such as *Reinvention* have to maintain themselves financially. By choosing to publish papers online, the costs involved with publishing are substantially reduced and, with undergraduate research becoming more established, potential sponsors and supporters are easier to identify. However, many undergraduate journals are open-access and therefore do not charge for subscriptions. This suggests a long journey before they reach the levels of stability afforded established academic journals who charge for their content.

The future of undergraduate publication is inextricably linked to the increasing prevalence and status of undergraduate research at a number of universities, in the UK and elsewhere. Both students and academics are, in our experience, in agreement that undergraduate journals are both desirable *and* necessary. This 'need' is variously identified as being intellectual, political and economic (not, of course, mutually exclusive categories) and we touched on some of these debates at the beginning of this chapter. One student author described undergraduate publishing as '. . . a brilliant idea, and it presents a deserved opportunity for undergraduates carrying out high-quality research to showcase their ability. Whenever I discuss the idea with other people, especially my peers, they seem really excited by the prospect of being a published author so the journal is obviously tapping into a desire within the undergraduate community'. If higher education within the UK is to provide a national Research Experiences Programme for undergraduate students (Thrift, 2008) and treat students as 'partners' rather than customers as Paul Ramsden (2008) advocates, it is vital an outlet exists for the work being undertaken. Undergraduate research voices will otherwise never be heard.

Reinvention, for its part, is actively participating in national and international conferences to raise awareness of undergraduate research. This enables critical engagement and debate with others undertaking similar ventures at other institutions. Wherever possible, conference papers are co-written and presented by students and staff, maintaining the commitment to collaboration beyond the administrative work of the journal and further embedding undergraduates in a range of research activities. Publications such as this edited book, and others written by the *Reinvention* team, also form a vital part of propagating a culture in which undergraduate research is encouraged and supported. Links with other undergraduate publications have been generated both in the UK and internationally and relationships fostered with colleagues internationally, through the journal's International Advisory Board. Members of this body support and encourage innovative teaching and learning initiatives, particularly undergraduate research activities. Vitally, such support contributes to ensuring that undergraduate research and publishing form a central part of the HE agenda, both now and in the future, so that appropriate structures and funding mechanisms are put in place to secure the future of such initiatives. Undergraduate publishing in isolation, as we have shown, provides significant opportunities for individual students; increasing confidence in research and writing skills, facilitating opportunities for collaboration with other students, academics and administrative staff, and providing vital experience whether or not students pursue a research career. However, the benefits of publishing undergraduate research can never be fully realized unless support is provided by a culture in which undergraduate research is funded and integrated into the wider research community.

The *Reinvention* journal provides an opportunity to trial alternative models of staff–student collaborative working practice but this experience is of limited value if its impact is not felt more widely in the academy. The long-term aim of any undergraduate journal, beyond merely surviving, must be to influence the culture it serves. The Reinvention Centre and the *Reinvention* journal have created 'a culture in which there is a presumption that all students have research potential' and, as noted in a previous editorial, 'without such a culture, undergraduate journals are unlikely to thrive' (Lambert and Metcalfe, 2009). After the publication of its fifth issue, we continue to believe that collaboration is one of the strongest aspects of *Reinvention*, giving students as well as staff the responsibility of developing the publication and providing an opportunity for staff and students to write collaboratively. However, as argued in this chapter, the question of collaboration is complex both in theory and in practice. While our experiences and evaluative data point overall to the values of collaboration, our discussion has also raised difficulties and challenges that we hope will continue to provoke discussion within higher education.

Notes

[1]   Seventy-four CETLs are funded by the Higher Education Funding Council for England (HEFCE) to the amount of £315 million over five years from 2005–06 to 2009–10. This represents the largest ever single funding initiative in teaching and learning. The purpose of CETLs is to promote 'excellence' across all subjects and aspects of teaching and learning in higher education. For further information see http://www.hefce.ac.uk/NEWS/HEFCE/2000/funding.htm

[2]   The Reinvention Centre for Undergraduate Research is a collaborative Centre for Excellence in Teaching and Learning (CETL) based between the Department of Sociology at the University of Warwick and the School for the Built Environment at Oxford Brookes. In 2005 the Reinvention Centre was awarded £500,000 recurrent over five years, and £800,000 capital funding. Further information on the Reinvention Centre is available at www.warwick.ac.uk/go/reinvention. The work of the centre and centre members covers a range of progressive pedagogies. The article represents the views of the authors.

³ A list of these is available at www.warwick.ac.uk/go/reinvention/resources/
   profile_and_dissemination.pdf

References

Banks, C. (2008), 'Editorial', *Diffusion: The UCLAN Journal of Undergraduate
    Research*, 1, (1&2), 5–6.

Benjamin, W. (1973), 'The author as producer', in W. Benjamin (ed.),
    Understanding Brecht. Bristol, UK: NLB.

Bioscience Horizons (2009), 'Editorial', *Bioscience Horizons*, 2, (2), i.

Boden, R. and Epstein, D. (2006), 'Managing the research imagination?
    Globalisation and research in higher education', *Globalisation, Societies and
    Education*, 4, (2), 223–236.

Boyer, E. (1990), *Scholarship Reconsidered: Priorities of the Professoriate*. San Francisco:
    Jossey-Bass.

Boyer Commission on Educating Undergraduates in the Research University
    (1998), *Reinventing Undergraduate Education: A Blueprint for America's Research
    Universities*. Stony Brook: State University of New York at Stony Brook. Retrieved
    28 April 2010 from http://naples.cc.sunysb.edu/Pres/boyer.nsf/

Ellis, H. (2009), 'Research and publications by students and junior doctors',
    Journal of Student Medical Sciences, 1, (1).

Ferrari, J. and Davis, S. (2001), 'Undergraduate student journals: perceptions and
    familiarity by faculty', *Eye on Psi Chi*, 5, (2), 13–17.

FKUC (Furthering Knowledge of Undergraduates in the Community) (2005),
    '*Universities PLC? Enterprise in Higher Education*'. Documentary film, retrieved
    28 April 2010 from www.warwick.ac.uk/go/reinvention/filmspublications/
    universitiesplc

Freire, P. (1970), *Pedagogy of the Oppressed*. London, UK: Penguin.

Gilbert, S. (2004), 'Should students be encouraged to publish their research
    in student-run publications? A case against undergraduate-only journal
    publications', *Cell Biology Education*, 3, (1), 22–23.

Henkel, M. (2000), *Academic Identities and Policy Change in Higher Education*.
    London, UK: Jessica Kingsley.

Higher Education Funding Council for England (HEFCE) (2010), *Research
    Excellence Framework*. Retrieved 28 April 2010 from http://www.hefce.ac.uk/
    Research/ref/

Hodgkiss, A. and Handy, C. (2007), 'The 'criminal face effect': physical
    attractiveness and character integrity as determinants of perceived criminality',
    Reinvention: a Journal of Undergraduate Research, Launch Issue, retrieved 26 June
    2009 from http://www.warwick.ac.uk/go/reinventionjournal/pastissues/
    launchissue/paper1

Lambert, C. (2007), 'Exploring new learning and teaching spaces', *Warwick
    Interactions Journal*, 30, 2, retrieved 1 January 2009 from www2.warwick.ac.uk/
    services/cap/resources/pub/interactions/current/ablambert/lambert.

Lambert, C. and Metcalfe, D. (2009), 'Editorial: The Importance of Great
    Expectations', *Reinvention: a Journal of Undergraduate Research*, 2, (1), retrieved

21 August 2010 from http://www2.warwick.ac.uk/go/reinventionjournal/
issues/volume2issue1/editorial

McCulloch, A. (2009), 'The student as co-producer: an alternative to the student
as consumer metaphor', *Studies in Higher Education*, 34, (2), 171–183.

Metcalfe, D. (2007), 'The launch of an undergraduate research journal',
Reinvention: a Journal of Undergraduate Research, Launch Issue, retrieved
18 October 2009 from http://www2.warwick.ac.uk/fac/soc/sociology/rsw/
undergrad/cetl/ejournal/issues/launchissue/editorial/.

Metcalfe, D. (2008), 'Involving medical students in research', *Journal of the Royal
Society of Medicine*, 101, (3), 102–103.

Moore, R. (2008), 'Assessment of diet, activity budget and daily path-length
of Sri Lanka's endemic Western Purple-faced Leaf Monkey (*Trachypithecus
vetulus nestor*) in a human modified environment', *Reinvention: a Journal of
Undergraduate Research*, 1, (2), retrieved 27 June 2009 from http://www2.
warwick.ac.uk/go/reinventionjournal/issues/volume1issue2/moore

Naidoo, R. and Jamieson, I. (2005), 'Empowering participants or corroding
learning? Towards a research agenda on the impact of student consumerism in
higher education', *Journal of Education Policy*, 20, (3), 276–281.

Neary, M. and Thody, A. (2009), 'Learning landscapes: designing a classroom of
the future', in L. Bell, H. Stevenson and M. Neary, (eds), *The Future of Higher
Education: Policy, Pedagogy and the Student Experience*. London, UK: Continuum,
pp. 30–41.

Neary, M. and Winn, J. (2009), 'Student as producer: reinventing the student
experience in higher education', in L. Bell, H. Stevenson, and M. Neary (eds),
The Future of Higher Education: Policy, Pedagogy and the Student Experience. London,
UK: Continuum, pp. 126–138.

Ramsden, P. (2008), *The Future of Higher Education. Teaching and the Student
Experience*. Retrieved 29 June 2009 from http://www.dius.gov.uk/policy/
documents/teaching_and_student_experience_131008.pdf

Reinvention Centre (2009), *Students at Work: Learning to Labour in Higher
Education*. Retrieved 28 April 2010 from www.warwick.ac.uk/go/reinvention/
filmspublications/studentsatwork

Robbins, D. (1988), *The Rise of Independent Study: The Politics and Philosophy of
an Educational Innovation, 1970–1987*. Buckingham, UK: Open University
Press.

Schwartz, R. (1997), '*McGill Journal of Medicine* (MJM): an international forum
for the advancement of medical science by students', *New England Journal of
Medicine*, 336, 885–886.

Slaughter, S. and Leslie, L. (1997), *Academic Capitalism: Politics, Policies and the
Entrepreneurial University*. Baltimore, USA: The Johns Hopkins University
Press.

Thrift, N. (2008), *Research Careers in the UK: A Review*. Retrieved 30 June 2008
from http://www.dius.gov.uk/policy/documents/Nigel%20Thrift%20
contribution%20to%20HE%20Debate.pdf

WASS Collective. (2007), 'Gender transformations in higher education',
Sociological Research Online, 12, (1), retrieved 25 July 2009 from http://www.
socresonline.org.uk/12/1/lambert.html

Wilding, D. (2008), 'The educational experiences of Gypsy travellers: the impact of cultural dissonance', *Reinvention: a Journal of Undergraduate Research*, 1, (1), retrieved 27 September 2009 from http://www2.warwick.ac.uk/go/reinventionjournal/volume1issue1/wilding

Chapter 13

Exploring Students' Perceptions of Research in the Learning Environment: A Partnership to Enhance Our Understanding of the Undergraduate Student Experience

Brad Wuetherick and Lisa McLaughlin

In her installation address as President of the University of Alberta (UofA) in 2005, Dr Indira Samarasekera dared the academic community to create an enhanced student learning environment built on discovery, where students and staff come together as partners to work on humanity's grand challenges. This challenge was indicative of a growing movement on campus, mirrored on many campuses around the world, to examine the student learning environment more closely, particularly in light of the perceived imbalance between teaching and research felt by many – staff and students alike – to be a major issue in higher education.

> The human spirit thrives on discovery. We must integrate discovery into all aspects of learning. The 'Great University' of the twenty-first century must involve students in exploring our grand challenges. What might they be? Will we be able to conquer the next great frontier – the human brain? How do language, music, dance and philosophy shape our beliefs? Will we eradicate disease? Will we retain our vitality as we age? Will computers become ubiquitous and invisible? How will we satisfy our need for sustainable energy? Will we mitigate climate change? Will civil wars ever end? How will we preserve the world's great cultures? What is the nature of the universe? Are we alone? Our students, graduate and undergraduate, must acquire a capacity for creativity and social ingenuity by tackling questions like these.
>
> (Samarasekera, 2005)

This chapter explores two separate studies investigating students' perceptions of the role research plays in the undergraduate learning environment, undertaken through a partnership between the UofA Students' Union and the university administration represented by the Vice-President (Research)'s Research Makes Sense for Students initiative. In exploring these studies, the chapter will reflect on the importance of three aspects of staff–student partnerships – individual staff–student partnerships through undergraduate research opportunities (which forms the primary context for this chapter), the development of inclusive scholarly communities that embrace all undergraduate students as partners in discovery, and the institutional partnerships possible between university administrators and students' unions to enhance the undergraduate student experience.

Context

The UofA, one of Canada's largest research universities, has in recent years undergone a significant transformation in the proportion of externally sponsored research revenue as part of the overall institutional consolidated budget, mirroring the situation at many research universities around the world. The recent UofA academic plan *Dare to Discover* argues that a research-intensive environment defines a qualitatively different educational experience for undergraduate students, who are the primary vehicles for bringing the institution's research and scholarship into our communities (University of Alberta, 2006). This has resulted in an institutional focus on, and commitment to, discovery learning in all its forms, including but not limited to undergraduate research opportunities. The Research Makes Sense for Students initiative of the Office of the Vice-President (Research) focused on raising the awareness of student involvement in research, to promote the importance of research-based learning, and to work with faculties and departments to explore ways to embed research experiences for students more effectively in the learning environment.

In 2005, the Vice-President (Research) established a working group to explore what was currently being done across campus related to integrating teaching and research. The working group membership included a number of interested staff from across the institution and, typical of many UofA committees, the student associations. The report of this working group was then presented across campus, including to the Students' Union's council and the institution-wide Committee on the Learning Environment (University of Alberta, 2005a). Subsequently, the Students' Union initiated two separate survey research projects involving a number of partners on campus to assess the undergraduate student experience at the UofA and students' perceptions of the learning environment. In the context of an ongoing institutional discussion about the role of research in undergraduate education, the Students' Union approached the Office of the Vice-President (Research) to collaborate in assessing undergraduate students' perceptions of the role of research therein. This partnership seemed logical given both parties' interest in providing a high-quality educational experience for undergraduate students and the increased focus on the integration of research and teaching at the undergraduate level.

It is important to note that this collaboration between the Students' Union and university administration reflects a long tradition of student involvement in institutional governance at the UofA, and also reflects the productive relationship between student leaders and university administration at all levels of the institution. This culture of collaboration and mutual respect has developed at the UofA over many years, and may not be represented fully at other higher education institutions. This tradition of collaboration, and reflections on how both university administration and student leaders can work to enhance the partnership, will be explored later in this chapter.

Individual staff–student research partnerships
Two decades have passed since Boyer challenged the US and global higher education system to move 'beyond the tired old research vs. teaching' debate (Boyer, 1990, p. ix), yet the role of research in the undergraduate learning environment is still a hotly contested issue. Universities in the twenty-first century must balance complex teaching and research mandates. Just as the leading researchers can, at times, continue to be exempted from teaching undergraduate classes to focus on their research, undergraduate students can also still find themselves removed from research at the fore of their disciplines (Boyer Commission, 1998). There is a growing consensus that an undergraduate education needs to ensure students graduate with higher order skills that prepare them for today's increasingly supercomplex society and economy (Barnett, 2000). Barnett has articulated a future where universities must implement new pedagogies, in particular focused on research-based learning, that develop critical academic dispositions in students and enable students to strive 'to become authentically their own persons' (Barnett, 2005, p. 7).

While it has been argued that an increased emphasis on highly focused disciplinary research has had large-scale negative effects on the delivery of an effective general education for all undergraduate students, it has also been argued that universities must move towards a more research-based teaching and learning model as we struggle to develop students' academic dispositions, in areas like research and inquiry, to enable them to thrive in the supercomplexity in which they find themselves today (Pocklington and Tupper, 2002; Healey and Jenkins, 2009). Most higher education institutions are trying to increase the exposure of undergraduate students to research both inside and outside of the classroom through various individual, departmental or institutional initiatives aimed at improving the undergraduate learning environment (Jenkins and Healey, 2005; Jenkins et al., 2007). Yet even in institutional contexts where attempts are made to involve students in research-based learning, students still report that they feel 'at arm's length' from the world of university research (Brew, 2006, p. 52).

Globally, there has been no shortage of focus on the undergraduate learning environment, thanks in part to the increasingly public debate of institutional data on tools such as the National Survey on Student Engagement (US and Canada) and comparable tools in Australia (Australasian Survey on Student Engagement, AUSSE), England (National Student Survey), and in other national contexts. Measures within these tools, including staff–student ratio, level of academic challenge, or the level of student engagement inside and outside of the classroom, are positively correlated to high-impact educational practices such as research-based teaching and learning (Kuh, 2008). As a result, we have seen a shift (or at least an attempted shift) towards a research-based teaching and learning environment across the higher education sector internationally. The question, however, still remains:

> What are the motivations for [bringing teaching and research more closely together]? Is this just a bid on the part of research-intensive universities to prop up the research enterprise, or a cry from less research-focused institutions to ensure that a wedge is not drawn between research and teaching institutions?
>
> (Brew, 2003)

One of the motivations for bringing teaching and research closer together can and should be the importance of staff–student partnerships in higher education. There is a well-established literature that has explored the impact that research partnerships between individual undergraduate students and researchers can have on students' personal and professional development (Hunter et al., 2007; Hunter et al., 2010). The benefits students experience through these individual staff–student partnerships in research can include increased confidence, cognitive and technical skill development, problem-solving and critical thinking development, clarification of future career or educational opportunities, and an understanding of how knowledge is created (Brew, 2006; Hunter et al., 2007, Hunter et al., 2010). These partnerships also have the potential for benefiting the staff involved through, for example, increased research productivity in both the area of data collection and the dissemination of results, increased coherence and integration between their teaching and research roles, and opportunities to recruit postgraduate students (Brew, 2006).

The impact of individual staff–student partnerships that arise from opportunities to participate in undergraduate research can be transformational for the students involved in the partnerships. While perhaps not completely typical, when interviewed on the importance of undergraduate research, Professor David Schindler, one of the most prolific researchers at the UofA, stated that an undergraduate research experience changed the course of his life. He said:

This is how students learn what [staff] really do, rather than taking courses focused on learning skills. I myself switched from engineering physics to ecology because of a summer (research) job. I would never have followed this path if I had not . . . I myself published two papers from work that I did as an undergraduate, one in *Science* and one in *Nature*. As a result, I got a Rhodes Scholarship and went on to a career that has been very rewarding . . . [Since becoming a staff member] I have had several undergraduate co-authors on several papers. Several of my undergraduate assistants have gone on to become professors and scientists, some of them rather famous.

(University of Alberta, 2005b)

While few experiences may be as profound as this example, there are several research studies that attest to the transformational impact that participating in a staff–student research partnership can bring for both staff and student participants, even though there can be variability in the experience due to a number of factors (Nagda et al., 1998; Brew, 2006; Hunter et al., 2007; Kim and Sax, 2009; Hunter et al., 2010).

There are, however, both real and perceived barriers to implementing individual staff–student research partnerships, including limited time of both academics and students, lack of appropriate physical infrastructure and equipment, constraints in the curriculum needed to prepare student partnerships in research, insufficient rewards and incentives for participating academics, and an institutional research culture that discourages undergraduate participation or 'confines undergraduate students to the fringes of academia' (Brew, 2006, p. 91). There are additional dangers associated with students engaged in undergraduate research opportunities where their experience is highly negative, for a number of possible reasons including poor mentoring or engagement from staff, which might turn students with significant potential off from research (Nagda et al., 1998). The increased commodification of education in the minds of many students, and the focus on employability as an outcome of their university degree, also presents a challenge to motivating students to participate in undergraduate research opportunities (Kneale, 2009).

Research project

Both surveys undertaken as part of the partnership between the UofA Students' Union and university administration explored undergraduate students' priorities in terms of their overall learning environment at the UofA, including but not limited to their perceptions of, and experiences with, research. Previous studies exploring student perceptions of research found that the motivation and interest a student felt in a subject area often arose from their perceptions of staff enthusiasm, which arguably had its roots in the staff member's research interests (Jenkins et al., 1998). Students, however, still perceived research activities as an 'extra' to the primary requirement of a university – a quality undergraduate learning environment. Jenkins et al. (1998) reported that students place a higher priority on the need for teaching staff who are available, able to communicate course content effectively, and involve and interest students in the subject, rather than on staff research activity.

Shock has been expressed regarding the 'level of alienation that some students expressed' in terms of their connection to the research environment in universities, even when they appreciate the importance of staff research as an activity in their institution (Zamorski, 2002, p. 419). Zamorski's research, which interestingly also arose out of a partnership with her institution's Students' Union, reported that students feel disconnected as stakeholders in the research process, and perceive that they have access to research only as a product. This has left students with little understanding of the nature of academic work, often reporting difficulties when they actively participate in the research process (Zamorski, 2002). Robertson and Blacker (2006, p. 227) found that, while some students have a sense of proximity to and participation in research, others express frustration at how 'research is hidden from them.' They argue that student frustration manifests when participation in the academic community is delayed and when they are unable to reconcile their perceptions of their current learning environment to their perceptions of the research community (Robertson and Blacker, 2006).

Recent articles by Turner et al. and Healey et al. both concluded that, while students' awareness of research is high, the proportion of students who report experiencing research remains low (Turner et al., 2008; Healey et al., forthcoming). They do report, however, that a high proportion of students responded that they learn best when involved in some form of research or inquiry activity regardless of the institution's research intensity. Healey (2005a, p. 193), in summarizing the literature examining student perceptions of research, has reported that students perceive clear benefits from staff research, including enthusiasm, credibility, and 'the reflected glory of being taught by nationally and internationally known researchers'. Disadvantages reported by students included staff unavailability, the lack of involvement in research activities, and staff research taking priority over their learning (Healey, 2005a).

In the specific context of the UofA, the primary motivation for the Students' Union to undertake the two studies as a partnership with the university administration was to facilitate a more thorough understanding of undergraduate students' educational experiences, including their attitudes towards and experiences with research. The first was a paper-based survey distributed in a cross-section of classes with responses elicited from 2484 students in 14 different faculties – a response rate of 69 per cent. The second was an electronic survey distributed to a representative sample of students on campus and had 1304 students respond from 14 different faculties – a response rate of 26 per cent. The balance between the various years of study was comparable across both surveys, as was distribution across disciplines and between genders. Rather than explore the results of each survey in detail, this chapter will highlight statistically significant results related to students' reported experiences with research and the place of research in students' priorities for a quality learning environment.

Results
Experiences with research
In asking students about their experiences of research as part of their learning environment, we identified representative examples of different ways of conceptualizing research-based teaching and learning (Healey, 2005b; Elsen et al., 2009). While acknowledging that there may be different ways of interpreting the term 'research', students were asked if they experienced one or more of the following: (i) engaging with a research project outside of a class, (ii) acting as a participant in a research project, (iii) learning research methods, (iv) having an instructor discuss research in class, (v) attending a research seminar or conference, or (vi) giving an oral paper/poster presentation outside of class. Approximately 55 per cent of respondents indicated that they had experienced both learning research methods and having an instructor discuss research in class. Less than 20 per cent of respondents indicated, however, that they had experienced attending a research seminar or conference (19%), conducting a research project (14%), or giving an oral paper/poster presentation (7%). Almost 80 per cent of respondents experienced at least one or more of these six different research experiences, while approximately 30 per cent of respondents reported three or more experiences. Almost all respondents in years 3 and 4 (over 95%) reported having at least one experience, while most first-year respondents (over 80%) reported having either zero or one experience with research. The types of research experiences espoused in the educational literature as being most influential for student learning were by far the fewest experienced, yet the proportion of students reporting these experiences represent significantly higher proportions than reported by Turner et al. (2008) and Healey et al. (forthcoming) at surveyed British universities.

The importance of appropriate communication between instructors and students when experiencing any aspect of research-based teaching and learning has been noted elsewhere, but is important in the context of these results (Turner et al., 2008). It would be reasonable, for example, to assume that by the end of the first year all students would have at least experienced having an instructor discuss research in their class – if not the instructor's own research, at least some research in the discipline, yet almost 20 per cent of respondents across all four years report not having any experiences with research. A simple change in how staff lecture, referencing the research underpinning their lecture content, in first-year courses might achieve this goal.

Students in academic faculties (Arts and Science) were significantly more likely to report three or more research experiences than those in professional faculties – such as Business, Law, Engineering, Nursing or Education. Further to that, significantly more respondents from academic faculties (~45%) reported that research experiences were an important or very important part of their learning environment, as compared with respondents from professional faculties (~32%). This difference in attitudes towards research between academic and professional programs is important considering the predominance of educational literature focusing on the research versus practice nexus in professional programs.

Students were also asked if having instructors discuss research in a way that is relevant to the course material was common. Just over 40 per cent of respondents reported that it was common or very common. In addition, students were asked to choose the characteristics most important to their assessment of their classroom teaching experiences, and only 10 per cent of respondents reported discussing research in a relevant manner to be among their top priorities. Students in academic faculties were again significantly more likely to report that research being discussed in a relevant manner was common or very common, as well as more likely to report that it was a high priority.

Place of research in students' reported priorities in a quality learning environment

As well as exploring experiences of research, the surveys explored students' perceptions of the role research plays in a high-quality learning environment. Students were asked to identify what characteristics were priorities in determining a quality learning environment, as well as what experiences with their instructors were both common as well as most important to their assessment of the learning environment. Students' responses showed a focus on two key elements – instructors who are good teachers and care about students' learning and the connection of their learning to a future career. Factors that reflect key aspects of student engagement, such as meaningful interaction with instructors and students, or the learning environment itself, including quality of facilities/technology or classroom size, ranked lower in their list of priorities. Some of the lowest-ranked priorities were those factors related to research and what might be expected in a research-intensive institution, including university reputation, opportunities to do research, and being taught primarily by full-time staff engaged in both research and teaching.

On the other hand, common experiences students have had with their instructors show a slightly different reality. Factors the educational literature has linked with research-based teaching and learning, such as instructor knowledge of and enthusiasm for the subject matter, were in the top four in terms of the respondents' experiences, and were the top two experiences in terms of overall importance. Overall, experiences that would reflect key aspects of student engagement, such as encouraging class participation, interaction with students, and making an effort to verify students' learning were among the lowest in terms of respondents' reported experiences, and, somewhat surprisingly, were among the lowest in terms of priorities.

Correlations between research-related variables and other variables were then run to determine if those respondents who rated research as more important had noticeable differences in other responses in the survey when compared to students who rated research as a lower priority. The learning environment characteristics rated among the most important by students who rated research as important included instructors encouraging feedback from students, discussing research in a way that is relevant to the course material, possessing a thorough knowledge of the subject matter they are teaching, and giving good feedback about learning on assignments and exams. Other results that were significantly different between the two groups of students included the importance of the university having a good reputation, experiences where the student was motivated to learn more, and their perception of the overall quality of their education experience. In terms of demographics, respondents prioritizing research were significantly more likely to be non-transfer (i.e. direct entry from secondary school), of urban origin, enrolled in academic faculties, and enrolled in academically specialized programs (i.e. honours).

Each respondent was given opportunities in both surveys to provide qualitative responses to further express their opinions about the issues addressed in the surveys. Negative responses related to the role of research focused primarily around two specific themes: respondents' perceptions of priority placed on research over teaching, and the inaccessibility of research opportunities for all students. Two representative comments were:

A majority of the time I feel that instructors just come to class to fulfill their requirement of teaching so that they can continue on with their research.

I had tried to find out who accepts volunteers for their labs/research, but they never reply. It seems impossible to get lab experience, which is really important for grad school and for future jobs in general.

Positive responses also focused primarily around two specific themes: respondents' perceptions of instructor enthusiasm based on their personal research, and the impact of research-based pedagogies on students' learning. Two representative comments were:

I . . . feel that professors' research endeavours have not interfered with their teaching ability. Many of my professors are teachers only second to researchers, but as of late, their zealous nature for the things they study manifests itself in how they teach, and it is interesting to get first-hand knowledge of groundbreaking science . . .

The most learning I did . . . was through field work and an undergraduate thesis. This is where I determined what I enjoyed and I learned that research does not require straight As.

The results of these studies reinforce Kuh's argument about the importance of research-based teaching and learning as a high-impact educational experience, and also attest to the fact that if students prioritize research experiences, it impacts on their prioritization of other aspects of the learning environment (Kuh, 2008). They also supported previous literature that students' perceptions of instructor enthusiasm and the overall quality of the institution are impacted by their perceptions of the role of research in the learning environment, while reinforcing the perception that research still ranks quite low on the overall priorities students identify as part of a quality learning environment. This emphasizes the need for effective communication with students about the role of research in their learning, and in particular the impact staff–student research partnerships can have on their undergraduate experience (Turner et al., 2008).

Moving towards an inclusive, scholarly, knowledge-building community

One of the significant challenges associated with providing opportunities for these types of transformational experiences for students is the cost associated with scaling these opportunities so that all students benefit from staff–student research partnerships. Jenkins and Healey, for example, argue for a move away from a few privileged undergraduate students having opportunities to engage in research, towards a more inclusive goal of undergraduate research opportunities for *all* students (Jenkins and Healey, 2007). One way that we can approach the idea of widespread staff–student partnerships in higher education is by providing opportunities for all students to become members of the scholarly community (whether at the disciplinary, departmental, faculty or institutional level). This can be viewed as a community-based staff–student partnership where staff and students participate as partners to create a scholarly learning environment for all students and staff. Brew (2006) argues for the development of inclusive, scholarly, knowledge-building communities that engage everyone from senior academic staff through to first-year undergraduates.

In order for this model of staff–student partnership to succeed, the hierarchy that is implicitly built into the organization of universities must be challenged, as must the definition of who can legitimately be a scholar. While 'inclusive' does not mean equal, Brew argues that it does mean 'valuing the contributions of each person no matter what their level of prior understanding and knowledge' (Brew, 2006, p. 163). We must critically reflect on the ways in which we enable not only undergraduate students, but also postgraduate students and contract instructors, to be a part of this scholarly community. Such an inclusive community would rely on the development of a culture of inquiry at the university, where staff and students collectively work in partnership to push forward the boundaries of knowledge (Brew, 2006; Rowland, 2006). As Smith and Rust argue, achieving a truly inclusive academic community would potentially require a significant restructuring of institutions into manageable subject or discipline groupings for all learning, teaching, research and administration, as well as a significant restructuring of formal and informal physical infrastructure where staff and students engage with one another (Smith and Rust, in submission).

Were this type of staff–student partnership at the community level to be successful, it would inevitably result in a profound transformation of universities. This type of transformation might merge Barnett's three key aspects of an inquiring university, where each of pedagogical and curriculum space (where new pedagogies may be attempted in order to enable students to strive 'to become authentically their own persons'), scholarly space (where academic staff 'pursue their own research interests in their own way'), and intellectual or discursive space (where the academic community is allowed to engage the wider community in order to contribute to social discourse) exist and interact (Barnett, 2005, p. 7). The results of this type of community staff–student partnership, in terms of realizing meaningful change in areas such as student engagement and the integration of research and teaching, could have a transformative impact on the overall undergraduate experience. Indeed, Gibbs has recently reported that internationally one of the common features of research-intensive academic departments with excellent teaching ratings is a high level of student involvement as members of the departmental community (Gibbs, 2007).

Building on a culture of collaboration to develop institutional staff–student partnerships

As has been mentioned, the two research projects that have been presented in this chapter were facilitated by a partnership between the UofA administration and the Students' Union. This partnership arose as a result of a shared interest in understanding and improving the educational experiences of students and the potential advantages of engaging both stakeholders from the outset, particularly in setting future policy directions related to the integration of research and teaching. In an age where most higher education institutions struggle to achieve true collaboration with their students' union, and in fact regularly find themselves in conflict, the UofA may serve as a model for institutional partnerships between university administration and students' unions that are built on mutual respect and concern for the well-being and experiences of all members of the academic community.

The role of students in the governance of universities has been debated and contested for decades, particularly following the rise of 'the student movement' in many countries during the 1960s (McGrath, 1970). Recent explorations of university governance, including specific examinations of the student role in governance, have resulted in repeated calls for a more inclusive and transparent involvement of students in the higher education decision-making process (Menon, 2003). We believe that student leaders play an incredibly important role in the successful governance of any university; however, we do not intend to discuss the importance of involving students in university governance here. Rather, we aim to explore the possibilities that might emerge from partnerships between university administration and student governments.

The UofA serves as a case study of what is possible when a partnership is formed between levels of student government and the university administration. The UofA has among the highest levels of student participation in major university committees and academic councils among all Canadian universities. In the past decade graduate and undergraduate student leaders at the UofA, working with the support of university administration, have played a leading role in completing major research projects exploring the student experience, including those discussed in this chapter, developing new university facilities, implementing major changes to tuition policy that benefit thousands of students, and providing essential academic and support services for students, among numerous other initiatives.

The culture of collaboration between the UofA administration and student governments has developed over decades and has been nurtured by a mutual respect for each other's roles, perspectives, opinions and positions. In addition, the experience and institutional memory of long-serving permanent Students' Union staff members has enabled this culture to transcend the annual change of student leaders. Such a partnership, contrary to what may be intuitively understood about student governments working closely with university administration – particularly by student leaders at institutions regularly mired in conflict – must recognize and respect the need for differences of opinion (e.g. the annual debate over raising tuition fees), but moves the organizations beyond confrontation to seek progressive ways to address issues of common interest to the benefit of all students and staff. As mentioned above, this level of staff–student partnership has worked to the benefit of university students and staff at the UofA for years.

The specific partnership reported in this chapter has had a profound impact on the future direction the UofA community has taken with respect to the integration of research, teaching and learning. The overall commitment to providing students with opportunities to benefit from staff–student research partnerships resonates throughout the university administration's strategic planning and policy documents. The Students' Union's own priorities were also shaped by this partnership, as represented by their recent submission to the new academic planning process at the UofA, which called on the institution to develop a specific undergraduate research office to help coordinate the opportunities for students to partner with staff on research.

In addition to benefiting the UofA administration and the Students' Union, partnerships such as this also have the potential to provide student leaders involved in students' unions with valuable experiences they may not otherwise have throughout their education. In this particular case, the partnership to undertake these two research studies enabled one of the authors (McLaughlin) to engage in the entire research process for the first time in, and at the end of, her undergraduate education. In accordance with the literature espousing the benefits of staff–student partnerships for students, this experience of being an active participant in research developed a unique set of knowledge and skills and has had a significant impact on her subsequent endeavours.

Conclusion and reflections

Developing a partnership between the Students' Union and the university administration to undertake the two research projects discussed in this chapter was a positive and beneficial experience for both parties. The partnership reduced costs and duplication of effort, provided access to resources and advanced knowledge of the subject matter, and facilitated a mutually productive working relationship in terms of addressing the integration of teaching and research at the UofA. Reflecting on the institutional impacts of this specific partnership presents some unique challenges in that both authors left their positions, with university administration and the Students' Union respectively, shortly after the projects were completed, one to a new role within one of the faculties on campus and the other because her term as an executive of the Students' Union ended. While difficulties completing the writing process for a project like this might also be expected due to the transient nature of undergraduate students, particularly arising from their graduation, and to the time lag between undertaking the study and completing the writing process, it was compounded doubly in this specific case due to the staff author switching institutions part-way through the process. Being prepared for such challenges when embarking on a staff–student research partnership is critical to the ongoing success of such partnerships. Both authors feel strongly that the staff–student partnership explored in this chapter was highly rewarding in terms of its impact both from the perspective of the individuals involved – staff and students alike, as well as from the ongoing relationship between the university administration and the Students' Union.

In order for institutions to address challenges related to creating a learning environment focused on research-based learning opportunities for all students, it is critical to understand the transformative role of staff–student partnerships in higher education. Individual staff–student partnerships can help to facilitate discovery research, while providing transformational opportunities for students to develop personally and professionally. Staff–student partnerships, in the form of an inclusive, scholarly, knowledge-building community, might help in creating a truly inquiring university where the overall student experience is profoundly transformed. And finally, institutional staff–student partnerships between university administration and student governments can work productively to improve all aspects of the institution for both staff and students.

Acknowledgements

The views expressed in this chapter reflect the perspectives of the authors only and do not reflect the current perspectives of the UofA Administration or the Students' Union. More information on the surveys can be found at the UofA Students' Union website (www.su.ualberta.ca). Dr Stanley Varnhagen was instrumentally involved in helping with this initiative.

References

Barnett, R. (2000), *Realizing the University in an Age of Supercomplexity.* London: Society for Research into Higher Education and Open University Press.

Barnett, R. (2005), 'Introduction'. In R. Barnett (ed.), *Reshaping the University: New Relationship between Research, Scholarship and Teaching.* London: Society for Research into Higher Education and Open University Press, pp. 1–8.

Brew, A. (2003), 'Teaching and research: new relationships and their implications for inquiry-based teaching and learning in higher education', *Higher Education Research and Development*, 22, (1), 3–18.

Brew, A. (2006), *Research and Teaching: Beyond the Divide.* New York: Palgrave MacMillan.

Boyer, E. (1990), *Scholarship Reconsidered.* Princeton: Carnegie Foundation for the Advancement of University Teaching.

Boyer Commission on Educating Undergraduates in the Research University

(1998), *Reinventing Undergraduate Education: A Blueprint for America's Research Universities*. Stony Brook: State University of New York at Stony Brook.

Elsen, M., Visser-Wijnveen, G., van der Rijst, R. and van Driel, J. (2009), 'How to strengthen the connection between research and teaching in undergraduate university education', *Higher Education Quarterly*, 63, (1), 64–85.

Gibbs, G. (2007), *Departmental Leadership of Teaching*. Presentation at the Learning Institute, University of Oxford, 8 February 2008.

Healey, M. (2005a), 'Linking teaching and research: exploring disciplinary spaces and the role of inquiry-based learning', in R. Barnett (ed.), *Reshaping the University: New Relationship between Research, Scholarship and Teaching*. London: Society for Research into Higher Education and Open University Press, pp. 67–78.

Healey, M. (2005b), 'Linking teaching and research to benefit student learning', *Journal of Geography in Higher Education*, 29, (2), 183–201.

Healey, M. and Jenkins, A. (2009), *Undergraduate Research and Inquiry*. York: Higher Education Academy.

Healey, M., Jordan, F., Pell, B. and Short, C. (2010), 'The research–teaching nexus: a case study of students' awareness, experiences and perceptions of research', *Innovations in Education and Teaching International*, 47, (2).

Hunter, A-B., Laursen, S. and Seymour, E. (2007), 'Becoming a scientist: the role of undergraduate research in students' cognitive, personal and professional development', *Science Education*, 91, (1), 36–74.

Hunter, A.-B., Laursen, S., Seymour, E., Thiry, H. and Melton, G. (2010), *Summer Scientists: Establishing the Value of Shared Research for Science Faculty and their Students*. San Francisco: Jossey-Bass (in press).

Jenkins, A. and Healey, M. (2005), *Institutional Strategies to Link Teaching and Research*. York: Higher Education Academy.

Jenkins, A. and Healey, M. (2007), 'Critiquing excellence: undergraduate research for all students', in A. Skelton (ed.), *International Perspectives on Teaching Excellence in Higher Education: Improving Knowledge and Practice*. London: Routledge, pp. 117–132.

Jenkins, A., Blackman, T., Lindsay, R., and Paton-Saltzberg, R. (1998), 'Teaching and research: student perspectives and policy implications', *Studies in Higher Education*, 23, (2), 127–141.

Jenkins, A., Healey, M. and Zetter, R. (2007), *Linking Teaching and Research in Disciplines and Departments*. York: Higher Education Academy.

Kim, Y. and Sax, L. (2009), 'Student-faculty interaction in research universities: differences by student gender, race, social class, and first-generation status', *Research in Higher Education*, 50, 437–459.

Kneale, P. (2009), 'Teaching and learning for employability', in H. Fry, S. Ketteridge and S. Marshall (eds), *A Handbook for Teaching and Learning in Higher Education: Enhancing Academic Practice*. New York: Routledge.

Kuh, G. (2008), *High-Impact Educational Practices: What They Are, Who Has Access to Them, and Why They Matter*. Washington, DC: Association of American Colleges and Universities.

McGrath, E. (1970), *Should Students Share the Power? A Study of their Role in College and University Governance*. Philadelphia: Temple University Press.

Menon, M. (2003), 'Student involvement in university governance', *Tertiary Education and Management*, 9, (3), 233–246.

Nagda, B., Gregerman, S., Jonides, J., von Hippel, W. and Lerner, J. (1998), 'Undergraduate student-faculty research partnerships affect student retention', *The Review of Higher Education*, 22, (1), 55–72.

Pocklington, T. and Tupper, A. (2002), *No Place to Learn*. Vancouver: UBC Press.

Robertson, J. and Blacker, G. (2006), 'Students' experiences of learning in a research environment', *Higher Education Research and Development*, 25, (3), 215–229.

Rowland, S. (2006), *The Enquiring University*. London: Society for Research into Higher Education and Open University Press.

Samarasekera, I. (2005), *Installation Address*. Edmonton: Office of the President, University of Alberta. Retrieved 28 April 2010 from http://www.president. ualberta.ca/speeches.cfm

Smith, P. and Rust, C. (in submission), 'The potential of research-based learning for the creation of truly inclusive academic communities of practice'.

Turner, N., Wuetherick, B. and Healey, M. (2008), 'International perspectives on student awareness, experiences and perceptions of research', *International Journal for Academic Development*, 13, (3), 199–211.

University of Alberta (2005a), *Creating a Foundation for an Inquiry-Based Life: Working Group Report on the Integration of Teaching and Research*. Edmonton: Office of the Vice-President (Research), University of Alberta.

University of Alberta (2005b), *Celebrating Undergraduate Research*. Edmonton: Office of the Vice-President (Research), University of Alberta.

University of Alberta (2006), *Dare to Discover/Dare to Deliver*. Edmonton: Office of the President, University of Alberta. Retrieved 28 April 2010 from http://www. president.ualberta.ca/daretodiscover.cfm

Zamorski, B. (2002), 'Research-led teaching and learning in higher education: a case', *Teaching in Higher Education*, 7, (4), 411–427.

Chapter 14

Breaking Research Boundaries: Academics and Undergraduates Engaged in Collaborative Research

Heather Sharp, Linda Stanley and Marie Hayward

Research collaborations between academics and students introduce a number of complex issues for those interested in exploring ways to promote genuine collaboration, rather than positioning students as the standard appendices to existing academic research or as research subjects. In particular, there are issues within academic–student collaborations that would not need to be taken into consideration with academic to academic (or peer) partnerships, for example, the dynamics of a profoundly noticeable power relationship and inexperience as opposed to proven research capabilities. This chapter examines challenges and satisfactions that were experienced through the collaborative work between a lecturer and undergraduate students engaged in writing a chapter for a core undergraduate course. These experiences are then analysed, providing a theoretical framework through which to look at ways to address key challenges faced during the collaborative process in order to nurture successes for future collaborations. Benefits such as development of a research culture as motivation to engage with further projects at the tertiary level are discussed further in this chapter.

The framework of analysis is set up as a pedagogy of critical student research; a term used here to describe the positive and emancipatory effects of students and academics collaborating in research, and is based on the theoretical underpinnings of the work of Kincheloe and Steinberg (1998a; 1998b), Bourdieu (1998), and Freire (2001). These theories are selected to inform the critique of academic–student collaboration, and to theorise about the particular case study presented in this chapter, applied within the contextual screen of first-year experiences and academic–student collaboration. While a type of taxonomy of collaboration to apply to achieve success or to structure a critical pedagogical approach to collaborating with students is not provided, it is anticipated that the points made in this chapter may be modified and applied to other academic–student collaborations.

First-year experience is an area of increasing interest among higher education researchers, particularly in the areas of curriculum improvement, and is increasingly seen as a transition year, providing opportunities to engage this specific group to achieve academic success (see, for example, the work of McInnes, 2002; Nelson et al., 2008). The involvement of the students in this project can be seen in light of their own personal positive first-year experiences. Involving students as 'full-fledged collaborator(s)' (McKinney, 2007, p. 44) has benefits such as increasing the quality of student–academic relationships, freedom to diverge academically and encouragement to aspire to exceed academic expectations. In part, this includes flow-on impacts of collaboration, which can be linked to increased feelings of self-efficacy (Bandura, 1995). Michael Fielding describes this as student voice, whereby '. . . transformation is more likely to reside in arrangements which require the active engagement of students and teachers working in partnership than those which . . . treat student voice as an instrument of teacher . . . purposes' (2004, p. 306). Self-efficacy, through student voice, was demonstrated through the evolving positive relationships between academic and undergraduate students, which led to increased participation in other areas of university life.

This chapter draws on the collaborative academic–student process of researching and writing a chapter for publication in Education for Healthy Communities: Possibilities Through SOSE and HPE (Austin and Hickey, 2007), a textbook used for a core undergraduate course in a Bachelor of Education degree. What enhances the interest of this project, and makes it significant for others considering similar collaborations, is that first-year undergraduate students participated with an early-career academic. This demonstrates that successful collaboration can occur prior to students becoming research higher-degree candidates, and that research experience as a coursework undergraduate student can positively acculturate students into academia. This chapter is structured to first locate itself within existing literature on first-year experience and the emerging field of transition pedagogies; it then contextualizes the collaboration within a critical pedagogical approach, before detailing the students' experience and then ending with a critique of the development of the relationship developed between the academic and students in view of potential and unintended exploitation.

Background

Context of initial collaboration
Inspiration for the collaborative idea originated from the academic's invitation, by colleagues, to contribute three chapters to a publication intended as a textbook. Academics from three universities were invited to participate, with the intention that the book would be used cross-institutionally by fourth-year teacher education students. The aim of the book was to provide both theoretical understandings of the two curriculum areas of Health and Physical Education (HPE) and Studies of Society and Environment (SOSE),

and some practical examples, through the inclusion of unit plans, of how these key learning areas (KLAs) could be taught in school classroom settings.

Of the three chapters the academic was invited to write, two were to be based on the theoretical underpinnings of SOSE. These were to describe and deconstruct the syllabus in order to inform students' emerging understanding of the curriculum and pedagogy of SOSE in schools. A third chapter was to be a sample unit plan, informed by research, that teacher education students could adapt to their own context in the classroom, or to use as a sample model to construct their own SOSE unit. The editors invited the academic to either write the third chapter, or it was suggested to approach a school teaching colleague to undertake this task if the workload was going to be too great.

The academic's interest in exploring ways to authentically incorporate learner-centred and constructivist philosophies of education into a meaningful, educative product that would enhance the experience of university students became the basis for including student participants. This interest was motivated by the particular demographics of the students on this campus, many of whom (over 50%) were from low socio-economic status (SES) backgrounds and/or first in family to attend a tertiary education institution, as identified in research findings from the first year of the campus' operation (Ballantyne et al., 2007). These findings were significant in understanding the particular needs these students have, particularly in the area of acculturating students into academic disciplines. These identified needs include high levels of student academic and social support. The students selected to participate in the project were representative of the larger student body demographic.

Pre-identification of the students who would participate in the collaborative exercise was completed by the academic, and based on two specific focuses. First, the interest in developing a sense of belonging for students on campus; and second, developing a research culture among students. Selecting students to participate in consideration of these focuses was done as a way to foster these aspects of self-development. This project was an opportunity to see the combination of a sense of belonging and intellectual engagement in practice, as well as a pragmatic approach to measure success when applied to a tertiary institution through an authentic project and at a sophisticated intellectual level. A resulting impact of the students' experiences and benefits in participating in this project can also be critiqued through Kincheloe and Steinberg's (1998b) *Eight Cognitive Benefits*, the topic of another paper detailing this experience through a critical pedagogy lens (Sharp et al., 2009). These benefits refer to the students' involvement in developing research capacities, willingness to increase participation in tertiary systems, and other intellectual and motivational factors.

The students who were approached to participate were specifically identified as they appeared, from an academic observer's perspective, to have not only adjusted to, but were also succeeding in, the intellectual challenges of tertiary study. Additionally, it was evident, from both in and out of class socializing, that a tentative peer group had been established involving a number of mature-age students. It was considered that this project could be a way to strengthen this peer connection (and also the friendship could potentially strengthen the project outcomes), thus establishing stronger university social and friendship links. An added consideration was that extending these friendship links could provide an authentic experience similar to those that occur regularly in schools, between teachers collaborating in order to create units of work.

Development of a research culture with these students is evidenced from the decision three of the students would make to enter the honours program, engaging with the rigours of undergraduate research of their own creation. Two of the students have also co-authored subsequent publications, and tentatively accepted offers of doctoral supervision from academics involved in other areas of their undergraduate studies.

The initial collaboration involved the students authoring the unit plan, with the academic as a support and guide not co-author. The next point of collaboration, writing about this experience, has developed from this and is more closely aligned with principles in the spirit of a Freirean alliance generating conditions which support 'the possibilities for the production or construction of knowledge' (Freire 2001, p. 30). In this atmosphere of mutual respect and enthusiasm for the ideals embedded, individual skills have been brought together for the benefit of the group effort. Essentially this alliance involves a greater level of encouragement towards student emancipatory practices, with the academic unobtrusively scaffolding structures of academic research and writing, encouraging the development of self-directed learning. Student willingness to engage with the rigours of academic research moved them towards *conscientisation* (Freire, 2001) as the students' and academic's inquiry has extended beyond the original project. Conscientisation, in the context of this chapter, refers to the process of social awakening the students and academic experienced as they started to critique the structural boundaries of academic research (see Freire, 2001 for an in-depth definition of this concept). Engaging with the early stages of conscientisation during the initial project has enabled both students and the academic to critique their different roles. While reflecting on the processes and outcomes at a higher level, as collaborative partners we are able to share successes and address weaknesses in a non-threatening environment in order to establish and maintain a research partnership that opens future scope and opportunities for continued research collaborations.

Scholarship of student–academic collaboration

In the main, published literature (Chang, 2007; Chang and Schmidt, 2007; Lawrence, 2002) on the topic of student and academic collaboration focuses on engaging students in research with the scope of the project generally predefined by academics. In these instances, the students take on the role of 'academic assistant', such as interviewer, scribe or note taker, field worker or research assistant. Additionally, generally the students taking on this type of academic assistant work are postgraduate students looking to gain experience in the tertiary education sector. These roles are, in themselves, important and provide students with a range of valuable experiences and skill sets, which can be used for leverage when pursuing academic and professional employment. Less common, however, is undergraduate student participation in research projects alongside academics. Where this project differs significantly from much of the published literature is that the students engaged in this research project were undergraduates and, with support from an academic, were able to lead the project (within a set boundary, predetermined by the scope of the book).

Identification of the levels of support the students needed in order to successfully carry out the different phases of the research and writing processes was undertaken at the commencement of the project, and renegotiated by the students and the academic at regular intervals throughout the duration of the project. The negotiations that took place were also informed by the professional experiences of the academic in supporting students in other non-research-based projects at secondary school level, and scaffolding students through to successful completion of coursework assessment at tertiary level. Even though the students were highly self-motivated and had responsibility for their chapter, their need for scaffolding and support to achieve success in this endeavour was evident.

Academic research in this area was new to the students, and an uncommon area for undergraduates to venture into. Therefore, providing materials as exemplars, suggesting research pathways and being a sounding board for ideas was an important aspect of the collaboration. This approach contributed not only to the success of the outcome, but also to the staged development of academic skills and experiences of the students. Creating an environment where open dialogue can occur, for example where questions can be posed without fear of humiliation, is an important aspect of working with students. Kincheloe and Steinberg (1998b, p. 234) support the scaffolding of students in research projects and write, '. . . teachers working with student researchers not only focus on what students know but what they don't know as well . . . Thus, it is important for humble teachers to talk with student researchers about what none of them know . . . this create[s] a safe classroom climate . . .' As the academic was also writing two chapters for the same textbook, it seemed appropriate to share the research plan and writing strategies used to construct the chapter, so that the students were able to learn possible ways to approach the writing of their own chapter. In addition, the students were shown drafts of the chapters and invited to comment on them, not only for appropriateness of communication to a student audience but also content substance. An indication of the developed efficacy and the strong rapport between the students and the academics was evident when the students *did* provide some honest and critical reviews of the chapter, which ultimately led to a strengthened publication.

First-year experiences

Transition pedagogies are increasingly becoming widely accepted as an area of importance when discussing the broader first-year student experience. In this way, focus is placed on the development of curriculum that meets the needs of the ever-diverse university student population, especially those from low SES backgrounds and other risk factors such as first in family to pursue higher education. The collaborative endeavour undertaken by the undergraduate students can be viewed as an extension of their first-year experience in two specific areas. First, the students had been observed to have successfully transitioned from previous education to the requirements of academic study; and second, this was an opportunity to begin the transition to research from coursework, and to engage in a process of acculturating students in research skills and attitudes. This acculturation meant that deeper relationships needed to be developed. Fostering an open, collaborative research relationship between academics and students requires a great deal of trust to be gained and then maintained. This type of collaboration occurs most effectively, from the perspective of Kincheloe and Steinberg (1998a, p. 8), with lecturers who are

> . . . comfortable with ambiguity [as they] are better equipped to establish a productive interaction between students and students and teachers. Such interaction heightens self-awareness, as student researchers are attuned to the power of their own words and those of others, and the nature of the contexts and codes and the ways they construct the meaning of communication.

Being comfortable with the ambiguity that surrounded the initial development stages of a unit of work, in this case that was to be the focus of the chapter, was not a difficult task, as the students had been carefully and specifically selected (although they did believe for quite some time that it had been a random selection) to participate. Having had experience teaching these students, being familiar with the standard of their work combined with their commitment to strive to achieve their academic best, and seeing their confidence develop through participating in class discussions and debates, made establishing trust in this new context a smoother transition than it otherwise might have been if the students were not so well known to the academic.

Building on from their discussion on open and collaborative research partnerships developing between teachers and students, Kincheloe and Steinberg (1998a) also report on the respect teachers give to their students when engaging them in meaningful work with real-world outcomes. Rather than the oft-cited need for students to respect their teachers (which has a number of ambiguous connotations), directing attention at teachers respecting students (Shor, 1992) leads to meaningful work being developed in which students can connect with their day-to-day learning. Kincheloe and Steinberg write: '[T]eachers operating on the basis of this critical system of meaning respect students enough to give them real work to do, research that matters . . . Research as real work involves teaching students to do work that historians, anthropologists or physical scientists perform' (Kincheloe and Steinberg 1998a, p. 15). In the case of this collaboration, the research and outcome the students produced was a real-world example of what school teachers need to do regularly in their classroom curriculum planning. Providing this truly authentic experience, not as an assignment which potentially no one other than themselves and the marker would read, but rather as a published outcome, meant the students' real work had a deeper meaning than otherwise may have been the case. This activity then also had the added pressure of ensuring that a high-quality chapter was written, with the unit of work carefully aligned to stated curriculum outcomes. In order to achieve this, the students were scaffolded and supported through the process by the academic, with existing relationships first strengthened, and then developed further.

Challenges of collaboration

Reasons for students accepting the request to participate in the project

What follows now, in this section, is a critical reflection of the student participants, in their own first-person voice. This critique is positioned within a critical pedagogy framework, indicative of their own emerging understandings of what it is to be an educator. Terms like 'our collaborative academic' are used as a phrase of respect towards Heather Sharp who provided this opportunity to develop academically.

Acceptance of the opportunity to participate in this endeavour was not just based on the challenge of doing something different, but rather based on the privilege of having been asked. At first, as students, we were overwhelmed by the possible ramifications of this project; manipulating and dividing our time while maintaining the focus of attention on our full-time studies and juggling family commitments. Each may have had a different personal reason to initiate engagement with this project, but as a collective group we were attracted by the challenge of producing work of a suitable standard to be included with the work of recognized academics. An added challenge was producing work of a standard that the audience, our student-teacher peers and the academics teaching the course this book was intended for, would regard as writing of the level of quality toward which we were aspiring. We set ourselves a challenge to create as professional and polished a document as we were capable of, and were wary of being perceived as amateurish. Our ultimate goal was to create a text that the editors could not refuse to include in the final publication on the basis of judgement of its quality. As sceptical as we had been, it came as a great surprise when the work we had undertaken was presented to us, unedited, in a book with our university's bookshop price tag on the back. The realization that our work was worth putting a price on indicated the value of our intellectual abilities, and became the culminating self-reflection for us. *Our* final edit had been accepted, and our work, our thoughts and our ideas had commercial and academic value.

Our initial impression was that our work would only be included, if at all, as a supporting appendix to a chapter our collaborating academic was writing. However, this was never the case, and our work was included, as originally planned by the academic, as a stand-alone case study that supported the theme of the textbook, educating students for healthy communities. This theme closely aligned with the Queensland Studies Authority's SOSE outcomes-based curriculum. Therefore, our unit of work included such themes as physical, mental and social personal development, care of the environment, changes that occur over time, and how the human need for land impacts on the natural environment.

With the theme for the chapter predetermined by the editors, we fumbled over the starting point, at which time some of us opted to approach our collaborative academic, seeking guidance and direction about the nature of the task at hand. That approach would have been our first attempt at engaging with the collaborative process, and the initial step in helping to partially dismantle the self-created boundaries within which we operated (Bourdieu, 1998). These boundaries were created to accommodate our comfort zones, a direct impact of the socialization processes we had each experienced in other education contexts, exposing as simulacrums of understanding, our adherence to the belief that universities operated within particular power discourses (Lawrence, 2002). For us, the nature of collaboration with an academic was still formulated on traditional hierarchical ideology derived from our assumed expectations of the power discourses which should have been present between ourselves, as students, and the academic.

This, coupled with our initial impression of the task, led us to incorrectly assume the academic would take on the dominant voice within the project, directing us to produce an academically focused text that would be purposefully adapted to the topic. Approaching the project from this position we adopted a laissez-faire attitude about the content of the chapter, taking it for granted that the academic would interpose her expertise on our work, correcting any errors and adjusting our direction to suit the purpose of the task. It needs to be noted that this was never actually the case, nor the intention of the academic. Instead, the academic communicated her intent to involve us in a flexible and empowering pedagogical environment in which she did not abandon her authority, but modelled an emancipatory practice (Shor, 1992) to tease out our collective limitations (Giroux, 2005) and empower us enough 'to relate personal growth to public life' (Shor, 1992, p.15). Our voices were developed academically, empowering our intrinsic abilities to formulate our ideas into action. To facilitate this process, the academic took on a supportive role in which no one voice was dominant or dominated.

As first-year undergraduate students, our perceptions of collaboration intermingled with cooperative practices, as we had no distinguishing understanding of the difference between these two concepts. We had participated in a number of graded group assessments, but at that stage we participated in them cooperatively in order to use our individual strengths to generate a suitably high mark. Our motivation was overtly extrinsically driven towards our idea of success garnered from the acknowledgement of a higher grade. We rarely considered these assignments in relation to real-life situations, even though some of them were, and so completed them in some instances without due consideration of the potential learning from each assessment piece. Task completion was delegated individually in a jigsaw format, the pieces of which were to be joined together closer to the required submission date for a brief editing. Delegation of tasks was also done as an exchange of expertise in keeping with Bourdieu's notion of 'symbolic alchemy' (1998, p. 100) through which the power relationships central to this notion negotiated whose expertise was valid, and validated.

Without formally acknowledging that collaborative work may have had a particular format, we engaged with it both personally and academically through the willingness of supporting one another's differentiated work patterns (Bond and Thompson, 1996), which, although they were different, did complement each other with the work they produced. One of the challenges we faced was transcending from working cooperatively, a harmonious process through which we had previously harnessed individual strengths for the betterment of group assessment outcomes, to working collaboratively, a process in which we could feel free to digress with each other in a mentally stimulating and mutually supportive environment, while also disavowing the necessity of having an acknowledged designated leader. Initially, we approached the research cooperatively; tentative, but eager to be involved and to involve each other. It was only in the later stages of the project that we developed the sort of supportive work environment that indicates the transition to collaborative research (Bond and Thompson, 1996).

Other discourses impacted on the student–student aspect of the collaboration, with one such discourse, gender, impacting on the structure of the group dynamics in the early stages of the project. As we were all mature students who had completed school education over a quarter of a century ago, our traditionalized terms of reference for the gender locations each of us occupied (Wood, 2007) saw us place the sole male (who is very assertive) into a leadership position at the commencement of the project. It was unconsciously assumed that gender would take priority in the leadership of our collaboration. However, this socially generated scenario did not run for the entire duration of the collaboration, due in part to a number of personal issues that occurred, and so we revised our beliefs on the need for a male leader (Giroux, 2005) and completed the project as a cohesive and collaborative group.

One final challenge was the recognition of signature authorship. As our collaborating academic did not actually participate in the writing process, instead acting in a supportive capacity and then as *critical friend* by assisting with the editing, she was not acknowledged in the authorship details. All names were included, but instead of being acknowledged in order of workload contribution or alphabetically, once again we allowed the stereotyped gender roles in which we operated (Wood 2007) to dictate that the male be acknowledged first (Bond and Thompson 1996). This is now acknowledged as an area of blindness in the collaborative process, and furthermore exemplifies the necessity to ensure that issues such as authorship are determined in the early stages of collaboration.

Current collaborative efforts between the students and academic are markedly different to the initial one. The students have developed as researchers, both are currently pursuing honours research projects in which collaborative skills are used and expanded. The academic has also expanded her expertise in research. Experiences, both past and present, have consolidated the academic motivation (intrinsic and extrinsic) in all three members of this partnership, encouraging the expansion of consideration for future academic endeavours. Taking on board lessons learnt, as detailed throughout this section, has contributed to the success of more recent collaborations, and has provided a positive environment for ongoing collaborative endeavours.

A summary of the benefits enjoyed as a result of inclusion in this endeavour:

- Provision of an entry point into the world of academia through the visible identification of student abilities and capabilities commensurate with the rigours of engaging in research.
- Empowerment to take on leadership roles, and to breach the boundaries of traditionalized education, exercising authority as stakeholders in the educational experience (Shor, 1996). Ira Shor (1996) discusses power-

sharing as a way for teachers to empower their students, and through that process of empowerment to encourage students to become critically aware of the educational benefits of negotiating the boundaries between 'being unconsulted curriculum-receivers to becoming collaborative curriculum-makers' (Shor, 1996, p. 200). To facilitate these processes the academic provided 'the option for students to be leaders and stakeholders in the process, which means they can occupy the enabling center of their educations, not the disabling margins' (Shor, 1996, p. 200). The relationship that continues to develop between the three authors of this text very closely mirrors Shor's philosophy.

- Dissolution of the myth of power related to institutional hierarchies. As mature-age students, the expectation of the power relationships it was assumed should have been evident in such a situation started to dissolve because the academic did not demand acknowledgement of that power.
- Increased participation in campus life. Having seen the benefits of inclusion in the educational experience, the students began, and continue, to volunteer for various activities on their campus, as well as standing for elected positions on the University Council and the Student Representative Council, allowing both students to continue encouraging students on campus to participate and take ownership of the dynamics of their campus life.

These points clearly demonstrate the positive flow-on effects of the outcomes of genuine collaboration between academics and students, especially when considered in terms of participants being able to offer their newly developed skills and confidence to the student body in general, and to do so in a sophisticated, as distinct from token, manner. However, power dynamics in a multi-level collaboration cannot be ignored and disqualified from such endeavours, even though in this instance they were not obvious to the student participants.

Conclusion

This section addresses learning points that resulted from our collaboration. Witnessed by the academic, the transformative process that the students engaged in was an exciting and unplanned aspect of the collaboration. The empowering effect participating in this type of research project has on other aspects of the students' academic lives is referred to by Kincheloe and Steinberg (1998a, p. 2) as their ability to

> . . . gain a power literacy – that is, the ability to recognize the ways power operates to create oppressive conditions for some groups and privilege for others. Thus, students as researchers gain new ways of knowing and

producing knowledge that challenge the commonsense views of reality with which most individuals have grown so comfortable.

In this case, the practical impact this reality had on the students was to develop their confidence and critical thinking skills, and it began a process of critiquing the hidden (and not so hidden) power structures of the institution, encouraged them to join various student groups and participate voluntarily in events both as a group and on occasion as individuals. This developed efficacy, noticed by other students, has led them to advocate on behalf of other students to actualize real change for their peers, rather than simply tokenistic representation on boards and committees which have a mandatory student representative. Where participation on boards and committees could lead to a potentially tokenistic representation, the students have developed sufficient self-efficacy to challenge this arrangement and to voice their views at meetings, leading to a stronger, more meaningful experience, for which they have been commended by academic and community representatives on the same boards.

Although critical thinking skills are used every day within the banalities of normal existence, the significance of the outcomes of engaging in processes to improve these skills was not apparent to the students at this time. Entry into the world of academia was not yet an aspiration, not even a pathway that had been given any credibility or indeed conscious thought. However, through the engagement with critical thinking skills they were positioned to '. . . no longer see themselves as the passive receivers of expert produced knowledge' (Kincheloe and Steinberg 1998b, p. 239). From this juncture they developed the critical skills necessary to create their own knowledge, allowing openness to opportunities that furthered their capacity for intensive intellectual engagement.

The leadership role a lecturer can play in developing students scholastically and as an aspect of supporting students in their emerging research journey, is to 'involve students in an analysis and clarification of their goals and dreams' (Kincheloe and Steinberg 1998a, p. 2). This did not occur during the initial collaboration; however, positive relationships between the lecturer and the students continued to be developed in the time afterwards, leading to in-depth discussions about critical education topics and guidance on practical education experiences. This relationship has continued, despite now being in different institutions across two different states; and it was the initial collaboration that provided an avenue for the connection between lecturer and students to develop and continue beyond institutional boundaries.

The benefits of effective collaboration with consideration of the intellectual, social and emotional well-being of students have been explored, including hurdles that needed to be overcome, negotiated boundaries, and issues of exploitation during the process of collaboration. This provides an outline of key issues for consideration when academics and students engage in authentic collaborations. This collaborative exercise between the academic and the students involved in the original project is written with the benefit of having worked collaboratively already, with this chapter providing an opportunity to put the lessons learnt into practice. Many publications addressing the topic of academic–student collaborations or students as researchers are authored by the academic or teacher involved. We maintain that this practice continues to silence students and treat them as a type of subaltern 'Other'. Instead, by co-authoring we acknowledge the strengths each of us as individuals brings to the collaboration and support each other in strengthening our weaknesses. A 'pedagogy of critical student research' (Kincheloe and Steinberg 1998a, p. 19) has developed from the initial project and continues to be nurtured and built upon as collaborations continue.

References

Austin, J. and Hickey, A. (eds) (2007), *Education for Healthy Communities: Possibilities Through SOSE and HPE*. Frenchs Forest, Australia: Pearson Education.

Ballantyne, J., Todd, N. and Olm, T. (2007), 'The first-year experience: perceptions of students at a new campus'. Paper presented at the HERDSA National Conference, Adelaide, South Australia, July, 2007.

Bandura, A. (1995), *Self-Efficacy in Changing Societies*. Cambridge, UK: Cambridge University Press.

Bond, C. and Thompson, B. (1996), *Collaborating in Research*. Canberra, ACT: Higher Education Research and Development Society of Australasia.

Bourdieu, P. (1998), *Practical Reason*. California: Stanford University Press.

Chang, H. (2007), 'Making connections: an international student's perspective', in A. D. Thompson, H. Chang and I. Sabin (eds), *Faculty Mentoring: The Power of Students in Developing Technology Expertise*. Charlotte: Information Age Publishing, pp. 34–37.

Chang, H. and Schmidt, D. (2007), 'Faculty technology mentoring: major trends in literature', in A. D. Thompson, H. Chang and I. Sabin (eds), *Faculty Mentoring: The Power of Students in Developing Technology Expertise*. Charlotte: Information Age Publishing, pp. 31–34.

Fielding, M. (2004), 'Transformative approaches to student voice: theoretical underpinnings, recalcitrant realities'. *British Educational Research Journal*, 30, (2), 295–311.

Freire, P. (2001), *Pedagogy of Freedom: Ethics, Democracy, and Civic Courage*. Lanham, MD: Rowman and Littlefield Publishers.

Giroux, H. A. (2005), *Border Crossings: Cultural Workers and the Politics of Education* (2nd edn). New York: Routledge.

Kincheloe, J. L. and Steinberg, S. R. (1998a), 'Students as researchers: critical visions, emancipatory insights', in S. R. Steinberg and J. L. Kincheloe (eds),

Students as Researchers: Creating Classrooms that Matter. London, UK: Falmer Press, pp. 2–19.

Kincheloe, J. L. and Steinberg, S. R. (1998b), 'Making meaning and analyzing experience: student researchers as transformative agents', in S. R. Steinberg and J. L. Kincheloe (eds), *Students as Researchers: Creating Classrooms that Matter.* London, UK: Falmer Press, pp. 228–244.

Lawrence, J. (2002), 'Academics and first-year students collaborating to access success in an unfamiliar university culture', in L. Thomas, M. Cooper and J. Quinn (eds), *Collaboration to Widen Participation in Higher Education.* Oakhill, UK: Trentham Books Limited, pp. 213–238.

McInnes, C. (2002), 'Signs of disengagement? Responding to the changing work and study patterns of full-time undergraduate students in Australian universities', in J. Enders and U. Teichler (eds), *Higher Education in a Globalising World: International Trends and Mutual Observation.* Dordrecht, Netherlands: Kluwer Academic Publishers, pp. 175–190.

McKinney, K. (2007), 'The student voice: sociology majors tell us about learning sociology', *Teaching Sociology*, 35, (April), 112–124.

Nelson, K. J., Kift, S. M. and Clarke, J. A. (2008), 'Expectations and realities for first-year students at an Australian university'. Paper presented at the 11th Pacific Rim First Year in Higher Education (FYHE) Conference, 'An apple for the learner – celebrating the first-year experience', Hobart, Tasmania, June–July, 2008.

Sharp, H., Stanley, L. and Hayward, M. (2009), 'Critiquing undergraduate student participation in academic research using Kincheloe and Steinberg's Eight Cognitive Benefits'. Paper presented at the HERDSA National Conference, Darwin, Northern Territory, September, 2009.

Shor, I. (1996), *When Students Have Power: Negotiating Authority in a Critical Pedagogy.* Chicago: The University of Chicago Press.

Shor, I. (1992), *Empowering Education: Critical Teaching for Social Change.* Chicago: The University of Chicago Press.

Wood, J. T. (2007), *Gendered Lives: Communication, Gender and Culture* (7th edn). United States: Thomson Wadsworth.

Chapter 15

Collaborating for Staff–Student Partnerships: Experiences and Observations

Sabine Little, Heather Sharp, Linda Stanley, Marie Hayward, Pat Gannon-Leary, Peter O'Neill and Jane Williams

The process of developing this volume has been a long and laborious one. An initial call for chapters was needed in order to gauge what work was happening where, and whether such work warranted an edited book on the topic of staff–student partnerships in higher education. Furthermore, it was felt that, since the collaborative writing model was still fairly novel, a case would need to be made in advance, with strong contributions across the field, before a publisher was found. This meant that initial work on the book began in summer 2007. And while such time spans are by no means unusual in the world of academic publishing, they offer all sorts of complications to a project seeking to bring together staff and students, giving both an equal opportunity to share their ideas and experiences. Many chapters have, on an individual basis, touched on the advantages and challenges such a collaboration presented; this final section seeks to summarize these experiences, offering an honest reflection on the overall process, and an observation or two from Sabine's perspective as editor. The chapter, like the rest of the book, has been written collaboratively, but the contributions, at least in part, were more haphazard, with an open invitation to all authors to contribute, via a collaborative writing tool. In some cases, co-authors are quoted directly, in order to indicate the context within which a contribution has been made, especially where a discussion section from the online document has been tied together through the editorial process. Other sections have been collaboratively authored and are presented as such. By way of structure, this chapter will look at the challenges raised throughout the book in turn, including the power relationships inherent in staff–student collaborations, and resulting issues around exploitation; the benefits of working in partnership, and challenges caused by student (and in some cases, staff) transience. The chapter finishes on considerations relating to the creation of a space – whether intellectual or literal – for staff–student partnerships to prosper.

Staff–student partnerships as exploitation?

The question of power has been raised repeatedly throughout this volume, and from different perspectives (see e.g. Chapters 1, 2 and 11). Heather Sharp, Linda Stanley and Marie Hayward have explored the concept of research collaboration as exploitation in greater detail, as part of this chapter.

Collaborative research between partners where there potentially exists an unequal power relationship due to either unspoken power relationships or explicit hierarchical structures needs to be examined in order to determine whether collaboration, rather than exploitation, has occurred. This examination can include factors such as quality of experience, fairness in workload and equity of recognition for research output. In discussing the potential exploitation that can occur between academic researchers and teachers in schools, Ladwig (1991) makes the claim that

> 'collaborative educational research' as it is currently practised by some educational researchers is minimally 'collaborative' and, in fact, exploitative. [and that] mechanisms of symbolic control in educational research [can] lead to the systematic exploitation of teachers (Ladwig, 1991, p. 111).

Throughout this book, staff and students have collaborated on writing up their experiences – whether as part of an 'organized' research project, or as part of a reflective process following an educational enhancement initiative. Looking at various models and critiques of such staff–student collaborations allows us to think about the extent to which the way we work can indeed be considered a 'partnership'.

It can be argued, as Ladwig (1991) does, that research involving either unequal partnerships or between those with completely separate roles (for example, academics and school teachers) can often result in a type of exploitation due, in part, to the different levels of importance placed on research outputs by, for example, employers and promotion panels. If applying Ladwig's notion of exploitation through collaboration to this context whereby the academic is placed in a position of institutional power, required by employment conditions and the nature of academic work to generate quality research outputs; and the students are placed in a position of institutional unimportance in relation to research outside of specific course requirements, there exists a potential for exploitation to occur. In some chapters, staff and students had no traditional hierarchical connection (e.g. where students involved were Student Union officers, or had already graduated). In others, however, staff had 'curricular power' over students, and, at the same time as extracurricular writing for the chapter took place, the staff would assess students for work completed as part of the curriculum. Is it possible to separate the two, or is the underlying implication of hierarchy and power always such that, if in doubt, the student will defer to the member of staff?

From the anecdotal evidence of working on this book, this was not always the case. In some cases, the student partners took the lead, including most of the communication with co-authors and the editor. Several chapters point towards the concept of partnership as allowing both (or all) partners to work to their strengths – in most cases, navigating the world of writing for publication will be more familiar to staff than to students.

What does or does not constitute exploitation when staff and students work together is a difficult issue to tackle. Certainly, when academics are considering partnering with undergraduate students, measures need to be taken to avoid using students as a novelty to research or as a way to validate personal teaching success. If students are in a position that makes it difficult to 'opt out' of an invitation for staff–student collaboration, the issue of power and hierarchy enters into the discussion.

Exploitation, however, is not necessarily a one-way street. In recent years, there has been an increase in pressure placed on academics to publish articles in high-ranking, peer-reviewed, international journals. Increasingly, government funding is seen to be linked to quality research outputs, meaning that first and sole authorship of papers is highly regarded both for institutional and professional benefit. In addition, academics are increasingly encouraged to seek cross-institutional and transnational collaborations in order to strengthen their research profile. In collaborating with students, both these factors, therefore, can be seen to limit academics' opportunities to engage in research at this level. So, equity of collaboration, a factor considered important in avoiding student exploitation, comes at a cost to the academic in having to first share authorship, and second to ensure students are sufficiently mentored to achieve high-quality results, *if being genuinely collaborative.*

Furthermore, once we put aside the often ingrained assumption that students would always and by default constitute the weaker or disadvantaged half of a partnership, and allow for the idea that many students are entrepreneurial, enthusiastic and strategic about their education, then we might admit that students do have chances to 'exploit' working with staff as partners, benefiting from expertise, developing new skills, putting themselves in a position where, in an increasingly difficult world of employment, they can show that they have 'the edge', whether the career path they contemplate is in academia or not.

Interestingly, we don't view this as exploitation. We view it as students learning the trade, and welcome their interest and engagement. In other fields, such as trade for example, the term 'partnership' implies mutual benefits, but this, too, is rarely, if ever, termed 'exploitation'. When staff and students work together, then, whether in educational enhancement or research, does the application of the term 'exploitation' imply the lack of knowledge of what each partner is letting themselves in for? If this is the case, then for all parties to have made explicit the terms of the partnership will be one of the most important aspects of collaboration. These terms should include:

1. being very explicit about the intentions of collaborations and the roles of each participant
2. informing the students that participating in collaborations is a process of acculturation into academic research
3. demonstrating a very clear research path and opportunities for the students, for example, graduation to honours or research higher degrees
4. ensuring that authorship of published texts is properly attributed and placement of authorship dependent on intellectual input and effort alone
5. mentoring in other areas of opportunities that may arise, for example, supporting students to submit sole-authored papers to conferences, acting as a sounding board, guide and mentor so that students can develop skills to act independently in fields of research
6. being honest about workload and expectation of success. Not all writing gets published, some pieces intended as journal articles end up as internally circulated working papers, or get resurrected years later as part of a different piece of research. Staff and students working on this book had to do a fair amount of work *before* it got accepted by a publisher, drafting a chapter outline for the proposal. If unsuccessful, no doubt some author teams would have pursued different avenues for publication; others might simply have discarded the idea of writing collaboratively.

If staff and students also engage with each other in the more traditional teacher–student role, one assessing the other, clear boundaries and good communication are even more key to a partnership where each member feels fully represented.

Transience as a barrier to staff-student partnerships

Nearly all chapters in this book have been affected by transience – most often, the students involved have left the course and begun employment (both in academia and in unrelated fields). In two cases, members of staff have moved on to new posts. Some students have kept up their involvement despite taking on employment, but others have moved on, engagement with employment substituting engagement with education. For staff members, who are often the permanent fixpoint trying to engage and enthuse a constant stream of new students, this can be both frustrating (because a constant change in step is required) and enthusing (because there is a steady income of new ideas and enthusiasm). Manor (in Manor et al., 2010) finds the positive in such transience when he explains:

> I'm already 20 years old and in a couple of years the majority of students who helped write this book will have moved beyond college to be teachers and other professionals. We will no longer know what it's really like to be a student or how students really learn. The study of education will always need newer, more diverse student voices (p. 8).

If a 20-year-old student feels that he will be out of touch with the student voice soon, then what hope can staff have to consistently stay in touch with student needs, without consistently engaging with students? And what better way might there be to engage with students and understand them, than to work with them? Slack (2003) warns of the dangers of a top-down approach, with governmental goals and decisions being imposed on the education system, rather than current needs and ideas informing these decisions. However, for students to be able to participate fully in educational discourse, a certain apprenticeship will need to take place. From Sabine's work at CILASS (Centre for Inquiry-based Learning in the Arts and Social Sciences), students engaged in learning and teaching enhancement reported an improved understanding of how the university works, and appreciation for certain rules and regulations that had been imposed by staff (exactly the type of understanding, in fact, which caused frustrations for Niamh Collins in Chapter 7). The students who had thus engaged over the course of one or two years, however, would then leave, and new students were recruited in their place. Many other chapters in this book are about one-off projects, rather than ongoing practice. How, then, do we retain student expertise in learning and teaching enhancement, while at the same time making space for new ideas and thoughts from incoming students?

From Sabine's perspective, the answer lies in students recruiting students. At the beginning of her work on staff–student partnerships, she worked with a group of ten students on potential scenarios for collaboration. Her suggestions included student-led workshops, conference presentations, research papers and events. Her suggestions were met with incredulity, and, in some cases, fear. The consultation model ('We'll show you our outputs and you tell us what you think') seemed to make this first group of students feel far more comfortable than the idea of taking the lead and putting forward ideas.

Four years on, there was still a considerable turnover in students year on year, and yet, all of the above activities were now firmly implemented in the students' work. The status quo of what is and isn't 'done' had shifted for both staff and students, and continued to shift, despite the turnover. This has been achieved by involving current students in the recruitment and training of the next 'cohort', and a logistical plan that encourages collaboration between outgoing, remaining and incoming students. A long handover period ensures new students get to see outgoing members in action, see how they engage with staff, and gradually take over their role, until the outgoing member leaves.

This works well for continuous engagement in learning and teaching, at departmental level for example, or for annual events such as a staff–student conference. For longer-term projects such as research, the internal processes such as ethical review procedures, or indeed external deadlines such as grant application deadlines, mean that one student (or group of students) might be involved in the developing of a research proposal, and another with the conducting and/or writing up of the research. This process is less than ideal; and doubtless results in a decreasing feeling of 'ownership' on the students' part. In most cases, however, this can be overcome by planning research outputs differently, in a way that allows students who are leaving to be directly involved in the dissemination process, such as at a conference where 'ongoing research' may be discussed.

Transience, however, can be more than physical. In any environment that includes a partnership or collaboration, individuals may 'move on', intellectually speaking. External pressures might mean that one planned outcome might change to another, or that aspects of the collaboration are postponed or even shelved. Conflicting timetables for staff and students are not naturally conducive to collaboration, with different pressure points for examinations, preparation, marking, etc., and different priorities for holiday periods. Pat Gannon-Leary raised the following issues within the collaborative writing space:

> Lack of opportunities for informal interaction, absence of dedicated 'non-contact' time for reflection and planning, and pressured individual workloads constrain attempts at working together.
>
> Co-authors overburdened with their own schedules and deadlines, leaving little time to devote to the common good.
>
> Non-attendance by co-authorship personnel at meetings and low engagement has the potential to create problems in the future if they disagree with decisions taken and wish to make subsequent changes.
>
> Lack of liaison personnel and of leadership with drive, direction and commitment can undermine a co-authorship.

All these examples are, in their own way, examples of 'transience', in the sense of 'transient engagement' with the topic or question at hand. Viewed from this perspective, most partnerships are transient in the sense that each individual's focus is only partially on the 'common enterprise' (Wenger, 1998), and divided among the needs of the individual and several communities. In collaborations which are entirely between members of staff or entirely between students, the shared language and knowledge that members of a community use as a 'shorthand' description to highlight issues and problems already exists. In staff–student partnerships, additional communication is needed to navigate gaps left by 'intellectual transience' – planning around deadlines, within the timeframes of institutional requirements (e.g. deadlines for working papers which are to go before a specific committee, etc.). Finding a space within which collaboration can still take place, and ensuring that all partners feel that they 'know where they stand', and benefit from working with each other, is therefore a vital aspect to be considered, if we want staff–student partnerships to succeed.

Benefits of staff–student collaboration

Throughout this book and the literature (see, e.g. Werder and Otis, 2010), staff and students comment on the enjoyment of working together to have a positive impact on education. Although 'enjoyment' is often sadly underrepresented on a list of possible benefits, impact evaluation at the University of Sheffield (Levy et al., 2010) has shown that staff working with students on curriculum design and development have found themselves motivated by the students' enthusiasm. One student working with staff, in turn, said that the opportunity to work in educational enhancement allowed them to re-engage with their learning and become enthused with their subject again, a stance that has been echoed many times by the nearly 100 students Sabine has worked with over the years. Noyes (2005) points out that students who are becoming disengaged or who are disenchanted with their educational experience tend to 'come back on board' if they think that they matter to the institution and that they are doing something worthwhile. Mann (2001) suggests that students 'be enabled through the responses of solidarity, hospitality, safety and the redistribution of power' (p. 18) in order to facilitate 'the will on the part of students to invest themselves in their engagement with thinking, self and action' (Mann, 2001, citing Barnett, 1997, p.171–2). Obviously, not all students working in staff–student partnerships for educational enhancement are necessarily disengaged to start with – often, staff interested in teaching and students interested in having an input into their education will find each other. In these cases, the benefit of the collaboration is not so much in rediscovering a certain enthusiasm, but instead in the pleasure of working with like-minded people. Peter O'Neill (see Chapter 5) describes their collaboration thus:

The Evolving Essay is a project which, I think, all of us enjoyed enormously, from the initial conversations where the idea was generated, throughout the actual online project, during subsequent reflections and joint staff–student conference presentations, and during the actual drafting of the final essay. The project – from initial idea to final draft of the essay – has taken three years, but I don't think that this particular project has ever seemed like a burden. Even when deadlines neared and personal lives intruded, making drafting impossible, we all felt committed to the project and confident that it would be finished. And even now that the final publication of our [chapter] brings some closure, we still find ourselves thinking of future possibilities. Amid the often isolating nature of academia – especially in the non-scientific fields – collaborating on a project has been a pleasure. Clearly, we should be doing more of this!

Jane Williams (see Chapter 6) tells a similar story:

> [. . .], all three of our student authors commented on how much they enjoyed the project and how they valued the processes they were engaged with. We look forward to July (the main project period) when we know we will work with our medical students – they are really inspiring, innovative, committed and this in turn motivates us and we go to great lengths to support them in their endeavours. And then again, September, when we mark their completed projects and read their reflective accounts. It's not work!

Motivation, then, is a clear benefit, and not a surprising one. In looking at how these benefits were achieved, the right attitude towards the collaborative experience seems to be key. Although laying out the terms of the collaboration is mentioned above, it seems not all staff–student collaborations need such guidelines in order to be successful. In fact, both Peter O'Neill and Jane Williams comment that they never officially considered the 'who is staff, who is student' conundrum, nor any potentially related power issues. It is perhaps interesting that both chapters are involving online environments, where traditional hierarchies might be more easily disregarded. As Peter puts it, '[m]ore than in "real life", everyone is equal and people are judged by their words, not by their credentials'. Still, the attitude with which staff–student partnerships are approached seems to have considerable impact on the benefits that may be taken away. Jane comments:

> I'm not sure we ever saw it as a collaboration. We didn't set out to collaborate or set up a partnership. It was something that evolved from one student developing online learning materials and the partnerships and initiative as a whole have grown from there. It wasn't until there was a call for abstracts for this book that we really saw this as a partnership; again it was something that evolved quite naturally. [. . .] Interestingly, it wasn't until we responded to the call for abstracts [for this book] that we began to think about partnerships and if we hadn't I don't think we would have realized or unravelled the levels of partnerships that exist – more like an

intricate web of players, [or indeed, a] community of practice (Wenger, 1998). It's been truly fascinating and has spawned lots of new research ideas and projects.

Not all author teams have used the term 'community of practice', although a fair number of them have. The connotations related to working in such a community, however, are present in virtually all chapters in this book. Heather Sharp, Linda Stanley and Marie Hayward cite as a benefit

the knowledge that at a future stage the collaborations between academics and students will result in academic to professional or academic to academic collaborations once the students have graduated, and potentially providing a link for the academic to the professional field in order to engage in practice-based research.

Such knowledge, and the interpretation of staff–student partnerships as a way to induct students into the world of academia is akin to Wenger's idea of 'peripheral participation' in the community of practice, with the understanding that students would gradually increase their participation as they pick up the shared language of the field (e.g. educational development, curriculum design, scholarship of teaching and learning, etc.). This, however, does not easily chime with the idea of equality – do (and should) students join staff in the academic 'community' or is it up to staff and students to explore, jointly, where a collaborative community for students and staff might exist?

Conclusion – a community around partnerships in teaching and learning

A number of author teams have – either in their reflections, or in direct communication with Sabine as editor, commented on how challenging they found the writing of the chapter. Without citing what was, in part at least, confidential communication, it becomes obvious that 'finding common ground' may actually be easier than previous sections have suggested. When Northedge (2003) considers the challenge students face before they have picked up the language which allows them to express their opinions in line with accepted vocabulary of the academic community, this challenge could easily be extended to include staff, too, many of whom have never in detail discussed their teaching style, or tried to put the 'philosophy' behind their teaching approach into words.

Jane Williams shares challenges along these lines, which have nothing to do with staff–student collaboration at all:

Personally, writing the chapter was challenging, being a scientist and wanting to show imperative of proof, [. . .] no random controlled trials! and using narrative. This is a particular issue facing medical education research at the moment – that learning is 'messy' and takes place in localized, rich contexts.

When author teams put themselves forward for this book, it was not necessarily just the students who had doubts about finding the right academic 'voice' with which to write. And while working together when all partners are developing their understanding might be more frightening, it is also significantly more 'equalizing'. Both staff and students have experience of their role as teachers and learners, but neither will necessarily have had to make that experience explicit to an external audience (e.g. readers), and locate it within the literature. This mutual exploration of new knowledge was not a common denominator for all chapters, but unfamiliarity with the literature around staff–student partnerships, for example, was raised often enough in communication to believe in the value of joint, genuine exploration as a means of putting into words often implied experiences in learning and teaching. The collaborative inquiry process which is inherent to identifying new common ground and situating one's own experiences of staff–student partnerships in the existing field around the topic has doubtlessly helped at least some author teams to 'gel'.

This chimes rather well with existing literature on future universities (see, e.g., Brew, 2006; Rowland, 2006; Boyer Commission, 1998), where 'everyone [. . .] should be a discoverer, a learner' (Boyer Commission, 1998, p. 9). Joint exploration, whether called 'inquiry' (Chapters 1, 2, 6, 8, 11 and 14), 'enquiry' (Chapters 2, 3, 4 and 12), 'discovery' (Chapters 1 and 13) or indeed 'exploration' (Chapter 10), features significantly throughout this volume, as does the acknowledgement of the various expertises, experiences and knowledges staff and students bring to the partnership. From some teams, there was a clear indication that the notion of who was staff and who was student never really entered their minds, until they had to discuss the matter for the chapters in this book. Others, however, had to struggle harder to ensure the student and the staff voices were equally represented. Some, by their own admission, have not managed it entirely. Yet all have reported that the *process* they underwent has been a rewarding one – in some cases, an opportunity to formalize and discuss an intervention or project where the process did not come under scrutiny until it had to be described for others. But a description was necessary in order to communicate with a growing 'Community Around Partnerships In Teaching And Learning', and so, unable to resist the acronym CAPITAL, we hope that the book is seen as an investment in the ever-growing community of people – learners, teachers, staff, students, educators alike – who collaborate in order to understand education from a holistic perspective, and, together, seek to enhance it.

References

Barnett, R. (1997), *Higher Education: A Critical Business*. Buckingham: Society for Research into Higher Education and Open University Press.

Boyer Commission on Educating Undergraduates in the Research University (1998), *Reinventing Undergraduate Education: A Blueprint for America's Research Universities*. Stony Brook: State University of New York at Stony Brook.

Brew, A. (2006), *Research and Teaching: Beyond the Divide*. New York: Palgrave MacMillan.

Ladwig, J. G. (1991), 'Is collaborative research exploitative?', *Educational Theory*, 41, (2), 111–120.

Levy, P., Reilly, N., Nibbs, A. and Little, S. (2010), *Final Evaluation Report of the Centre for Inquiry-based Learning in the Arts and Social Sciences (CILASS) to the Higher Education Funding Council for England (HEFCE)*. University of Sheffield: CILASS.

Mann, S. (2001), 'Alternative perspectives on the student experience: alienation and engagement', *Studies in Higher Education*, 26, (1), 7–19.

Manor, C., Bloch-Schulman, S., Flannery, K. and Felten, P. (2010), 'Foundations of student-faculty partnerships in the scholarship of teaching and learning: theoretical and developmental considerations', in C. Werder and M. Otis (eds), *Engaging Student Voices in the Study of Teaching and Learning*. Sterling, VA: Stylus, pp. 3–15.

Northedge, A. (2003), 'Enabling participation in academic discourse', *Teaching in Higher Education*, 8, (2), 169–180.

Noyes, A. (2005), 'Pupil voice: purpose, power and the possibilities for democratic schooling', *British Educational Research Journal*, 31, (4), 533–540.

Rowland S. (2006), *The Enquiring University*. London: Society for Research into Higher Education and Open University Press.

Slack, K. (2003), 'Whose aspirations are they anyway?', *International Journal of Inclusive Education*, 7, (4), 325–335.

Wenger, E. (1998), *Communities of Practice: Learning, Meaning and Identity*. Cambridge: Cambridge University Press.

Werder, C. and Otis, M. (2010), *Engaging Student Voices in the Study of Teaching and Learning*. Sterling, VA: Stylus.

Index

Lightning Source UK Ltd.
Milton Keynes UK
UKOW041448070912

198650UK00003B/14/P